encountering
the HOLY
SPIRIT in
Every Book of the Bible

DAVID DIGA HERNANDEZ

DESTINY IMAGE® PUBLISHERS, INC.

P.O. Box 310, Shippensburg, PA 17257-0310

"Promoting Inspired Lives."

This book and all other Destiny Image and Destiny Image Fiction books are available at Christian bookstores and distributors worldwide.

Cover design by Eileen Rockwell
Interior design by Terry Clifton

For more information on foreign distributors, call 717-532-3040.

Or reach us on the Internet: www.destinyimage.com

ISBN 13 TP: 978-0-7684-1732-6
ISBN 13 EBook: 978-0-7684-1733-3
ISBN HC: 978-0-7684-1734-0
ISBN LP: 978-0-7684-1735-7

For Worldwide Distribution, Printed in the U.S.A.
1 2 3 4 5 6 / 21 20 19 18

DEDICATION

I dedicate this book to Pastor Benny Hinn, who is to me a mentor, a friend, and a father in the faith. Thank you, Pastor Benny, for the rich and unparalleled teachings that the Lord has anointed to lay a foundation for my understanding of the Person of the Holy Spirit. To Jesus belongs the glory. I will steward well the impartation that I have received. I will boldly and unapologetically preach the saving and healing Gospel of Jesus Christ in the power of the Holy Spirit.

With love and honor,
David Diga Hernandez

CONTENTS

Introduction	The Search for the Spirit	1
Chapter 1	The Nine Symbols of the Spirit	7
Chapter 2	The Holy Spirit in Genesis	36
Chapter 3	The Holy Spirit in Exodus	45
Chapter 4	The Holy Spirit in Leviticus	56
Chapter 5	The Holy Spirit in Numbers	61
Chapter 6	The Holy Spirit in Deuteronomy	65
Chapter 7	The Holy Spirit in Joshua	69
Chapter 8	The Holy Spirit in Judges	77
Chapter 9	The Holy Spirit in Ruth	84
Chapter 10	The Holy Spirit in First Samuel	91
Chapter 11	The Holy Spirit in Second Samuel	93
Chapter 12	The Holy Spirit in First Kings	96
Chapter 13	The Holy Spirit in Second Kings	102
Chapter 14	The Holy Spirit in First Chronicles	106
Chapter 15	The Holy Spirit in Second Chronicles	109
Chapter 16	The Holy Spirit in Ezra	112
Chapter 17	The Holy Spirit in Nehemiah	117
Chapter 18	The Holy Spirit in Esther	119
Chapter 19	The Holy Spirit in Job	122
Chapter 20	The Holy Spirit in Psalms	124
Chapter 21	The Holy Spirit in Proverbs	129
Chapter 22	The Holy Spirit in Ecclesiastes	132
Chapter 23	The Holy Spirit in the Song of Solomon	135
Chapter 24	The Holy Spirit in Isaiah	138
Chapter 25	The Holy Spirit in Jeremiah	142
Chapter 26	The Holy Spirit in Lamentations	145
Chapter 27	The Holy Spirit in Ezekiel	147
Chapter 28	The Holy Spirit in Daniel	151
Chapter 29	The Holy Spirit in Hosea	153
Chapter 30	The Holy Spirit in Joel	156
Chapter 31	The Holy Spirit in Amos	158
Chapter 32	The Holy Spirit in Obadiah	163

Chapter 33	The Holy Spirit in Jonah	166
Chapter 34	The Holy Spirit in Micah	169
Chapter 35	The Holy Spirit in Nahum	171
Chapter 36	The Holy Spirit in Habakkuk	174
Chapter 37	The Holy Spirit in Zephaniah	176
Chapter 38	The Holy Spirit in Haggai	178
Chapter 39	The Holy Spirit in Zechariah	181
Chapter 40	The Holy Spirit in Malachi	186
Chapter 41	The Holy Spirit in Matthew	188
Chapter 42	The Holy Spirit in Mark	191
Chapter 43	The Holy Spirit in Luke	193
Chapter 44	The Holy Spirit in John	195
Chapter 45	The Holy Spirit in Acts	199
Chapter 46	The Holy Spirit in Romans	203
Chapter 47	The Holy Spirit in First Corinthians	208
Chapter 48	The Holy Spirit in Second Corinthians	212
Chapter 49	The Holy Spirit in Galatians	215
Chapter 50	The Holy Spirit in Ephesians	218
Chapter 51	The Holy Spirit in Philippians	220
Chapter 52	The Holy Spirit in Colossians	223
Chapter 53	The Holy Spirit in First Thessalonians	224
Chapter 54	The Holy Spirit in Second Thessalonians	226
Chapter 55	The Holy Spirit in First Timothy	230
Chapter 56	The Holy Spirit in Second Timothy	232
Chapter 57	The Holy Spirit in Titus	234
Chapter 58	The Holy Spirit in Philemon	235
Chapter 59	The Holy Spirit in Hebrews	237
Chapter 60	The Holy Spirit in James	240
Chapter 61	The Holy Spirit in First Peter	242
Chapter 62	The Holy Spirit in Second Peter	245
Chapter 63	The Holy Spirit in First John	246
Chapter 64	The Holy Spirit in Second John	248
Chapter 65	The Holy Spirit in Third John	251
Chapter 66	The Holy Spirit in Jude	253
Chapter 67	The Holy Spirit in Revelation	257
Conclusion	Who Is This Holy Spirit?	259
Epilogue	Welcome, Holy Spirit	263

Introduction

THE SEARCH FOR THE SPIRIT

Can the Holy Spirit truly be found in every book of the Bible? The answer is *yes*! How could it be otherwise? How could the One who inspired every word written in both the Old and New Testaments not be found in the same?

I love the Holy Spirit, and I never tire of talking about Him. I'll never forget the day He touched my life. I was never to be the same again. I am forever ruined for anything less than the majesty of His presence. I'm driven by a holy obsession with the Spirit. Since the moment He first befriended me, I have sought to be a better friend to Him; I have sought to know His mind, power, and nature. Hungry to know more about the Person of the Holy Spirit, I asked Him to teach me. I told Him, "Teach me everything! I don't want to miss a thing about You!"

I had been faithful to steward all of the beautiful revelations the Lord had given me before—revelations concerning the Holy Spirit. I wrote them in books. I preached them in sermons. I taught them in lessons. I prayed them in prayers. I recorded them in both audio and video media. And the more I talked about the Holy Spirit, the more I realized that there was more to know. Sometimes, right in the middle of me preaching, the Holy Spirit would give me whispered instructions, spontaneous glimpses about His Person. Just when I thought that I had discovered all there was to discover about Him, I would find more—much more. Dear reader, the well of revelation will never run dry. There's that much to Him.

As I remained faithful to properly steward those revelations, the Lord poured even more into me. The more we use what He has given to us, the more He gives us to use. The Lord always gives us more as we steward His treasures well.

"Stewardship" = key

If you are faithful in little things, you will be faithful in large ones. But if you are dishonest in little things, you won't be honest with greater responsibilities (Luke 16:10).

I began to see the Holy Spirit in places of the Bible I had never before seen Him. Especially in the books of the Bible that are historic in nature, I did not anticipate finding Him. Nonetheless, He was there—He was there all along. True to His gentle and humble nature, He worked in subtle ways through mighty servants of God, faithfully nudging divine vessels across the plane of God's perfect will.

I wondered how I could have missed Him before so many times. After all, I had read those passages. Internally, I asked the Holy Spirit, "How did I miss You in the Scriptures so often? Why didn't You show me that You were there?" I sensed this message in response: "Because you never asked."

You see, the Holy Spirit does not make it His priority to testify of Himself. His primary message is the same as the Father's—their message is Jesus.

But I will send you the Advocate—the Spirit of truth. He will come to you from the Father and will testify all about Me (John 15:26).

This does not mean, however, that the Holy Spirit will never reveal His work, nature, or Person. It just means that His emphasis is Jesus. In fact, the closer you become to the Holy Spirit, the more you will love Jesus. A passionate love for Jesus is the ultimate sign of fellowship with the Holy Spirit. Still, there is nothing wrong with pursuing fellowship with the Spirit Himself.

May the grace of the Lord Jesus Christ, the love of God, and the fellowship of the Holy Spirit be with you all (2 Corinthians 13:14).

Encouraged by the truth of God's Word, I continued my search for the Spirit in the Scriptures. I asked myself, "Could it be that the Holy Spirit can be found, in one way or another, in every single book of the Bible?" Sure, we can find the types and shadows of Christ. But is the same true of the Holy Spirit?

Dear reader, why wouldn't that be the reality? After all, it is the oil which keeps the light of the lamp aglow. It is the Spirit who reveals Jesus and makes Him known. Where we see Jesus in action, we always see the Spirit at work. Where we see God's will being fulfilled through people, we also see the Spirit moving. The Word of God is a divine classic marked by the supernatural, traced out masterfully by the hand of the Spirit. It was His breath that carried the words of the prophets. It was His hand that guided those who recorded the very Word of God.

My contention is simple and, in my opinion, modest: there's something to be learned about the Holy Spirit or His work in every single book of the Bible.

His work, His Person, and His nature are emanating from every page of the Scripture. You just have to know how to look. When searching for the Holy Spirit in the pages of Scripture, I have found Him to be mentioned in three different ways: He is mentioned specifically, subtly, and symbolically.

SPECIFIC MENTIONS

When I write of the "specific mentions" of the Holy Spirit, I am refer-ring to the Bible's direct references to the Holy Spirit. For obvious reasons, the specific mention of the Holy Spirit is the easiest to find. Here is an example of a specific mention:

> *But you will receive power when the Holy Spirit comes upon you. And you will be My witnesses, telling people about Me every-where—in Jerusalem, throughout Judea, in Samaria, and to the ends of the earth* (Acts 1:8).

In the verse you just read, the Holy Spirit was named outright. There was no need for Him to be revealed from behind a symbol or a mystery.

The specific mentions of the Holy Spirit give us the clear and guiding truths about Him—these truths help us to see Him clearly where He might otherwise be missed. Upon those simple truths, we build a foundation for understanding Him in greater depth. So long as we follow the clear biblical revelations concerning the Spirit, we can avoid straying into the dangerous places of falsehood and superstition.

The specific mentions of the Spirit will prepare your heart to receive the mysteries of the Word, while protecting you from error. We must under-stand the clear biblical truths about the Holy Spirit before we are equipped enough to find Him symbolically.

SYMBOLIC MENTIONS

If you want to see the "symbolic mentions" of the Holy Spirit in the Bible, then you must pay careful attention to the Scriptures. The following are symbols of the Holy Spirit: wind, fire, oil, light, the dove, the cloud, the seal, water, and wine.

It is important to understand, however, that not every mention of those words in the Bible is a reference to the Holy Spirit. Sometimes "fire" just means "fire." Sometimes "wine" just means "wine," and so forth. We must also avoid forcing any meaning upon the Scriptures.

I'll write more on the symbols of the Holy Spirit in chapter 1 of this book.

SUBTLE MENTIONS

Subtle mentions of the Holy Spirit are references where, while the Holy Spirit might not be mentioned symbolically or specifically, His work or effects are seen in action. They are subtle in that the Holy Spirit's nature or ministry is seen at work—but there is no symbolic or specific mention of His title or name.

What we know of the Holy Spirit through the specific mentions can be used to familiarize ourselves with His work and nature. And in becoming familiar with His work and nature, we become more discerning in seeing the effects of His invisible hand.

For example, it is both rightfully and commonly pointed out that God is not specifically mentioned even once in the Book of Esther. But does this mean that we cannot see the Holy Spirit's guiding hand at work?

Was it not promised to us that the Holy Spirit would speak through us at pivotal moments?

For the Holy Spirit will teach you at that time what needs to be said (Luke 12:12).

For it is not you who will be speaking—it will be the Spirit of your Father speaking through you (Matthew 10:20).

Knowing that the Holy Spirit is the One who speaks through human vessels at divine moments, we can clearly see the Holy Spirit at work though Mordecai when he spoke those timeless and prophetic words:

If you keep quiet at a time like this, deliverance and relief for the Jews will arise from some other place, but you and your relatives will die. Who knows if perhaps you were made queen for just such a time as this? (Esther 4:14).

That is, of course, just one example of how a clear teaching about the Holy Spirit (Luke 12:12, Matt. 10:20) can be used to find the Holy Spirit carrying out His ministry in a subtle way (Esther 4:14).

Another example of a subtle mention of the Holy Spirit is the voice of God itself. When God speaks to His servants in the Old or New Testament, He does so by His Holy Spirit.

God spoke to Isaiah the prophet through the Holy Spirit:

And He said, "Yes, go, and say to this people, 'Listen carefully, but do not understand. Watch closely, but learn nothing'" (Isaiah 6:9).

How do we know that it was the Holy Spirit who spoke to Isaiah? Paul the apostle tells us so in the Book of Acts:

And after they had argued back and forth among themselves, they left with this final word from Paul: "The Holy Spirit was right when He said to your ancestors through Isaiah the prophet, 'Go and say to this people: When you hear what I say, you will not understand. When you see what I do, you will not comprehend'" (Acts 28:25-26).

The Holy Spirit spoke to the prophet Isaiah, but that isn't completely apparent if you read the Old Testament without a New Testament filter. Only after looking at that same portion of Scripture through the New Testament does the subtle mention of the Holy Spirit become an undeniable one.

Look also at the Book of Hebrews:

That is why the Holy Spirit says, "Today when you hear His voice, don't harden your hearts as Israel did when they rebelled, when they tested Me in the wilderness. There your ancestors tested and tried My patience, even though they saw My miracles for forty years" (Hebrews 3:7-9).

When did the Holy Spirit say that? He said it through King David in the Book of Psalms:

means quarreling

means testing

> *The Lord says, "Don't harden your hearts as Israel did at Meribah, as they did at Massah in the wilderness. For there your ancestors tested and tried My patience, even though they saw everything I did"* (Psalm 95:8-9).

So when the "Lord" or "God" speaks to people in the Old Testament, it's by the Holy Spirit. The same is true in the New Testament.

Those biblical examples are proof that the Holy Spirit can be discovered in places where He is not specifically or even symbolically mentioned. He permeates the Scripture.

And so, dear reader, I want you to ask the Holy Spirit, who is the Spirit of Wisdom and Revelation, to anoint you and prepare you to receive revelations. As I present you with specific, subtle, and symbolic mentions of the Holy Spirit, I will also tell you of my wonderful experiences with the Spirit of God. Let your faith come alive as you ready yourself to encounter the Holy Spirit in every book of the Bible.

Stewarding the Word of God:
1 Cor. 10:31

Chapter 1

THE NINE SYMBOLS OF THE SPIRIT

Mystery is in the very nature of God. Jesus taught in parables. The declarations of the prophets had, hidden within them, the secrets of the Christ. Our God is a God of wonder and unpredictability. Only those who walk in close fellowship with Him will come to truly understand His mysterious ways.

> *He made known his ways unto Moses, His acts unto the children of Israel* (Psalm 103:7 KJV).

The children of Israel knew God's acts and power. But Moses understood God's ways and nature. It is the nature of the Lord to reveal Himself incrementally in response to the faithfulness of the one who seeks Him.

> *If you look for Me wholeheartedly, you will find Me* (Jeremiah 29:13).

> *The secret of the Lord is with them that fear Him; and He will shew them His covenant* (Psalm 25:14 KJV).

> *Verily Thou art a God that hidest Thyself, O God of Israel, the Saviour* (Isaiah 45:15 KJV).

Why does the Lord cloud Himself with mystery? It's quite simple. The Lord *wants* to be sought.

> *His purpose was for the nations to seek after God and perhaps feel their way toward Him and find Him—though He is not far from any one of us* (Acts 17:27).

> *It is God's privilege to conceal things and the king's privilege to discover them* (Proverbs 25:2).

When asked why He spoke in parables, Jesus gave to His disciples this powerful response:

> *He replied, "You are permitted to understand the secrets of the Kingdom of Heaven, but others are not. To those who listen to My teaching, more understanding will be given, and they will have an abundance of knowledge. But for those who are not listening, even what little understanding they have will be taken away from them* (Matthew 13:11-12).

The nature of God is mysterious, and Scripture was born of the nature of God.

> *All Scripture is God-breathed and is useful for teaching, rebuking, correcting and training in righteousness* (2 Timothy 3:16 NIV).

All throughout the Bible, God speaks to us through clear, straightforward messages, as well as through hidden revelations. The hidden revelations become easier to discover as we grow in our understanding of the clear truths of Scripture.

Here I must emphasize this important point: always interpret the unclear verses of Scripture by the clear verses of Scripture and never the other way around.

When you are faithful to steward and rightly handle the written Word of God, the *now and alive* Word of God becomes activated. Secrets of the Spirit become unlocked and ready for you to open. Remember that Jesus promised, *"To those who listen to My teaching, more understanding will be given..."* (Matt. 13:12).

Stop for a moment and say, "Holy Spirit, help me to be faithful to the clear revelations that I might be trusted with the hidden revelations."

The thrilling truth is that in the Scripture, you will find meanings hidden in types, shadows, parallels, parables, and symbols. Just as Jesus is revealed symbolically—the spotless Lamb (see John 1:29; 1 Peter 1:19; Rev. 5:12), the Door (John 10:7), the Vine (John 15:1,5), the Bread of Life (John 6:35), the Light (Isa. 9:2; John 8:12), the Morning Star (2 Peter 1:19; Rev. 22:16), etc.—so the Holy Spirit is also revealed in symbolism.

Here in this chapter, I have listed for you what I call "the nine symbols of the Spirit." I'll use the symbols of the Spirit throughout this book.

But for now, I just want to present a short and simple summary of these nine symbols.

1. Wind
2. Fire
3. Oil
4. Light
5. The Dove
6. The Cloud
7. The Seal
8. Water
9. Wine

WIND

At the early age of eleven, I was born again. At the very moment of salvation, I received an immediate and intense desire to truly know Jesus. I wanted to see Him as clearly as I could. So within mere weeks of being born again, I had already developed a faithful and profound prayer life. There was something very special about my first several encounters with the Lord—they have marked my life in a way that I will never forget. Those encounters brought me into an awareness of God. Even up until this very moment, as I write this very sentence, I have an awareness of God's presence. That awareness, that deep knowing of God's reality, is potent. That's how powerfully He touched my life—the loving impressions of His power still abide with me after over a decade.

Although I make contact with the Lord on a daily basis and although He is faithful to make Himself known in each moment of each hour, I am still very fond of that time in my life. I would pray between four and eight hours a day, desperately seeking the face of God. I would pray when I awoke. I would pray throughout my day. I would pray before I fell asleep. Often, my pillow would be wet with tears because I would fall asleep sensing the nearness of the glory of God. I would also wake up in the early morning hours—2:00 A.M., 3:00 A.M.—to seek the Lord. I didn't have to set an alarm because the Holy Spirit would nudge me out of my sleep. I could almost feel His hand pulling me out of bed. He would call to me—I could sense His joy and excitement as He invited me to know His presence. I would wake to hear His voice gently speaking, "Pray." I wouldn't allow myself to hesitate or even think about hesitating, for I knew the persuasive power of the flesh. I had trained myself to immediately respond—with a spiritual reflex—to the Holy Spirit's prompting. And I never regretted responding to Him.

One night, after falling asleep while singing worship songs to the Lord and asking for a divine encounter of any sort, I awoke to a beautiful experience in the Holy Spirit's presence. I mean that the presence of the Lord was revealed with such severity that the sense of it startled me out of my deep sleep.

This is the best way I can word it: I felt like God breathed into my being.

Gasping, I awoke to sense my body being filled with a refreshing and strong air. I felt life fill me. There was something electric, something energetic moving through me. I've described it as the same feeling one experiences when one drinks very cold water, except I felt this in my breath. My skin tingled, and I became wide awake. I sat up and looked around my room. My room was covered in the quiet of a holy stillness. I sensed the Lord so near to me in that moment.

I pondered the significance of that event. As to what change or transformation took place within me in that moment, I could only guess. "Perhaps," I wondered, "I was graced with the lovingly playful side of the Spirit's nature and the Spirit was just saying, 'Hello.' Or maybe God performed some hidden work within me, though hard to specifically identify."

While looking back on that strangely wonderful experience and reflecting on its significance, this is what I sensed God communicate to me: "The same Spirit in Jesus is the same Spirit in you, so the same breath in Jesus is the same breath in you."

That night, I had encountered the Holy Spirit in a special way. He revealed Himself to me as a breath. The Holy Spirit is the breath of God, the wind of Heaven.

In the Old Testament, the word for "spirit" is *ruach*. The Hebrew word *ruach* can mean "spirit," "wind," or even "breath." In the New Testament, the word for "spirit" is *pneuma*, which can also mean "spirit," "wind," or "breath." Of course, as far as the words and languages, there is much more to it than that, but for the sake of simplicity, just note that *ruach* and *pneuma* can mean "spirit," "wind," or "breath."

The Holy Spirit comes as a mighty wind from Heaven.

Jesus had resurrected and ascended. As instructed by Jesus, His followers gathered together in one place. Eagerly they waited for the One Jesus had promised to send. I can't even begin to imagine what sort of excitement hovered about such a faith-filled atmosphere. The followers of Jesus had seen Him heal the sick. They had seen Him raise the dead. They had witnessed His might and authority in the expelling of demonic powers. They had heard His life-altering teachings. Every promise He had made to them He faithfully kept. So, they fully expected Him to keep His promise in sending the Holy Spirit.

> *Once when He was eating with them, He commanded them, "Do not leave Jerusalem until the Father sends you the gift He promised, as I told you before. John baptized with water, but in just a few days you will be baptized with the Holy Spirit"* (Acts 1:4-5).

Obediently, they awaited the arrival of His promise. They must have imagined all sorts of different scenarios. They must have talked among themselves, speculating on what exactly Jesus had in store for them. "Who do you suppose Jesus is sending to us? How does the Holy Spirit look? What will He tell us when He arrives? Will He descend from the heavens, or will He just appear before us as Jesus did several times?"

Indeed, there was a holy anticipation among the people. They had been so blessed as to witness the coming of the promised Messiah. Now, they were privileged to wait upon the Holy Spirit. And as the people of God waited, the Holy Spirit came upon them. He showed up *suddenly.*

> *On the day of Pentecost all the believers were meeting together in one place. Suddenly, there was a sound from heaven like the roaring of a mighty windstorm, and it filled the house where they were sitting* (Acts 2:1-2).

I love the way the King James Version describes the coming of the blessed Holy Spirit. It describes His arrival as being accompanied by *"...a sound from heaven as of a rushing mighty wind..."* (Acts 2:2 KJV). The sound came from Heaven, and it rushed through the believers who had gathered. I love that the Holy Spirit arrives suddenly. The ordinary can become extraordinary at the turn of a second. When the Holy Spirit shows up, the evidence of His presence is immediate and intense. Like a wind, He comes from seemingly nowhere and whirls through the atmosphere.

The Holy Spirit is the wind from Heaven.

> *The wind blows wherever it wants. Just as you can hear the wind but can't tell where it comes from or where it is going, so you can't explain how people are born of the Spirit* (John 3:8).

The Holy Spirit is also the breath of God; He is the breath of life that sustains all living beings.

> *And the Lord God formed man of the dust of the ground, and breathed into his nostrils the breath of life; and man became a living soul* (Genesis 2:7 KJV).

> *The spirit of God hath made me, and the breath of the Almighty hath given me life* (Job 33:4 KJV).

The Holy Spirit sustains all life, not just for the redeemed, but also for the unredeemed.

> *Thus saith God the Lord, He that created the heavens, and stretched them out; He that spread forth the earth, and that which cometh out of it; He that giveth breath unto the people upon it, and spirit to them that walk therein* (Isaiah 42:5 KJV).

The Holy Spirit proceeds from the depths of God. This is why, when imparting the Holy Spirit to His followers, Jesus *breathed* upon them.

> *Then He breathed on them and said, "Receive the Holy Spirit"* (John 20:22).

The Holy Spirit is symbolized by wind and breath.

However, this does not mean that every time you read the words *breath* or *wind* in the Bible that you will see a connection to the Holy Spirit. For example, in First Kings 19:11, Elijah the prophet comes into contact with a mighty wind sent by God. However, that mighty wind was not in and of itself divine in nature.

> *"Go out and stand before Me on the mountain," the Lord told him. And as Elijah stood there, the Lord passed by, and a mighty*

windstorm hit the mountain. It was such a terrible blast that the rocks were torn loose, but the Lord was not in the wind (1 Kings 19:11).

Even though we see a form of the word *ruach* in the verse above, the wind mentioned is not symbolic for the Holy Spirit, for *"...the Lord was not in the wind"* (1 Kings 19:11).

By contrast, we see that the Lord was in the whirlwind encountered by Job:

Then the Lord answered Job from the whirlwind (Job 40:6).

So it's important to be attentive in how you interpret potentially symbolic Scriptures. Still, wind and breath are powerful symbols of the Holy Spirit.

Wind and breath represent the refreshing nature of the Holy Spirit's presence, His unpredictable ways, His invisible but obvious involvement in your life, and His power, which sustains all life. He is the wind of Heaven, the breath of God, and the breath of life. Therefore, breath and wind can be symbolic of the Holy Spirit.

FIRE

My family roots run deep into the grounds of revival. I am a fourth-generation Christian and a third-generation minister of the Gospel. I grew up hearing stories of the supernatural power of God at work throughout our family generations. I grew up hearing accounts of divine rescues, unusual occurrences, miraculous healing, angelic encounters, and improbable outcomes. My family endured trials of all sorts, heartache of the most painful kind, and challenges from every side. But through it all, God proved Himself to be good. With every story I heard, I learned of God's faithfulness to His Word, the certainty of His promises, and the might of His power. I could go on and on telling you stories about the guiding hand of God. However, for one reason or another, one story in particular has impacted me more profoundly than most of the others.

While attending a service at a small church in Maywood, California, my grandparents and my father, who was ten years old at the time, witnessed an unusual work of the Holy Spirit.

As I am told, the church was in a season of revival. Miraculous healing occurred on a regular basis, people worshiped the Lord with a holy fervency, and, most importantly, many unbelievers found radical, immediate transformation through the miracle of salvation. Although the church was faithful to the call of ministry, there was nothing in particular that any man did to start that revival. It was purely a sovereign move of God, a fresh wind that had arrived from seemingly nowhere.

At one service in particular, the people of God were worshiping in an atmosphere bathed in God's glory. There was a rich invisible weight that had settled upon the sanctuary, and a joy-filled energy pulsed about the air. Exalting the name of Jesus through song, jubilant people danced around the tiny building.

The worship was exciting but not chaotic, moving but not driven by emotion. There was a true touch of Heaven upon the place. The service was in progress when something strange happened.

There was a pounding at the back door—someone was knocking persistently. That persistent knock went unanswered for only a few seconds before the doors were bumped open. The violent sound of the doors hitting the walls was loud enough to draw the attention of some of the worshipers. Rushing through the door with axes in their hands and gear attached to their bodies, a group of firemen entered the room. Initially vigilant and excitable in demeanor, the firemen soon appeared bewildered. They glanced around the room and slowly began to relax their readied stances.

One of the church members approached them to see what had brought them to the church. The firemen explained the reason for their visit.

While the church was worshiping, neighbors began to call the fire department. People around the neighborhood saw smoke and flames coming out of the church building. "The church is on fire!" the people reported. However, when the firemen entered the building, they saw no visible source for the flames and the smoke.

"We don't see any fire here," one of the firemen remarked. One of the church members replied, "Yes, there is a fire here, but it can't be put out by any man. It's the fire of the Holy Ghost."

That occurred at their church more than once.

The fire of God is not a force or an energy. The fire of God is not passion or emotion. The fire of God isn't even revival. The fire of God is a Person—the Holy Spirit.

In the Book of Acts, within the same narrative where we read of the Holy Spirit descending from Heaven along with the sound of a mighty rushing wind, we also see another symbol of the Holy Spirit recorded:

> *Then, what looked like flames or tongues of fire appeared and settled on each of them* (Acts 2:3).

The presence of the Lord is often described as being like or accompanied by fire, as mentioned in the Book of Exodus:

> *And the angel of the Lord appeared unto him in a flame of fire out of the midst of a bush: and he looked, and, behold, the bush burned with fire, and the bush was not consumed* (Exodus 3:2 KJV).

The Lord is described as having eyes of fire. Think about that! You can see the Lord's fiery Spirit through His eyes.

> *His body also was like the beryl, and His face as the appearance of lightning, and His eyes as lamps of fire, and His arms and His feet like in colour to polished brass, and the voice of His words like the voice of a multitude* (Daniel 10:6 KJV).[1]

In his letter to the Thessalonians, Paul the apostle gives an important warning about stifling the work of the Holy Spirit. But it is his use of the word *quench* that tells us of the Holy Spirit's fiery nature:

> *Quench not the Spirit* (1 Thessalonians 5:19 KJV).

In the Greek, that word *quench* is *sbennumi*, which means "to extinguish"—as in to extinguish a fire. It's the same exact word used in the following verse from Ephesians:

> *Above all, taking the shield of faith, wherewith ye shall be able to quench all the fiery darts of the wicked* (Ephesians 6:16 KJV).

Furthermore, when telling of the promised baptism of the Holy Spirit, John the Baptist uses the word *fire* to describe that baptism:

---

1   See also Revelation 1:14; 2:18; 19:12.

I baptize with water those who repent of their sins and turn to God. But someone is coming soon who is greater than I am—so much greater that I'm not worthy even to be His slave and carry His sandals. He will baptize you with the Holy Spirit and with fire (Matthew 3:11).

In the Old Testament, God demonstrated the fact that He was with His people through a fire that hovered over the tabernacle.

On the day the Tabernacle was set up, the cloud covered it. But from evening until morning the cloud over the Tabernacle looked like a pillar of fire (Numbers 9:15).

In the New Testament, the Holy Spirit, the fire of God, dwells in His new temple—your body.

Don't you realize that your body is the temple of the Holy Spirit, who lives in you and was given to you by God? You do not belong to yourself (1 Corinthians 6:19).

Fire represents the Holy Spirit's righteous nature. It speaks to His purity, judgment, and His refining presence. Thus, fire can be symbolic of the Holy Spirit.

OIL

When I was sixteen years old, I attended Tuesday night prayer meetings taught by my aunt, Esther Bloom. A mighty woman of prayer, she was used of the Lord to help lay the foundations of prayer in my life. Every Tuesday, she would pick me up from my house and drive me in her red sedan to her class.. She taught about intercessory prayer, spiritual warfare, hearing God's voice, and many other intriguing spiritual topics. Those prayer meetings had a special grace upon them. We would pray for hours, without agenda, asking for the Lord to reveal Himself to us. There was a divine kiss upon the meetings. The presence of the Lord was very evident.

It was at those Tuesday night meetings that I also was taught the importance of the anointing oil. One of the regular prayer meeting attendees made a batch of anointing oil just for the prayer team. Wanting to take from the divine atmosphere we were enjoying, the team and I prayed over that oil and asked the Lord to place a tangible deposit of His power upon it, just like He did with the cloth that touched Paul's body.

> *When handkerchiefs or aprons that had merely touched his skin were placed on sick people, they were healed of their diseases, and evil spirits were expelled* (Acts 19:12).

To this day, I can still remember the oil's sweet smell. I would use that oil everywhere I went to minister. In fact, I would use that oil in my home. I would apply it to the blankets in my bed and ask the Lord to envelope me in His presence as I slept—and indeed, I would have dreams in which God would speak clearly to me.

Before preaching, I would anoint my clothes. Before praying, I would apply the oil to the doorway and walls of my room. Before laying hands on the sick, I would place it on the afflicted. My prayers were childlike, and God honored them.

I had a Bible that I also anointed with the oil. I would use that Bible to preach publicly and study privately. I said to the Lord, "Let Your power be so strong upon me that people who touch this Bible receive from it."

At a Bible conference, I had set that Bible down on a chair to save my seat. Someone in my church group thought that I had forgotten my Bible so they picked it up for me. When they did, they came up to me, exclaiming, "Diga, I picked up your Bible to bring it to you, and when I did, I felt a strong heat rush up my arms. My body is tingling all over. I feel the power of the Holy Spirit."

I have many stories like that. It's amazing how easily one can access the spiritual realm with simple acts of faith and obedience.

Now, of course, there is nothing spiritual about oil itself. The power is found in the faith that people exercise when using the oil. But what oil represents is of biblical significance. For example, in the Book of James, we are told that anointing oil can be used in praying for the sick:

> *Is any sick among you? let him call for the elders of the church; and let them pray over him, anointing him with oil in the name of the Lord: And the prayer of faith shall save the sick, and the Lord shall raise him up; and if he have committed sins, they shall be forgiven him* (James 5:14-15 KJV).

The Bible doesn't say that the oil will heal the sick; it says that "the prayer of faith" heals the sick. Prayer and faith, not oil, produce results. However, faith is exercised when we obey God. So the use of oil *in obedience and faith* can produce results. The faith behind our obedience, not the act itself, is what activates power and pleases the Lord. The Lord uses the oil to help us release our faith, and He has used it for quite some time.

There is an ancient ritual recorded in both the Old and New Testaments. In this ritual, specially made oil was poured ceremoniously over the one who was "being anointed." When this oil was poured, sprinkled, or dabbed onto an object, animal, or person, the same was understood to be set aside for a special purpose.

God's servants would apply the oil as instructed for many different purposes. When applying the oil to people, it would be poured upon the head.

Kings were anointed.

> *Now the Lord said to Samuel, "You have mourned long enough for Saul. I have rejected him as king of Israel, so fill your flask with olive oil and go to Bethlehem. Find a man named Jesse who lives there, for I have selected one of his sons to be My king."...So as David stood there among his brothers, Samuel took the flask of olive oil he had brought and anointed David with the oil. And the Spirit of the Lord came powerfully upon David from that day on. Then Samuel returned to Ramah* (1 Samuel 16:1,13).

Prophets were anointed.

> *Then anoint Jehu grandson of Nimshi to be king of Israel, and anoint Elisha son of Shaphat from the town of Abel-meholah to replace you as My prophet* (1 Kings 19:16).

Priests were anointed.

> *Clothe your brother, Aaron, and his sons with these garments, and then anoint and ordain them. Consecrate them so they can serve as My priests* (Exodus 28:41).

Special holy items and places, such as altars, were anointed.

> *Each day you must sacrifice a young bull as a sin offering to purify them, making them right with the Lord. Afterward, cleanse the altar by purifying it; make it holy by anointing it with oil* (Exodus 29:36).

When a person was anointed, it was because they were being appointed to a divinely given place of leadership and influence. The oil was used to consecrate, purify, and mark them as unique servants of God. The ritual took place only once at the initiation for their newfound position of authority.

But when God sent Jesus, He did not mark Him, consecrate Him, or position Him with the typical anointing ritual. For that ritual was only symbolic for what was to come. God marked and anointed Jesus, not just with oil, but with the Holy Spirit.

> *And you know that God anointed Jesus of Nazareth with the Holy Spirit and with power. Then Jesus went around doing good and healing all who were oppressed by the devil, for God was with Him* (Acts 10:38).

The anointing oil was a foreshadowing of the Holy Spirit. Just as oil was poured from above and onto the head of those appointed, so the Holy Spirit is poured out from above onto the head of the Church—Jesus Christ.

> *The Spirit of the Lord is upon me, for He has anointed me to bring Good News to the poor. He has sent me to proclaim that captives will be released, that the blind will see, that the oppressed will be set free* (Luke 4:18).

You and I today are not anointed with oil but with power and the Holy Spirit.

> *But you have an anointing from the Holy One, and all of you know the truth* (1 John 2:20 NIV).

The oil represents the Holy Spirit's presence and power, His mark upon the one who receives Him. So, oil can be symbolic of the Holy Spirit.

LIGHT

I once had a prayer team visit my house to pray. While praying over my desk (where I studied the Word), an anointed woman of God saw a vision. She said, "I was praying over your room when I saw your Bible sitting open on your desk. So I started to anoint your desk and Bible. Then I saw the verses in the Bible begin to illuminate. In the spirit, I saw you studying. And as you studied, the verses were being illuminated."

What that woman saw in the spirit was the work of the Holy Spirit. The Holy Spirit illuminates the Word, and that illumination is not just for me—it's for you, dear reader.

Before I began to know the Holy Spirit as a friend, when I didn't even truly consider Him as a Person, I struggled to understand the teachings of God's Word. I was able to comprehend biblical doctrines, memorize Bible passages, and even appreciate the beauty of the Scriptures. Yet I lacked in how I received the revelation of God's Word. There was no life to my devotion. Because my mind would so easily wander, I would read long portions of Scripture only to stop and have to start again. I would often forget the context, misunderstand the ideas, and struggle to find any application for the truth I received.

Even knowing the Word, my spiritual mood would often shift as I failed to grasp the nature of God. Reading the Word of God was more of a discipline than anything else. Though discipline in the Word is certainly needed, I didn't want my devotion to the Word to be *just* a discipline. Sure, reading the Word benefited me. And yes, it helped me to grow. But something wasn't quite right. Something was missing, and I knew there had to be more.

One day, while reading the Word, I came across a portion of Scripture in the Book of James. I'll never forget the moment I first read it. It was life altering. I read this verse:

> *If you need wisdom, ask our generous God, and He will give it to you. He will not rebuke you for asking* (James 1:5).

Dear reader, I know that to most that verse may not appear all that thrilling, but when I read it, for me, that verse became *alive*! Something about it just pulled my soul. I felt God speaking to me.

Through that verse, the Lord was offering to me understanding of His precious Word. He was inviting me to ask for His wisdom. The very moment I read that passage, I stopped to pray. "Lord," I spoke softly, "Your Word says that if I lack wisdom, I can ask You for it. So I'm asking You to give me wisdom. Help me to understand Your Word."

That was the day the Holy Spirit introduced me to Himself as the Teacher.

But when the Father sends the Advocate as My representative—that is, the Holy Spirit—He will teach you everything and will remind you of everything I have told you (John 14:26).

On that day, the Holy Spirit offered me His help in knowing the Word, and everything changed.

Ever since then, when I read the Word, I can sense the Holy Spirit standing alongside me, and I can hear Him teaching me. I'm telling you—only He can truly reveal His Word. The Holy Spirit has helped me move beyond comprehension and into revelation. Comprehension and revelation are very different. One is received in the natural mind, the other in the mind of the spirit. My personal time in the Word is no longer dry and tedious; it's refreshing and exciting.

The Holy Spirit's guidance in the Word has even changed my ministry. The teaching of the Word, aside from the miracles, is what drew the crowds to Jesus (see Luke 5:15). I model my ministry after His. So this ministry is built on God's Word and the Spirit's teaching. So much can be built on the foundation of solid teaching and revelation. With the Holy Spirit as your Teacher, you can become filled with the Word to where it begins to pour out of you, and that will attract people to your ministry. Why? Because people are so hungry to know the deeper things of God. They want substance, and substance is hard to find. True substance of the Word, true knowledge of the Bible, is a rare treasure. So few ever take the time to get into the Word.

The illumination of the Holy Spirit can become the magnet of your ministry. That is one of the reasons why it's so important that we rely upon the Holy Spirit to teach us.

And that's what I've learned to do—just yield to my Teacher. Since the moment I read that verse in James until now, the revelations haven't ceased. The Holy Spirit is faithful to reveal His Word. It's purely supernatural. The ability to know the truth is beyond human reasoning. We need the illumination of the Holy Spirit.

When I think of such illumination, I'm reminded of apostle John. What awe and wonderful terror must have filled the yielded being of John as he stood in the realm of the Spirit to witness the majestic sight of God's throne room. Like the deep sea or the ever-expanding cosmos, the presence of the Lord can be so beautiful that it's frightening.

Then as I looked, I saw a door standing open in heaven, and the same voice I had heard before spoke to me like a trumpet blast. The voice said, "Come up here, and I will show you what must happen after this." And instantly I was in the Spirit, and I saw a throne in heaven and someone sitting on it. The one sitting on the throne was as brilliant as gemstones—like jasper and carnelian. And the glow of an emerald circled His throne like a rainbow. Twenty-four thrones surrounded Him, and twenty-four elders sat on them. They were all clothed in white and had gold crowns on their heads. From the throne came flashes of lightning and the rumble of thunder. And in front of the throne were seven torches with burning flames. This is the sevenfold Spirit of God (Revelation 4:1-5).

The Book of Revelation offers us spiritual symbolism and apocalyptic imagery unlike anywhere else in the Bible. However, it's in verse 5 that we see the Holy Spirit both symbolically and specifically mentioned.

The Book of Revelation describes the sevenfold Spirit of God as *"seven lamps of fire burning"* (Rev. 4:5 KJV). At first, I planned on using this Bible verse to support my description of the Holy Spirit as fire. But upon further reflection, I found that Revelation 4:5 was most suitable as a description of the Holy Spirit as light. Yes, the Holy Spirit is a refining, consuming fire. However, in Revelation 4:5, the lamps *themselves* are said to be the sevenfold Spirit of God, not the fire.

Lamps give light, guidance, and clarity. In the same way, the Holy Spirit brings about illumination in the life of the believer. The Holy Spirit gives illumination through:

Revelation of the Word of God (see John 14:26)

Revelation of the ways of God (see 1 Cor. 2:10-12)

Revelation of the will of God (see Acts 16:6-7)

The Word of God contains the written foundational truths concerning God's will (desires, plans) and God's ways (nature, character). However, there are certain aspects of God's will that only the Holy Spirit can reveal to you—especially when those aspects have to do with specific things in your life and ministry. The same goes for the ways of God. God's ways—or nature—can only be truly understood by the Holy Spirit.

The more that the Holy Spirit illuminates the Word of God, the more you can see the ways and will of God. The Holy Spirit illuminates your mind and your spirit. As a guiding lamp, the Holy Spirit enables you to see with your spiritual sight.

> *But you are not like that, for the Holy One has given you His Spirit, and all of you know the truth* (1 John 2:20).

The lamp speaks to the illuminating nature of the Holy Spirit. Lamps or light can be symbolic of the Holy Spirit.

THE DOVE

What does the Holy Spirit look like? We are given descriptions of Jesus and the Father, but rarely do we see a description of the Holy Spirit. Today, His body is your body, but the Holy Spirit appeared in physical form in the Gospels. Yes, the Bible gives a physical description of the Holy Spirit!

The Gospels each record the spectacular events in the life of Christ. Although they will often vary in the *way* they describe an event, they do not ever contradict one another. Matthew, Mark, Luke, and John each describe the event of Jesus's baptism in the same way. During the baptism of Jesus, the Holy Spirit descended upon Him like a dove. This agreement upon the *way* they described the Holy Spirit indicates to me that what they saw was a literal description and not a figurative description. Those who witnessed the heavenly display literally saw the Holy Spirit, in the shape and likeness of a dove, descend upon Jesus.

> *After His baptism, as Jesus came up out of the water, the heavens were opened and He saw the Spirit of God descending like a dove and settling on Him* (Matthew 3:16).

> *As Jesus came up out of the water, He saw the heavens splitting apart and the Holy Spirit descending on Him like a dove* (Mark 1:10).

> *Then John testified, "I saw the Holy Spirit descending like a dove from heaven and resting upon Him"* (John 1:32).

Luke's Gospel confirms the literal way in which the Holy Spirit came upon Jesus. He makes it clear that the Holy Spirit took on the form of a dove *bodily*:

> *and the Holy Spirit, in bodily form, descended on Him like a dove. And a voice from heaven said, "You are My dearly loved Son, and You bring Me great joy"* (Luke 3:22).

Other Scriptures in the Bible symbolically speak to the pure, innocent, and undefiled nature of the Holy Spirit:

> *I sleep, but my heart waketh: it is the voice of my beloved that knocketh, saying, Open to me, my sister, my love, my dove, my undefiled: for my head is filled with dew, and my locks with the drops of the night* (Song of Solomon 5:2 KJV).

> *I am sending you out like sheep among wolves. Therefore be as shrewd as snakes and as innocent as doves* (Matthew 10:16 NIV).

Like the dove, the Holy Spirit is elegant, pure, and gentle. As such, the dove can be symbolic for the Holy Spirit.

THE CLOUD

Kathryn Kuhlman was a uniquely anointed woman of God. I only had the opportunity to receive from her ministry through biographies, stories from those who experienced her ministry, and, of course, classic videos from her program and miracle services. Even through secondary means, I have found her ministry to be a powerful one.

The way she graced the platform, the manner in which she ministered the deep truths of God's Word, the childlike posture she took in worshipful adoration of Jesus—those, among many other things, made it evident to me that she was very close to the Holy Spirit. You can see the joy of the Holy Spirit on her face, and I've heard only a few talk about the Holy Spirit like her. She truly was a friend of the Holy Spirit. She rarely had to lay hands upon any who were sick. The presence of Jesus surrounded her so powerfully that many were healed just sitting there, listening to her preach the Word.

While speaking about Miss Kuhlman with those who attended her services in person, I learned that her meetings were "glorious" and "unlike anything else." Pastor Ralph Wilkerson, who was somewhat of a mentor to Miss Kuhlman, told me about her: "She didn't pretend to be spiritual; she was spiritual. She was unique and never tried to be anybody else."

Concerning the ministry of Miss Kuhlman, I heard stories of miracles. I read of her powerful revelations. I also heard stories about how, when she would walk into rooms, the whole atmosphere would shift. The power of the Holy Spirit rested upon her being. Among the most intriguing stories I heard about her were the eyewitness accounts of the visible cloud that would descend upon her platform as she ministered. Yes, there was a visible cloud that would surround her. Some even say that her face would light up like a light bulb. When I think of those manifestations, I am reminded of Moses, who would fellowship with the Lord in a cloud.

> *Then Moses climbed up the mountain, and the cloud covered it. And the glory of the Lord settled down on Mount Sinai, and the cloud covered it for six days. On the seventh day the Lord called to Moses from inside the cloud. To the Israelites at the foot of the mountain, the glory of the Lord appeared at the summit like a consuming fire. Then Moses disappeared into the cloud as he climbed higher up the mountain. He remained on the mountain forty days and forty nights* (Exodus 24:15-18).

It was in that cloud that Moses received, among many other instructions, commands on how to build the tabernacle. While in the cloud, Moses shared such a close relationship with God that his face would often shine.

> *Then all the people of Israel approached him, and Moses gave them all the instructions the Lord had given him on Mount Sinai. When Moses finished speaking with them, he covered his face with a veil. But whenever he went into the Tent of Meeting to speak with the Lord, he would remove the veil until he came out again. Then he would give the people whatever instructions the Lord had given him, and the people of Israel would see the radiant glow of his face. So he would put the veil over his face until he returned to speak with the Lord* (Exodus 34:32-35).

Reading and hearing of the manifested glory of God stirs within my heart a desire to know God in a deeper way. So often I cry, "Show me Your glory, Jesus! Reveal Yourself to me. I want to know You more. Let Your cloud surround me too." Dear reader, I know that you too desire to draw closer to God.

Now, here's the wonderful news! The same cloud that enveloped Moses and Kathryn Kuhlman dwells in you. For that cloud is the Holy Spirit. The Holy Spirit is God's abiding presence. He was the cloud that guided the children of Israel through the wilderness.

> *The Lord went ahead of them. He guided them during the day with a pillar of cloud, and He provided light at night with a pillar of fire. This allowed them to travel by day or by night* (Exodus 13:21).

In the same way that the Holy Spirit guided the children of Israel through the wilderness, so He guides you today. To stay within the will of God, simply follow the Holy Spirit. There's a saying I have that I use whenever I sense God changing my direction in life or ministry. I say, "The Cloud is moving."

This same cloud also filled the temple where the priests were ministering. The power of the glory of God was so overwhelming that the priests were unable to stand in it.

> *It came even to pass, as the trumpeters and singers were as one, to make one sound to be heard in praising and thanking the Lord; and when they lifted up their voice with the trumpets and cymbals and instruments of music, and praised the Lord, saying, For He is good; for His mercy endureth for ever: that then the house was filled with a cloud, even the house of the Lord; so that the priests could not stand to minister by reason of the cloud: for the glory of the Lord had filled the house of God* (2 Chronicles 5:13-14 KJV).

The presence of the Holy Spirit also manifested in the form of a cloud at the transfiguration of Jesus.

> *But even as he spoke, a bright cloud overshadowed them, and a voice from the cloud said, "This is My dearly loved Son, who brings Me great joy. Listen to Him." The disciples were terrified and fell face down on the ground* (Matthew 17:5-6).

The cloud represents the Holy Spirit's guidance and glorious presence in your life. He surrounds you and reveals the glory of God. He rests on His new tabernacle, you. The cloud can be symbolic of the Holy Spirit.

THE SEAL

Sadly, many Christians are afraid of losing their salvation. For now, at least in this book, I will avoid the debate about whether or not one can lose his or her salvation. What I'd rather focus on here is the fact that many believers just simply do not understand the work of salvation.

Often, I receive very specific questions from very fearful people who are wondering if they have done something to lose their salvation. The questions vary in specifics but are exactly alike at the core. "Brother David, I listened to a worldly song, and I felt bad—have I lost my salvation?" "David, I spoke ungodly words in anger toward my spouse, and now I feel a weight of guilt on me. Did I lose my salvation?" "Brother David, I don't feel God near me anymore. Am I still saved?"

Not a single believer should live under the paranoia, the constant fear, of being cast away from God's salvation. We place much faith in the power of our misdeeds and not enough in God's ability to secure that which He has purchased.

What's even sadder is the fact that most people I try to counsel out of such paranoia are much too busied in the mind to pay any attention to the truth. The truth can liberate them from the religious weight of performance-based faith, but they don't pause to really receive that truth. They obsess over the details about their own specific errors and ignore the principles of truth that apply to all. They long for a specific assurance that what they have done in particular has not disqualified them from the family of God.

So, dear reader, please read this carefully: salvation is quite simple. Jesus did the work, and He just asks that you believe in His accomplishment. Of course, we must live righteously thereafter, but not in order to gain salvation. We don't live holy to be saved; we choose to live holy *because* we are saved.

Still, even knowing this information about the simplicity of salvation, many Christians live their lives in misery. They carry the weight of their sins and live in fear. They live in fear because they think their salvation depends on their performance, when it doesn't. Again, I must emphasize that I believe in holy living, and I believe that there are consequences to sin.

But that doesn't mean that the believer isn't going through a transformation. Perfection is a process.

Thankfully, we have the Holy Spirit to help us defeat the religious paradigms that can so easily infect the mind. He is the One who assures us that we belong to God. I daresay that convincing you of your new identity is one of His most important works.

The Holy Spirit is the "down payment" on your heavenly inheritance. Yes, Jesus paid the price in full for your salvation when He gave His life upon the cross. However, the Holy Spirit is God's guarantee that we will receive the salvation for which Christ died to give us. The day of redemption is a certain reality for you and me because we have the Holy Spirit.

And He has identified us as His own by placing the Holy Spirit in our hearts as the first installment that guarantees everything He has promised us (2 Corinthians 1:22).

Because we have the Holy Spirit, we can be assured that we belong to God, and because we belong to God, we can be assured of all He has promised to give us and do for us through Jesus Christ. The Holy Spirit is your mark and guarantee. He is God's pledge and seal of promise upon you.

In Jewish wedding culture, the father of the groom would usually be the one who picked the bride for his son. After the father of the groom found whom he believed to be the choice bride, he would approach the bride and her family. There would be a written marriage agreement made. After the written agreement was finished, it was customary for the father of the groom to give a gift to the father of the bride. That gift acted as a deposit for the bride. It was a promissory note, a guarantee of the groom's intentions to marry. Once that deposit was made, the intent to marry would become official.

The Jewish wedding traditions, like many of the Jewish traditions, mirror the spiritual realm.

Just as the father of the groom selects the bride, so God the Father has chosen to give the Church to His Son. And just as the father of the groom leaves a gift representing a promise, so God fills you with His Holy Spirit, His divine promise.

While here upon the earth, we receive many things from the Lord. And many people, when they get to Heaven, will be saddened to discover what they could have experienced while here on earth. Still, not everything that God has promised us concerning our salvation can be experienced here and now. For example, the new glorified bodies we will receive cannot now be obtained. So, the Holy Spirit is God's seal of promise in you, guaranteeing that you will eventually receive it all!

> *For we will put on heavenly bodies; we will not be spirits without bodies. While we live in these earthly bodies, we groan and sigh, but it's not that we want to die and get rid of these bodies that clothe us. Rather, we want to put on our new bodies so that these dying bodies will be swallowed up by life. God Himself has prepared us for this, and as a guarantee He has given us His Holy Spirit* (2 Corinthians 5:3-5).

> *In whom ye also trusted, after that ye heard the word of truth, the gospel of your salvation: in whom also after that ye believed, ye were sealed with that holy Spirit of promise, which is the earnest of our inheritance until the redemption of the purchased possession, unto the praise of His glory* (Ephesians 1:13-14 KJV).

The seal represents the certainty that we receive from the Holy Spirit. Despite what our emotions tell us, despite what the lies of the enemy tell us, despite what our own human reasoning tells us, we know that we belong to God because of the Holy Spirit, the seal of the promise of salvation. The seal, the Holy Spirit, is God's fear-defeating, peace-giving promise to us, the assurance of our own salvation. The seal can be symbolic of the Holy Spirit.

WATER

I must have been fourteen years old the first time I went to see Pastor Benny Hinn minister in person. Before that, I had read a few of his books and watched him on television. The service took place in Anaheim, California, at what was then called the Arrowhead Pond Arena. My grandfather was the one who drove me to the arena. For weeks, I had looked forward to the service. I recall Pastor Benny on his television program saying that something special was going to happen at that particular service, and I believed it. In fact, I just knew it. I was filled with faith and expectation.

Being that this was the first time I had ever gone to hear Pastor Benny minister, I did not know that showing up "on time" was actually showing up "late." Thousands had stood in line several hours before the service was to begin.

Unfortunately, we weren't even on time by normal standards. A sensitive family matter had delayed us by a couple hours. So, by the time we arrived, the service was already in progress. Still, when we pulled up to the venue, there were hundreds of people outside, shuffling in to find seats. So, we weren't a part of the early crowd, and we weren't a part of the "on time" crowd. We were a part of the "arrived at the service in the middle of Pastor Benny's sermon" crowd.

Mind you, we still had to park. I began to wonder if we would even be able to find seats.

As soon as we parked, I got out of the car and began to move toward the arena entrance. My hurried steps created a noticeable distance between me and my grandfather. I stopped so that the gap would close. I didn't want to seem too excited, but I think he could tell that I just wanted to get into the arena. As much as I wanted to move quickly, my grandfather's intentional, slow-paced steps were actually setting me up for a divine encounter that would alter the course of my life.

Eventually, we got out of the parking garage, moved beyond some disgruntled protestors, and made our way into the arena foyer. "There are no seats on the floor," an usher informed us. "Go upstairs." So we moved to the next level. There just so happened to be a couple of seats available for us on that level. When we sat down, Pastor Benny had already been ministering. I recall him talking about a Muslim family that had encountered Jesus in a supernatural way.

An hour or two passed—heavenly worship, deep teaching of the Word, awe-inspiring miracles. I didn't want that service to end. As it came to a close, the atmosphere in the arena shifted. Certainly, there was already a very evident manifestation of the Holy Spirit's presence—you could sense Him all around the room. But it seemed as though the air was charged with power. Pastor Benny then boldly spoke out, "I want every preacher of the Gospel to get down here!" At first, I hesitated because of my age, but something deeper within me said, "You're a preacher. Go!"

I hurried down to the front, but because of where I was sitting, I wasn't able to get there before the large crowd. On both sides of the platform there was a staircase. People were being ushered up those staircases to receive prayer from Pastor Benny. I said, "Lord, please, let me go up there and receive."

Because of the way the crowd pressed behind me and in front of me, I found myself pinned between the crowd and the platform. I wasn't being crushed, but I was being pushed aside. There was no way I was getting to that staircase. I paused for a moment to try to figure out how I could get on the platform, and in that moment of pause, I realized that my body was vibrating. I thought I was cold but soon realized that what I was feeling was the power of God.

The choir sang, "Holy, holy, holy are You, Lord," as Pastor Benny moved back and forth across the platform laying hands on people. The platform was high enough to level with my neck. So I just stood there, looking at the people receiving from the Lord, my body still trembling. I could literally feel a current moving across the floor of the platform. It was as if there was a river on that stage.

I looked up onto the platform and noticed a couple of ushers. Somehow, I made eye contact with one of the ushers, and he just reached out his hand. I don't know who that man was, but he for some reason decided to break protocol and pull me up onto the stage. As I got onto the platform, I felt the power of God intensify. Not only was my whole body shaking—it was going numb.

The ushers moved me forward. I looked ahead and saw Pastor Benny making his way back toward my side of the platform. His nose was red, and he was praying in tongues. I closed my eyes and focused on receiving from the Lord. I felt Pastor Benny gently touch the side of my face—he didn't push or even nudge me.

The next thing I knew, I opened my eyes and was looking up at the arena ceiling. Then I looked down to see my legs shaking under the power of the Holy Spirit. Then, I was off of the floor and looking straight forward again—I was being picked up by the ushers. As they escorted me off the stage, I felt refreshed. I felt like someone had dunked me in a cold river. I looked around to see other people on the floor shaking. They were too overcome with God's power to be able to walk back to their seats.

Something special happened for me that day. I received an impartation from the river of God. Had I been one minute earlier or one minute later, I wouldn't have been on that platform. Something changed in my ministry from that day forward. Looking back, I can't help but describe what I experienced as a refreshing moment in the river of the Spirit.

We all, from time to time, enter into the place where we find ourselves spiritually tired and drained. The demands of living, paired with a waning prayer life, can produce a dryness of the soul. Sometimes we wander into dry places because we tend to neglect spiritual matters. You may find yourself in places that are dry, like the desert. In the spiritual desert, you become tired, frustrated, weak, and apathetic. Responsibilities and needs, like the intense heat from the beaming sun, drain you of vitality.

Life can sometimes be like a desert, but the Holy Spirit is always like a river.

> On the last day, the climax of the festival, Jesus stood and shouted to the crowds, "Anyone who is thirsty may come to Me! Anyone who believes in Me may come and drink! For the Scriptures declare, 'Rivers of living water will flow from His heart.'" (When He said "living water," He was speaking of the Spirit, who would be given to everyone believing in Him. But the Spirit had not yet been given, because Jesus had not yet entered into His glory.) (John 7:37-39)

The presence of the Holy Spirit brings life. His nearness is refreshing and restores the vitality of your soul. Because the waters flow from your spirit within, you never have to worry about emptying your source.

The Holy Spirit is not only represented by refreshing rivers of living water; He is also represented by rain (side note: this is also why the cloud is a symbol of the Holy Spirit; the cloud brings the rain).

The prophet Joel prophesied the coming of rain. He was referring to natural rain, but he went on to prophesy that God would "pour out" His Spirit. The mentioning of the Spirit and rain together creates this clear symbolic parallel—the Holy Spirit is the rain of Heaven.

> Be glad then, ye children of Zion, and rejoice in the Lord your God: for He hath given you the former rain moderately, and He will cause to come down for you the rain, the former rain, and

the latter rain in the first month.... And it shall come to pass afterward, that I will pour out My spirit upon all flesh; and your sons and your daughters shall prophesy, your old men shall dream dreams, your young men shall see visions: And also upon the servants and upon the handmaids in those days will I pour out My spirit (Joel 2:23,28-29 KJV).

Water cleanses, quenches, refreshes, and gives life. The Holy Spirit cleanses your soul, quenches your spiritual thirst, and refreshes your being. Wherever the rivers and rain of the Holy Spirit touch, there is life.

Jesus replied, "Anyone who drinks this water will soon become thirsty again. But those who drink the water I give will never be thirsty again. It becomes a fresh, bubbling spring within them, giving them eternal life" (John 4:13-14).

Water represents the Holy Spirit's ability to refresh us, quench our spiritual thirst, cleanse us, and bring forth life wherever He flows. He is the rain of Heaven, and He is the living river that flows from within. Water can be symbolic for the Holy Spirit.

WINE

One of the first videos I ever posted on YouTube featured footage from a service that I held in the state of Pennsylvania. The service was a youth and young adult service, and it was one of the first in which I ever ministered. In the video, you can see the power of the Holy Spirit touching spiritually hungry teens and young adults.

At one point in the service, all I asked people to do was to say the name "Jesus," and when they did, they fell under the power of God. Many of them began to laugh as they received the Holy Spirit's touch.

Another time, I was praying over someone who battled with severe depression. She told me that it had been years since she laughed—truly laughed. I simply prayed, "Lord, take away this depression and fill her with Your joy." Then, a heat rushed over her body, she fell to the floor, and she began to burst out in laughter. There was nothing bizarre or "off" about it. She truly was receiving joy.

In fact, the joy she was experiencing was so powerful that the people in the congregation began to laugh. People weren't moving about in chaos or howling with belligerence. They were simply laughing. The presence of the Holy Spirit brought joy, and that joy brought laughter. It was that simple. They received the wine of Heaven.

Admittedly, I've seen many abuse the notion that the Holy Spirit gives us joy. You too might have seen the abuse—people acting belligerent and wacky. They display fleshly behavior and claim to be "under the joy of the Spirit" or "drunk in the Spirit." But the existence of the counterfeit isn't a cause to reject the genuine. Sure, there are those who become wacky, bizarre, and disorderly. However, there are also *genuine* moves of the Holy Spirit in which people become so filled with joy that they cannot help but laugh. I will concede this: when "holy laughter" becomes the long-term emphasis of a ministry or individual, that's when you get into the flesh. But, still, that doesn't mean that the Lord can't give us laughter and joy by His Holy Spirit. The joy of the Holy Spirit can be a beautiful display of God's power if it's not exaggerated or abused by the flesh.

And while a life of drunkenness is clearly and adamantly condemned in the Scripture, wine can represent prosperity, joy, and the Holy Spirit. In the Book of Ephesians, Paul the apostle instructs the Church to avoid drunkenness and instead to experience the infilling of the Holy Spirit:

> *Don't be drunk with wine, because that will ruin your life. Instead, be filled with the Holy Spirit* (Ephesians 5:18).

The believer does not need wine to experience joy. Wine can only give unfulfilling counterfeits of what the Holy Spirit offers. The Holy Spirit is the wine of Heaven.

In the Book of Acts, when the Holy Spirit came upon the New Testament Church, those who saw the Holy Spirit's influence on the believers assumed that they were drunk.

> *But others in the crowd ridiculed them, saying, "They're just drunk, that's all!" Then Peter stepped forward with the eleven other apostles and shouted to the crowd, "Listen carefully, all of you, fellow Jews and residents of Jerusalem! Make no mistake about this. These people are not drunk, as some of you are assuming. Nine o'clock in the morning is much too early for that"* (Acts 2:13-15).

Of course, the Holy Spirit does not come to make us senseless and silly; He makes us sharp and bold. Many have abused those verses in Acts to defend bizarre and ungodly behavior. I believe in the joy and power of the Holy Spirit, but much of what we see on display today is just the flesh.

So what was it that made the onlookers assume that the believers were drunk? It's because they were acting under a new influence. They were behaving abnormally. They were speaking and moving in a way that was different. No, they weren't belligerent, but they were bold! They weren't incapacitated, but they were joyful.

The Holy Spirit is compared with wine, not because He brings foolishness and chaos, but because He brings boldness and joy. Just as people receive wine in celebration, so are we to receive the Holy Spirit with gladness. His presence, like wine, marks the occasion.

Wine represents the joy, prosperity, and boldness brought about by the Holy Spirit. It too can be symbolic of the Holy Spirit.

HOLY SPIRIT SYMBOLISM

Symbolism is a powerful way that God speaks to us through His Word. So, it's important that no interpretation or meaning be forced upon the Scriptures and that all conclusions agree with the clear teachings of the Bible. To keep the scales balanced, it's also important to be attentive to what the Bible says so that you can see the effects of the invisible hand of the Holy Spirit at work. He fills the Scripture, and knowing His symbols will help you find Him.

Chapter 2

THE HOLY SPIRIT IN
GENESIS

THE SPIRIT OF CREATION—*Genesis 1:2*

The Holy Spirit creates and brings new beginnings.

In the beginning was the Word, and the Holy Spirit was with Him also (see John 1:1; Gen. 1:2). Genesis 1:2 is the very first verse of the Bible that mentions the Holy Spirit. You can't even get past the second verse of the first book of the Bible before you witness the Holy Spirit's power in action.

> *The earth was formless and empty, and darkness covered the deep waters. And the Spirit of God was hovering over the surface of the waters* (Genesis 1:2).

We find Him in the creation narrative. He is the ancient Spirit of God, the breath at the beginning.

> *By the word of the Lord were the heavens made; and all the host of them by the breath of his mouth* (Psalm 33:6 KJV).

The Holy Spirit not only was involved in the act of creation—He was crucial to the act of creation.

We know this because the Scripture tells us that the Holy Spirit "hovered" above the face of the deep. The word *hovered* in the Hebrew is *rachaph*, which means "to flutter, move, shake, or brood." The verb gives us an image of a bird. In this case, I imagine a dove, one of the symbols of the Person of the Holy Spirit.

Like a dove, the Holy Spirit brooded, fluttered, and hovered over the surface of the waters.

In reference to a bird, "to brood" means "to sit on eggs in order to hatch them." Brooding is the incubation of an egg. The Holy Spirit brooded over the face of the deep to incubate creation.

> *By faith we understand that the entire universe was formed at God's command, that what we now see did not come from anything that can be seen* (Hebrews 11:3).

The Scripture tells us that all of creation was brought forth from the Word of God. God's voice carried the complex code that would, so to speak, program all that exists today. Everything is under the command of His Word. Even the *laws* of the physical universe must obey Him. And why wouldn't they? After all, it was His voice that put them into place. Every molecule in your body, every bit of matter in this universe, time itself, and the fabric of space were all brought forth by the Lord's Word.

The Holy Spirit incubated the very commands of the Father; He brooded over that Word and caused it to become creation. The potential of all that would be—every star, every mind, every possibility—was incubated by the Holy Spirit. He fluttered over the Word of God.

In the beginning, God the Father spoke the Word over the face of the deep, where the Holy Spirit hovered. The Holy Spirit took the seed of the Word of God and moved upon it, causing all of creation to come into existence.

Sadly, God's creation fell into the abyss of sinful dismay. Turning from the privilege of fellowship with God, man chose to act contrary to God's commands. Stemming from the disobedience of Adam and Eve, sin eventually grew among humanity. So God, for the sake of His own righteousness and the future of the human race, had to begin anew. He chose to utterly destroy all life on earth, except for a select few who demonstrated righteous living in the sight of God.

Noah, his family, and small groups of each kind of animal were all spared from the flood that God used to cleanse the earth. God instructed Noah to build an ark within which the chosen few were to take refuge from the destructive waters. Eventually, the flood waters began to recede. However, it wasn't until 150 days after the flood began that Noah's ark came to rest on the mountains of Ararat. Noah and all who were aboard the ark waited patiently for the waters to recede enough for dry land to appear. Later, in an attempt to find dry ground, Noah used the birds aboard the ark.

After another forty days, Noah opened the window he had made in the boat and released a raven. The bird flew back and forth until the floodwaters on the earth had dried up. He also released a dove to see if the water had receded and it could find dry ground. But the dove could find no place to land because the water still covered the ground. So it returned to the boat, and Noah held out his hand and drew the dove back inside. After waiting another seven days, Noah released the dove again. This time the dove returned to him in the evening with a fresh olive leaf in its beak. Then Noah knew that the floodwaters were almost gone. He waited another seven days and then released the dove again. This time it did not come back (Genesis 8:6-12).

Here again we see the dove involved in a beginning. Creation was beginning again, and the dove is seen participating in the inception of a new genesis. Seeking the place fit for a new beginning, Noah released the dove from the ark. The dove flew about in search of the new creation—the land where all things could begin again. The third time that the dove was released from the ark, it disappeared. It was never again seen. It flew away in search of the place to begin a new creation. It was never described as returning to the ark, because it found dry land.

Now think of the powerful symbolism here. The Holy Spirit brooded over the face of the deep at the beginning. Creation falls. God desires to begin again. Then, we see a dove flying away from the ark in search of a place to begin again. It sought to land in the place of the new creation.

Genesis does not record the dove landing on dry land. From the perspective of the biblical narrative, we never see the dove landing.

That is, we never see it landing until much, much later.

Matthew's Gospel shows us a dove descending upon the One who would help creation truly begin again. Announcing the dawn of the new creation, the Holy Spirit descends upon Jesus like a dove.

After His baptism, as Jesus came up out of the water, the heavens were opened and He saw the Spirit of God descending like a dove and settling on Him. And a voice from heaven said, "This is My dearly loved Son, who brings Me great joy" (Matthew 3:16-17).

So the Holy Spirit brooded over creation in the Book of Genesis. We see that He is present at the beginning of the Old Testament. And He is seen again at the beginning of the New Testament during the baptism of Jesus.

In the beginning, the Holy Spirit brooded over the face of the deep, announcing the creation of all things. Then the Holy Spirit came upon Jesus, signaling to the world that God was once again creating. His resting upon the Master was the hailing of the new creation—not a creation of the material but a new creation of the spiritual within the hearts of people. The new creation, the transformative miracle of salvation at work within the hearts of men, is revealed when the Word of the Gospel is met with the convicting power of the Holy Spirit.

Together, the Word and the Spirit equal creation. That's what the Holy Spirit does—He takes the Word and creates with it.

Dear reader, this is a powerful truth. Wherever you have the Word and the Spirit, you have creation. Jesus, the Word made flesh, was filled with the Spirit. That's why when Jesus spoke, there was creative power. He could multiply food, fortify the limbs of the lame, restore sight to blind eyes, and even raise the dead.

He wants to create in you. He wants to craft your being into the image of Jesus. He wants to create in you and for you.

He broods over every promise of God. He broods over every prayer you utter. He broods over every declaration that God has made concerning you. In faith, now, turn to Him. He doesn't just hover about you. He dwells within you, longing to bring about the new creation, longing to manifest the will of the Father in your life, longing to create on your behalf. Let Him create again and form the image of Jesus in you.

NAME CHANGER—*Genesis 17:5*

What's more, I am changing your name. It will no longer be Abram. Instead, you will be called Abraham, for you will be the father of many nations (Genesis 17:5).

The fifth letter of the Hebrew alphabet, the letter *Hei*, can represent the breath of God. It was the letter added to the name Abram, causing it to become Abraham. God breathed His Spirit into Abram's name, forever transforming his name and nature.

THE SPIRIT OF THE DREAMER—*Genesis 41:38*

The Holy Spirit gives, reveals, protects, and fulfills dreams.

When I was eleven years old, the Lord showed me my future. He showed me that I would be in the healing ministry. He showed me that I would use media and books to reach people. He showed me that I was to emphasize evangelism. He even showed me details like what television networks I would air my programs on, what key Christian leaders I would meet, and how I was to structure the ministry itself.

No, He didn't show me *every* detail, and walking the path He revealed to me still requires a lot of faith. But, by the Spirit, I did catch a glimpse of my future in ministry. So deep within I knew that the Lord wanted me to leverage media and television for the sake of the Gospel.

In 2012, I stepped out in faith and announced that my ministry was beginning a funding campaign to create a television production studio. At that point, I had already made some connections with certain television networks, but airtime was by no means a guarantee. So it was faith—it was all faith. All I really had was a God-given dream and a ministry infrastructure that He told me how to build.

During the campaign, I grew frustrated at the pace of our fundraising. Many people would make commitments and then disappear, never fulfilling their commitments. I was thankful for those who were partnering with me in the endeavor to reach more souls through television and media, but I admit that I was growing discouraged.

I did everything I knew to do. My team and I raised funds. We organized. We mailed letters, sent e-mails, and posted social media statuses. But our campaign fund hardly grew. I felt as though I was pressing my hands up against a giant boulder. I knew that if I could just get the thing moving, the momentum would pick up.

Some people mocked me. Others "rebuked" me for raising money for the Gospel. Even pastors I looked up to came out against me. Some of my spiritual heroes told me that what I was trying to do was impossible and that I was better off waiting until I was more "seasoned" in the faith.

All I knew is that God had spoken to me. I didn't know how the dream would come to pass, but I knew it would. I just knew it.

It was during those discouraging months that I went to Northern California to minister at a small church in a relatively small city. The pastor of that church was also a business owner—and a very successful one at that. He was known for being a generous giver to the Gospel.

I ministered at his Sunday morning service. During that service, I had done only what I had always done. I simply ministered the Word to the believers, preached the Gospel to the lost, and ministered healing to the sick. But during that service, there was a special moment that occurred. With hands lifted and voices raised, the congregation and I just sang to the Lord. Again, I must emphasize that I did nothing different than what I normally do when I minister. But the Lord's presence came to overshadow that place in an obvious way. The Holy Spirit's presence became so tangible, so thick, that people began to weep. All over the building, people were weeping.

I opened my eyes to see how the Lord was touching His people, and when I did, I saw the pastor. He had tears streaming down his face. He was being profoundly moved by the Holy Spirit.

There was a connection being made between the pastor and our ministry that day. His heart was so moved that months later, he wrote a check to our ministry that was enough to fund the building of our first production studio. Again, I did nothing out of the ordinary. It was all God.

Looking back, the man who wrote the check told me, "You know, Diga, that's not normal. God connected us. We're covenant." When I asked him why he gave such a large amount to our ministry—the largest gift he had ever sown into a ministry—he explained, "It was God. It was just God."

Throughout the years, the Holy Spirit protected that dream, and eventually He brought it to pass. When I was told what I was to do for the Lord, I didn't have the connections, the equipment, the expertise, or even the money to do it. All I had was a dream from the Lord, and He brought it to pass.

When I think of dreams and dreamers, I think of Joseph. The Scripture tells us that Joseph had the Holy Spirit.

So Pharaoh asked his officials, "Can we find anyone else like this man so obviously filled with the spirit of God?" (Genesis 41:38)

Joseph didn't begin in favor with Pharaoh. He began with just a couple of dreams from the Lord.

Now Joseph was favored over his brothers by his father, Jacob. This favor was demonstrated in the giving of a colorful coat from Joseph's loving father.

Jacob loved Joseph more than any of his other children because Joseph had been born to him in his old age. So one day Jacob had a special gift made for Joseph—a beautiful robe (Genesis 37:3).

Joseph's brothers were provoked to envy, and that envy became deep hatred for Joseph. The Scripture tells us that Joseph's brothers couldn't even bring themselves to utter a single word of kindness toward him (see Gen. 37:4). The hatred of his brothers should have discouraged Joseph from sharing his divine dream with the family, but Joseph shared the dream anyway.

One night Joseph had a dream, and when he told his brothers about it, they hated him more than ever. "Listen to this dream," he said. "We were out in the field, tying up bundles of grain. Suddenly my bundle stood up, and your bundles all gathered around and bowed low before mine!" (Genesis 37:5-7)

The dream stirred the embers of hatred within the hearts of Joseph's brothers. They all understood its meaning—that Joseph would rule over his brothers. Already filled with disdain for Joseph, the brothers were agitated by the sharing of such an audacious dream. They hated him more for it.

Again, Joseph had a dream. This time, it was about him ruling over not just his brothers, but his mother and father also.

Eventually, the jealousy of Joseph's brothers would influence them to do something desperately hateful. Originally planning to kill Joseph, the brothers changed their minds and instead sold Joseph into slavery after ripping away his colorful coat.

To hide their sin, the brothers took Joseph's coat, dipped it in the blood of a young goat, and convinced their father that Joseph had been killed by a wild animal.

Joseph found himself in the service of a man named Potiphar, but circumstances led him to become unjustly imprisoned. While in prison, Joseph accurately interpreted the dreams of two fellow inmates, a baker and a cup-bearer (who both served Pharaoh directly).

And they replied, "We both had dreams last night, but no one can tell us what they mean." "Interpreting dreams is God's business," Joseph replied. "Go ahead and tell me your dreams" (Genesis 40:8).

Through the interpretation of the dreams, Joseph was able to correctly prophesy that the cup-bearer would be restored to his position at Pharaoh's side in three days' time, while the baker would be executed in three days' time. In exchange for interpreting the dreams, Joseph asked one thing:

And please remember me and do me a favor when things go well for you. Mention me to Pharaoh, so he might let me out of this place (Genesis 40:14).

But when the cup-bearer was restored to his position three days later, he had forgotten to mention Joseph to Pharaoh. It wasn't until two years later that the cup-bearer remembered what Joseph had asked of him.

Two full years later, Pharaoh dreamed that he was standing on the bank of the Nile River (Genesis 41:1).

In that dream, Pharaoh saw seven healthy cows come out of the river, and then he saw seven scrawny cows come out of the river behind them. The scrawny cows ate the healthy cows. Pharaoh awoke and fell asleep again. Then Pharaoh had a second dream in which he saw seven heads of well-grown wheat appear on a stalk. Seven unhealthy heads of wheat then came and swallowed up the well-grown ones.

Those dreams so intensely troubled Pharaoh that he searched for someone who could interpret them.

The next morning Pharaoh was very disturbed by the dreams. So he called for all the magicians and wise men of Egypt. When Pharaoh told them his dreams, not one of them could tell him what they meant (Genesis 41:8).

It was then that the cup-bearer remembered Joseph.

Finally, the king's chief cup-bearer spoke up. "Today I have been reminded of my failure," he told Pharaoh.... There was a young Hebrew man with us in the prison who was a slave of the captain of the guard. We told him our dreams, and he told us what each of our dreams meant. And everything happened just as he had predicted. I was restored to my position as cup-bearer, and the chief baker was executed and impaled on a pole" (Genesis 41:9,12-13).

Joseph was released from prison, and he gave Pharaoh the interpretation of the troubling dreams. The dreams both meant the same thing: in the land of Egypt, there would be seven years of abundance and then seven years of famine. God had given Pharaoh a warning so that preparations could be made.

Pharaoh received the prophetic interpretation and appointed Joseph as second in command of all of Egypt so that he could help facilitate the preparations for the famine. And when Pharaoh had appointed Joseph, Joseph's dreams came true. Joseph's family found themselves under Joseph's rulership—just as had been foretold in Joseph's dreams.

So Pharaoh asked his officials, "Can we find anyone else like this man so obviously filled with the spirit of God?" (Genesis 41:38).

The Holy Spirit is the Spirit of the dreamer. He speaks to us in visions of the night, and He also speaks to our hearts in our waking hours. God feels and fulfills His desires through us by the Holy Spirit. The Holy Spirit presents the dream to you and works to bring it to pass. You only need to participate in His work through faithfulness and obedience. It's not your ability that will bring the dream to pass; it's the ability of the Holy Spirit within you.

When trying to obtain the resources to build my ministry's first television studio, I had done everything I knew to do, but it wasn't until the Holy Spirit decided to make a move that everything shifted.

The Holy Spirit will touch the hearts that need to be touched in order to bring the dream to pass. Just let Him work. For me, He touched the heart of a businessman. For Joseph, He touched the heart of Pharaoh. It wasn't my talent that captured the attention of my donor, and it wasn't Joseph's intellect that brought him into favor with Pharaoh—it was the Spirit of the Dreamer, the Holy Spirit.

The same Holy Spirit who rested upon Joseph lives within you. Let the dream be awakened in you, for the Spirit of God will surely bring it to pass.

Chapter 3

THE HOLY SPIRIT IN
EXODUS

THE FIRE OF EVANGELISM—*Exodus 3:2*

The Holy Spirit has and gives a passion for lost souls.

Although Joseph found favor with the Egyptians, his descendants—God's people—would eventually find themselves in slavery under the Egyptians.

> *Eventually, a new king came to power in Egypt who knew nothing about Joseph or what he had done. He said to his people, "Look, the people of Israel now outnumber us and are stronger than we are. We must make a plan to keep them from growing even more. If we don't, and if war breaks out, they will join our enemies and fight against us. Then they will escape from the country"* (Exodus 1:8-10).

The enslavement of the Israelites is a prophetic picture of humanity in sin. The human race wallows under the oppressive darkness of sin. Sin strips all of its prisoners of dignity, divinity, and destiny. Deep within, the soul of every person cries out for freedom, for deliverance. And we serve a God who can hear those cries.

Moses was tending the flock of his father-in-law when he came to encounter the Holy Spirit.

> *One day Moses was tending the flock of his father-in-law, Jethro, the priest of Midian. He led the flock far into the wilderness and came to Sinai, the mountain of God. There the angel of the Lord appeared to him in a blazing fire from the middle of a bush. Moses stared in amazement. Though the bush was engulfed in flames, it*

didn't burn up. "This is amazing," Moses said to himself. "Why isn't that bush burning up? I must go see it." When the Lord saw Moses coming to take a closer look, God called to him from the middle of the bush, "Moses! Moses!" "Here I am!" Moses replied. "Do not come any closer," the Lord warned. "Take off your sandals, for you are standing on holy ground. I am the God of your father— the God of Abraham, the God of Isaac, and the God of Jacob." When Moses heard this, he covered his face because he was afraid to look at God (Exodus 3:1-6).

Here we see the fire, the Holy Spirit's presence, appear before Moses. A voice speaks from the fire. Then, God declares His ability to see and hear the suffering of His people:

Then the Lord told him, "I have certainly seen the oppression of My people in Egypt. I have heard their cries of distress because of their harsh slave drivers. Yes, I am aware of their suffering" (Exodus 3:7).

Moses then discovers that God had chosen him to be used as the instrument of deliverance.

The fire of Heaven, the Holy Spirit, burns for the salvation of the oppressed. He can hear their cries.

There is no one on earth more passionate about the winning of the lost than the Holy Spirit. He desires to break the chains of sin from every soul. He is the Spirit of evangelism.

But you will receive power when the Holy Spirit comes upon you. And you will be My witnesses, telling people about Me everywhere—in Jerusalem, throughout Judea, in Samaria, and to the ends of the earth" (Acts 1:8).

What happens when the Holy Spirit comes upon you? The same thing that happened to Moses when he encountered the fire of God. The same thing that happened to the early Church that spread from Jerusalem and to the ends of the earth. They became witnesses. They became vessels of deliverance.

A sign that you have experienced a true encounter with the Holy Spirit is a passion to win souls. After coming into contact with the fire of God, Moses was determined to see God's people go free. Up until that time, he had spent decades in the mundane. All it takes is one touch from the Lord, a single moment with the Holy Spirit, to set your heart ablaze for the lost.

When you spend time with the Holy Spirit, His heart becomes your heart, His desires become your desires. You begin to see what He sees. You begin to hear what He hears.

Whenever I find myself in a crowded place, I look around at all the people moving in and out of my line of sight. I wonder where they are going and whether or not they know the Lord. My heart bends toward them, and I can hear their cries.

Can you hear the cry of the lost? Can you hear the cry of the drug-addicted, longing to be free from self-hatred and bondage? Can you hear the cry of the broken families, searching for a reason to hope again? Can you hear the cry of the suicidal, the self-righteous, the fearful, the per-verted, and the prideful? Can you hear the cry of a sin-bound people?

The Holy Spirit can. And when you come near to Him, your being also will be set aflame with a passionate love for the lost soul. You will burn with a holy dedication. You will become burdened with divine compassion. Your heart will ache with spiritual anguish. Everything in you will live to see just *one more* soul set free.

Like Moses, you've been appointed as a deliverer. You've been sent to a people. You've had contact with a fire. The Holy Spirit is the fire of evangelism.

THE PRECIOUS OIL—*Exodus 30:22-25*

There is a process to becoming surrendered under the Holy Spirit's power.

In my teen years, I so longed to be used by the Lord that I made the decision to separate myself from worldly cares. I didn't watch all the same things my friends watched. I didn't listen to all the same things my friends listened to. I didn't go to all the same places my friends went. I recall, on more than one occasion, walking out of a movie theater saying, "Lord, I will not compromise!"

I remember saying to the Holy Spirit, "Please, use my life for Your glory. Whatever it takes, Lord, use me. Whatever it costs, Lord, use my life. I just want Your presence and power. And when I feel the weight of the price I'll have to pay, remind me of this moment now. Remind me that I asked for this. Crush me as much as You need to, but Lord, whatever it takes, anoint me as much as I can possibly be anointed. I don't want to miss a single drop of oil."

To this day, when I face struggles, the Lord will remind me of that prayer I prayed. When the pressing comes, I remember that the power of God comes with a price. Your salvation is free, but the anointing will cost you everything. The price of the anointing is simply surrender. You want to know the key to power, honestly and truly? You have to die to self. Power is found in the death of the flesh.

I watched footage of Miss Kuhlman saying, "It costs everything. If you really want to know the price, if you really want to know the price, I'll tell you. It'll cost you everything. Kathryn Kuhlman died a long time ago. I know the day. I know the hour. I can go to the spot where Kathryn Kuhlman died."

How true that is.

The anointing is the power of God at work through you, and as you already know, the anointing oil is symbolic of the Holy Spirit. The anointing oil, a symbol for the Holy Spirit and His power, came with a price. The same is true of God's power. So what went into making the anointing oil? The Bible clearly tells us:

> Then the Lord said to Moses, "Collect choice spices—12 1/2 pounds of pure myrrh, 6 1/4 pounds of fragrant cinnamon, 6 1/4 pounds of fragrant calamus, and 12 1/2 pounds of cassia—as measured by the weight of the sanctuary shekel. Also get one gallon of olive oil. Like a skilled incense maker, blend these ingredients to make a holy anointing oil" (Exodus 30:22-25).

These are the ingredients of the anointing oil:

- Myrrh
- Cinnamon
- Calamus
- Cassia
- Olive Oil

Each ingredient speaks to how the Holy Spirit's power is produced in our lives. He is the costly anointing oil.

Myrrh

Myrrh is a gum-like substance that exudes from the bark of a shrub or a small tree. It was used for medicinal purposes and purification.

Myrrh represents purity.

The greater the purity within your life, the greater the power upon your life.

Make no mistake: the purity in your life matters. Time and again, I've seen servants of the Lord abandon their moral and spiritual purity to pursue things of the flesh. Although the effects do not show for quite a while, eventually those who practice ungodliness are exposed.

It's easy to be pure on a public platform, but the real power is found in secret purity.

> *Follow God's example, therefore, as dearly loved children and walk in the way of love, just as Christ loved us and gave Himself up for us as a fragrant offering and sacrifice to God. But among you there must not be even a hint of sexual immorality, or of any kind of impurity, or of greed, because these are improper for God's holy people* (Ephesians 5:1-3 NIV).

Yes, the anointing comes from the Holy Spirit, but your lifestyle matters. Your purity doesn't produce the anointing, but it does protect the anointing. Don't be deceived. The intensity of God's power in your life is directly proportionate to the purity in your life. The greater the purity, the clearer the prophetic. The greater the purity, the greater the miracles. The greater the purity, the heavier the glory.

Purity clears the flesh out of the way and allows the Holy Spirit to flow through you.

Cinnamon

Cinnamon represents sweetness.

Nothing will destroy the anointing on your life quite like bitterness.

What does bitterness have to do with lack of power? Think of the encounter that Peter and John had with a bitter sorcerer.

When they arrived, they prayed for the new believers there that they might receive the Holy Spirit, because the Holy Spirit had not yet come on any of them; they had simply been baptized in the name of the Lord Jesus. Then Peter and John placed their hands on them, and they received the Holy Spirit. When Simon saw that the Spirit was given at the laying on of the apostles' hands, he offered them money and said, "Give me also this ability so that everyone on whom I lay my hands may receive the Holy Spirit." Peter answered: "May your money perish with you, because you thought you could buy the gift of God with money! You have no part or share in this ministry, because your heart is not right before God. Repent of this wickedness and pray to the Lord in the hope that He may forgive you for having such a thought in your heart. For I see that you are full of bitterness and captive to sin" (Acts 8:15-23 NIV).

What was it that caused Peter to call the man bitter? Why was he so harsh in dealing with the sorcerer? I believe that Simon the Sorcerer was bitter with jealousy. He so desired to have what Peter and John had that he was willing to pay for it.

Was it wrong that he wanted God's power? Of course not. What made it wrong was *why* he wanted God's power. He wanted it for himself. He wanted it so that he could gain riches, status, and praise. That's what sorcerers seek to gain from power.

Bitterness is manifested in jealousy, and jealousy is manifested in competition. But sweetness is found when your motives are pure and your heart is free of carnal competition. If ever there was a crucial ingredient to the anointing oil, it would be this sweetness.

Unfortunately, bitterness finds its way into ministries. Ministers compete with ministers over social media followers, book sales, television ratings, church attendance, and pseudo-spiritual quotes. Dear God, no wonder the anointing is hard to find! Our preachers have turned into sorcerers.

Bitterness is counter-Kingdom, and competition is anti-Christ. I pray that God would slay the ambitions of an egocentric generation.

Let us obtain the sweetness of godly motives and do away with the bitterness of jealousy, ambition, ego, competition, and pretense. God will not anoint the bitter.

When Jesus received a bitter drink, He refused it even though it was mingled with myrrh (purity). Bitterness is so contrary to true ministry that Jesus will reject the bitter one, even if that one has moral purity. He'll reject the bitter one for use in the ministry, even if that one is otherwise pure.

And they gave Him to drink wine mingled with myrrh: but He received it not (Mark 15:23 KJV).

Sweetness, which is the absence of bitter jealousy and competition, allows the Holy Spirit to flow through you.

Calamus

Calamus is an Eastern plant, the Acorus calamus Linnaeus. Its stalk is cut, dried, and made into powder. That powder was used in some of the most expensive perfumes.

Calamus represents the fragrance of worship.

Our lives are a Christ-like fragrance rising up to God. But this fragrance is perceived differently by those who are being saved and by those who are perishing (2 Corinthians 2:15).

The Holy Spirit's presence is always within you. That's a biblical truth. So, worship isn't about bringing Him nearer to you; it's about you becoming more aware of Him. It is the awareness of the presence of God that makes one able to receive from it and sense it.

Worshipers live in the awareness of God's presence, and that awareness brings about the power of the Holy Spirit on one's life. That moment-to-moment awareness attracts divine appointments, divine favor, and divine connections. There is a fragrance around the people who worship the Lord continually. I learned early on that God favors those who worship Him. As a teenager in ministry, I would walk around and worship the Lord literally everywhere I went. I'm convinced that my worship caught His attention and helped shape the ministry early on.

Worship is of utmost importance. I heard a powerful man of God say, "If you have 60 minutes to pray, worship for 40."

Worship cultivates a place for the Holy Spirit to have His way. Worship allows the Holy Spirit to flow through you.

Cassia

The cassia plant had branches which held moisture. In order for it to grow properly or survive at all, it had to be rooted in wet areas, usually near a river.

Cassia represents roots or "process."

> *Oh, the joys of those who do not follow the advice of the wicked, or stand around with sinners, or join in with mockers. But they delight in the law of the Lord, meditating on it day and night. They are like trees planted along the riverbank, bearing fruit each season. Their leaves never wither, and they prosper in all they do* (Psalm 1:1-3).

You cannot rush God's process. Before God will use you, He will test you. Before God will reveal you, He will hide you. The anointing on your life, like the womb of a mother, will hide you in your development so that you live to see your birth.

Roots take time to grow.

I've heard many ministers say things like, "I want God to do a quick work with me" or "God is going to suddenly place me onto the scene." People who keep that sort of thinking rarely last long term. But the ones who say things like, "It's in God's timing" rarely fail. The process takes patience.

The deeper the roots, the more fruitful the plant.

To rush the process is to take away from the future quality of your ministry. When it comes to the long term, nothing will slow you down like a quick fix. Take the time to grow your roots deep into prayer and the Word.

When roots find their way into the ground, they have to go into isolated, dark places. That may be where you feel like you are right now. You might be saying, "Lord, I have so much to offer as a minister, but I feel like I'm hidden." The truth is that you probably feel hidden because you are hidden—and that's a good thing. It means your roots are going deep. The deeper the roots go, the darker it becomes around them.

This does not mean that you can't do anything for God right now; you can do something for the Lord in every season of life.

I'm talking about those times in life where you just know there's more and that "more" seems distant. In those times, it's important that you not resist the process. Process is a part of the preparation of the anointing.

Process allows the Holy Spirit to flow through you.

Olive Oil

To extract the oil from the olive, one must crush the olive. And before that, the olive must be shaken from the olive tree. The olive falls from the tree, its place of security and sustenance. Then pressure is applied to it, causing it to be crushed and to yield its oil.

This is what God does to us. Before He can use you, He must shake you from what is familiar and then crush you. He must disrupt all that makes you feel secure in order for you to see Him as your true source. Then He must press you until your image is marred, making way for the image of Jesus. It is the crushing, the pressure, that produces the oil. Trials and challenges, unwelcome as they may be, are your spiritual trainers.

> *Dear brothers and sisters, when troubles of any kind come your way, consider it an opportunity for great joy. For you know that when your faith is tested, your endurance has a chance to grow. So let it grow, for when your endurance is fully developed, you will be perfect and complete, needing nothing* (James 1:2-4).

When we are pressed by the pressures of life and ministry, we yield power, for God has made a deep deposit within you. If the Holy Spirit resides within you, then when you are pressed, His essence flows out of you. But again, you must be crushed if you are to yield such power.

Some say, "I have everything I need in Christ! I don't need to receive any more power." And they would be correct in saying so. However, the process of the precious oil isn't worked so that we might receive the Holy Spirit, but that He might flow from within us. For that to happen, one must be crushed. Think of the olive. The oil is already inside the olive, but it isn't until the olive is crushed that it yields the oil. And that oil, mixed with the other ingredients, becomes the precious anointing oil.

Today's pain is tomorrow's power.

Pressing allows the Holy Spirit to flow through you.

The Precious Oil

He is the One who empowers you unto every mighty work. He is the One who flows through you, transforming you and everyone you will ever influence. Like precious oil, He marks those who have been set aside for the purposes of God. He rests upon you. He is the precious oil. And when you allow yourself to be crushed to the point where you yield, He flows out of you. He is your purity. He is your sweetness. He is the fragrance that exudes from you, as you worship. He is the One who processes you in the hidden places of prayer, making you fit for use in God's intentional hands.

Through both the blessed and the trying times of life, let God work His process. When God processes you, the precious oil drips over into your life. That oil is the Person of the Holy Spirit.

THE EXPERT SPIRIT—*Exodus 31:1-6*

The Holy Spirit empowers us for the practical.

The Holy Spirit doesn't just empower us for ministry; He empowers us in all that we do. He wants to empower husbands, wives, mothers, fathers, business people, employees, and students.

The Holy Spirit is the Expert Spirit, and His touch improves every action of the believer.

When Moses went to meet with God at Mount Sinai, he wasn't just given commands for moral and civil duties; he also received a revelation of how the tabernacle was to be built. God gave him specific instructions on the crafting of the Ark of the Covenant, the gold lampstands, the incense altar, and the other furnishings of the tabernacle. Moses was even given instructions on how to craft the garments of the priests.

But to actually craft these things, God appointed certain men. They were men who were filled with the Holy Spirit.

> *Then the Lord said to Moses, "Look, I have specifically chosen Bezalel son of Uri, grandson of Hur, of the tribe of Judah. I have filled him with the Spirit of God, giving him great wisdom, ability, and expertise in all kinds of crafts. He is a master craftsman, expert in working with gold, silver, and bronze. He is skilled in engraving and mounting gemstones and in carving wood. He is a master at every craft! And I have personally appointed Oholiab son*

of Ahisamach, of the tribe of Dan, to be his assistant. Moreover, I have given special skill to all the gifted craftsmen so they can make all the things I have commanded you to make" (Exodus 31:1-6).

Even in the practical act of crafting, the Holy Spirit was involved.

The Holy Spirit is, literally, down to earth. He does not distance Himself from our practical living. He is an able Helper, not just in the matters of the supernatural, but also in the matters of the natural. He is God's empowering presence here upon the earth. He involves Himself in our day-to-day tasks and responsibilities; He desires to help you in all that you do.

We accept the fact that there is nothing too difficult for Him to perform but often lack the boldness to believe that there is nothing too small for Him to ignore.

To the business person, the Spirit is a business partner. To the parent, He is a wise guide. To the spouse, He is a counselor. To the student, He is a teacher. To all and in all, He is a helper and an expert.

Chapter 4

THE HOLY SPIRIT IN
LEVITICUS

THE SOVEREIGN FIRE—*Leviticus 9:24*

The Holy Spirit moves sovereignly.

Several years ago, I was watching a woman ministering on a Christian television channel. She ministered a powerful and profound word. Elegantly attired, she wore a classy black dress and carried herself well. She was poised, confident, and very magnetic.

After ministering her message, she moved out into the studio audience and proceeded to call people out so that she could give them prophetic words. I anticipated that the people would be moved by her prophetic declarations. I witnessed the opposite. Instead of nodding in the affirmative, the people responded to the woman's encouragements with bewildered facial expressions. One woman furrowed her eyebrows and slowly shook her head, indicating that the prophetic word wasn't exactly on point. To me, it appeared that the woman receiving the "word" felt awkward.

Since the prophetic wasn't exactly flowing, the woman preacher changed her approach. She then began to lay hands on the people. However, instead of seeing people falling under the power of God, I saw people being shoved backward into their seats. (It's one thing to lay hands aggressively with zeal and another thing to push so hard that people are bent over backwards.)

What I witnessed on my television was something that I had seen countless times before—human beings trying to force a move of the Holy Spirit.

Let me clarify: I'm *not* saying that we should not step out in faith to activate the power of God; I am saying that we should not step away from where God wants to go. When we don't see the Holy Spirit moving like we expect or desire, the answer isn't to try to make it look like Holy Spirit is moving. The answer is to find where the river is flowing and jump into that flow.

The Holy Spirit does the supernatural as we obey and do the practical. This kind of partnership between the minister and the Holy Spirit is found in the Book of Leviticus.

The Book of Leviticus is primarily a guide for the priests of Israel to follow. One of the major duties of those priests was the offering of sacrifice before the Lord on behalf of the people of Israel. The sacrifices were to be presented upon the altar. And it was upon that altar that the sovereign nature of the Holy Spirit was revealed.

For the first time, the priests performed their priestly duties. After presenting offerings of their own to the Lord, the priests gave offerings on behalf of the people of Israel. Among several kinds of offerings, the priests presented a burnt offering unto the Lord. When the priests began their work, they were met with a supernatural demonstration of the Holy Spirit's presence.

> *After that, Aaron raised his hands toward the people and blessed them. Then, after presenting the sin offering, the burnt offering, and the peace offering, he stepped down from the altar. Then Moses and Aaron went into the Tabernacle, and when they came back out, they blessed the people again, and the glory of the Lord appeared to the whole community. Fire blazed forth from the Lord's presence and consumed the burnt offering and the fat on the altar. When the people saw this, they shouted with joy and fell face down on the ground* (Leviticus 9:22-24).

As commanded, the priests presented their gifts upon the altar, but God was the One who sent the fire.

What is interesting is that earlier in the Book of Leviticus, the priests were given a strict instruction concerning the fire upon the altar:

> *Meanwhile, the fire on the altar must be kept burning; it must never go out. Each morning the priest will add fresh wood to the fire and arrange the burnt offering on it. He will then burn the fat of the peace offerings on it. Remember, the fire must be kept*

burning on the altar at all times. It must never go out (Leviticus 6:12-13).

The instructions were clear: never was the fire to be extinguished; it was to burn continually, indefinitely.

Here's what I noticed: the priests were never instructed to start the fire; they were simply instructed to keep the fire burning. The fire that burned upon the altar came directly from the presence of the Lord. The fire was started by God.

God didn't tell them to start that fire, because they were capable of starting only a manmade fire. They could not, through effort or persistence, spark a heavenly flame into existence. God didn't ask them to start the fire on the altar because they weren't capable of doing so—at least, not the kind of fire that was needed. The fire that was started was sovereignly sparked.

The Holy Spirit is the sovereign fire.

We cannot, by the will of men, stir Him to action. No measure of fervency can spark His consuming nature. It's not a matter of getting Him to come to us; it's a matter of us going to Him.

In due seasons, at divinely appointed times, God ignites the land. Sometimes He sets fire to a region, other times a nation. During these moves of God, souls are saved, the sick are healed, and the captives are released from the shame of their chains. Struggling to fully understand or appreciate the sovereignly kindled fires of the Spirit, we attach titles to these phenomena—revival, awakening, outpouring. Whatever one might come to call it, it's a beautiful demonstration of the Holy Spirit's power.

Some say that belief in these moves of God stagnates the activity of the Church. Their arguments employ tired clichés and recycled rhetoric. They chant the common idea, "If we wait around for revival, we'll never get anything done" or the especially overused, "You're waiting on God when God is waiting on you."

Of course, we are the Church. Of course, we must always be actively spreading the Gospel. We mustn't wait around for "revival," but believing in revival does not necessarily bind one to inactivity. You can both be active and still anticipate a coming move of God.

Besides, who cares about how people might abuse the hope of revival? What bearing does that have on the truth? Revival exists, whether people abuse the hope of it or not. Some say that looking to revival causes apathy; in me, the hope of revival inspires action. My point is that a hope should not be rejected simply because it is abused. The same is true of the hope of revival.

The truth is that God does send forth heavenly flames of His influence. Perhaps it's simply His response to the cries of His people. Perhaps it's just His divine timing. Perhaps it's a blending of the two. Regardless, there are certain occasions where God sovereignly pours out His Holy Spirit in a fresh and unique way. Sometimes, great awakenings come upon certain people, groups, or regions. But they always originate in the will of God.

And when God does send revival, He fully expects it to accompany a busy church. Revival is God's partnership with our labor, not His replacement of it. When the faithfulness of the Church connects with the sovereignty of God, true revival occurs.

Typically, those who claim, "I don't have to wait for revival; I am revival," as well as those who use the excuse, "I'm just waiting on God," both misunderstand the partnership between the Holy Spirit and the Church. Here's the truth about a move of the Holy Spirit: you can't cause it in your own power, but you can continue you it in your obedience.

Like the fire upon the altar, a move of the Holy Spirit cannot be started by man, but it can be stewarded by man. The priests were told to keep the fire burning. They didn't start the fire, but they were commanded to steward the fire. They were to keep the fire alive.

We ready the altar, and even reap some level of success in soul winning, all while busily and hopefully looking forward to the falling of the fire of revival.

Elijah too laid an altar before the Lord, and God vindicated his faith by sending forth a supernatural blaze (see 1 Kings 18:20-40). David also built an altar to which the Lord responded by sending fire from Heaven (see 1 Chron. 21:26). The same happened for Solomon (see 2 Chron. 7:1).

We cannot cause the fire, but it is our duty to continue with it.

That's the nature of the Holy Spirit—He is a fire proceeding from Heaven. We merely do our natural duties to set the altar, but how brightly He chooses to burn in any given moment is up to Him.

Your job is not to spark the flame; your job is to surrender. Only God can send the fire. Only He can release the Holy Spirit. God sends the fire; you steward it. God appoints the Holy Spirit; you welcome Him.

There's nothing any man or woman can do to choose to begin a sovereign move of God. There's not a single action one can take, no method one can apply, to bring about a move of God. It really is just the power of the Holy Spirit. The Holy Spirit chooses where and when to move. He watches to see who has truly laid an altar before Him. He searches for an offering, a sacrifice, a surrendered life to consume. He searches for a region to influence.

Be idle? No! Set the altar. Present the best offering—a surrendered life—before Him. Just know that the Fire is sovereign. The Holy Spirit is sovereign.

THE PURE OIL—*Leviticus 24:2*

Command the people of Israel to bring you pure oil of pressed olives for the light, to keep the lamps burning continually (Leviticus 24:2).

The oil that was to keep the lamps burning was pure oil. Just as the pure oil kept the light of the lamps burning, so the purity of the Holy Spirit keeps your witness and your testimony shining brightly. The purity in the way you live your life is a light for the world to see, and the Pure Oil Himself keeps that light burning.

Chapter 5

THE HOLY SPIRIT IN
NUMBERS

> *I will come down and talk to you there. I will take some of the Spirit that is upon you, and I will put the Spirit upon them also. They will bear the burden of the people along with you, so you will not have to carry it alone* (Numbers 11:17).

Impartation comes about by the Holy Spirit. Spiritual succession is spiritual, not of the natural. The anointing doesn't fall upon blood, and neither do mantles—they fall upon spirit. We don't receive the anointing by being related to someone in the natural. We don't receive the anointing by having a title. We don't receive the impartation of the anointing based upon man's standards of entitlement or "dues." We receive impartation by the Holy Spirit. He is the one who gives mantles.

THE DIFFERENT SPIRIT—*Numbers 14:24*

The Holy Spirit is unique, and so is everyone who fellowships with Him.

The first few years of my Christian life were key years, seasons of development that would shape me. Driven by a desire to receive all that Heaven had to offer, I sought ministries and people through which I could receive from the fountain of God's power. I searched for the rivers of the Spirit. I read books, attended services, and watched television broadcasts. I wanted to consume all that I could.

I found so many wonderfully unique voices. Some were quiet and pensive. Others were excitable and strong. I was so moved by the dramatic yet sincere sermons of Kathryn Kuhlman. I was thrilled as I watched Oral Roberts lay his hands upon the sick. I read of the unflinching, radical faith of Smith Wigglesworth. There are many streams of expression in God's great river of ministry. The Church is enriched with gifts, with lives that leave legacies of faith. I could name minister after minister, some known and some unknown, who deposited something of spiritual significance in my life.

In all my searching, I found this to be certain: those who love the Holy Spirit are different, peculiar.

Think of all the traits and personality types that God uses. The Church is a colorful and interesting display of the Holy Spirit's expressions. Each one of His servants can mark your life in a different way. There is no end to the spectrum. A vast array of anointed ministries is touching the earth—and you, dear reader, are counted among them. You too are different because you too love and know the Holy Spirit.

I've come to appreciate and celebrate the different nature brought about by the Holy Spirit. This different nature was also found in a man named Caleb, spoken of in the Book of Numbers.

The Book of Numbers continues the narrative left unfinished in the Book of Exodus. The children of Israel, camped around Mount Sinai, desire to enter into the Promised Land. They make preparations to enter and conquer the land of Canaan. Gathering intel for the battle ahead, twelve Israeli spies survey Canaan. When the spies return, ten of them speak in doubt, while two of them (Joshua and Caleb) speak in faith. Ten see the giants in the land and say that the land is impossible to take; two say that, with God's help, it is impossible to fail.

Because of the negative report of the ten faithless spies, fear spreads and infects the people. The people rebel and allow themselves to become doubtful and spiteful. They even talk about stoning Joshua and Caleb. So God punishes the people.

You will all drop dead in this wilderness! Because you complained against Me, every one of you who is twenty years old or older and was included in the registration will die. You will not enter and occupy the land I swore to give you. The only exceptions will be Caleb son of Jephunneh and Joshua son of Nun (Numbers 14:29-30).

Caleb was one of the exceptions. Because of his faith, he would enter the Promised Land.

What made the difference? Why was it that Caleb was able to see with the sort of faith that was pleasing to God? How was he able to see victory when others only feared defeat? What made him stand apart from the rest of the spies and the people?

But because my servant Caleb has a different spirit and follows Me wholeheartedly, I will bring him into the land he went to, and his descendants will inherit it (Numbers 14:24 NIV).

I love that. Caleb had a different spirit. He stood out from the others. Caleb's attitude and outlook were different. His faith was stronger than theirs. His vision was greater. So what made Caleb's spirit so different? I know it was the Holy Spirit. When your spirit is one with the Holy Spirit, faith is present. All the traits of the Holy Spirit attach themselves to your spirit because you are one.

But the person who is joined to the Lord is one spirit with Him (1 Corinthians 6:17).

The believer does not have two spirits. The believer has one Spirit. We are united with the Holy Spirit as one. Caleb had a different spirit because He had *the* different Spirit in him.

The Holy Spirit is the different Spirit.

Had Caleb been like all the others, he would have never entered the Promised Land. Be thankful for the different Spirit.

Had the people of Israel allowed the Holy Spirit to affect their spirits, they too would have seen with eyes of faith. The tragedy of the Book of Numbers is that it begins with people preparing to take hold of God's promise, but they ultimately miss out because of the posture of their spirits. Had they not allowed the flesh to dominate their thinking, they would have entered the Promised Land. Eventually, their generation would pass, and another would prepare to enter the Promised Land.

Those who have the Holy Spirit are peculiar, different, and extraordinary. We don't talk, think, or act like those who do not have a fellowship with Him. And the closer you draw to the Holy Spirit, the more different you become. We stand out and shine with the brightness of His glory. We may even anger people just by the way we exist. The people tried to stone Caleb, and people will come against you.

Don't ever allow the feeling of being different force you to distance yourself from the Holy Spirit. Let the people reject you before you reject the Spirit. Remember this: often what we see as man's rejection is God's protection. That peculiar nature won't isolate you; it will protect you. The different Spirit brings about holiness, not loneliness. The Holy Spirit won't allow you to mingle your spirit with anything that can bring contamination. The Holy Spirit doesn't make you pious or self-righteous, but He does make you different. If you fellowship with the Holy Spirit, even fellow believers might consider you a bit odd. I often say, "When you get saved, you lose your unsaved friends. But when you get anointed, you lose your lukewarm friends."

I wouldn't have it any other way. I've learned to embrace being different. That's where the power is. Call me weird, but I believe in miracles. Label me a fanatic, but I believe in the slain in the spirit phenomenon. Mock me, but that won't stop me from praying in tongues and laying hands on the sick. I love being different. I enjoy being unique. I don't want to sound and look like everyone else. Neither should you.

Never see your uniqueness as a weakness. Be thankful that He makes you different. What a joy, what a privilege it is to leave behind the dull and the typical for the colorful and the unpredictable. How blessed we are to see through His eyes of faith to see promise in the land of giants. How blessed we are to be different, to have the different Spirit.

THE SPIRIT IN JOSHUA—*Numbers 27:18*

The Lord replied, "Take Joshua son of Nun, who has the Spirit in him, and lay your hands on him" (Numbers 27:18).

Many believers are under the impression that the Holy Spirit did not fill people in the Old Testament. Joshua, a mighty leader of God's people, is one example of the infilling of the Holy Spirit in an Old Testament personality.

Chapter 6

THE HOLY SPIRIT IN
DEUTERONOMY

THE FIRE BY NIGHT AND THE CLOUD BY
DAY—*Deuteronomy 1:33*

The Holy Spirit guides us.

In the Book of Deuteronomy, Moses gives his final words to the people of Israel, who finally are preparing to enter the Promised Land. A generation has passed away (those who did not have faith and were punished in the Book of Numbers). Moses recounts, among many other things, the miraculous ways in which God brought Israel to this point. Moses mentions the fact that Israel was faithfully guided by a cloud in the day and a fire at night:

> *But even after all He did, you refused to trust the Lord your God, who goes before you looking for the best places to camp, guiding you with a pillar of fire by night and a pillar of cloud by day* (Deuteronomy 1:32-33).[1]

The cloud and the fire had guided God's people through the wilderness. Although Israel had wavered and rebelled, the fire and the cloud were faithful to guide them to God's promise.

Moses trusted the fire and the cloud for guidance, and he was never led astray. In fact, the fire and the cloud guided him—from start to finish—through his life. Think about this: it was from the fire that God

---

1 See also Exodus 13:21; Exodus 40:38; Numbers 9:15-16; Numbers 14:14; Nehemiah 9:12; Psalm 78:14; Psalm 105:39; and Isaiah 4:5.

commissioned him, called him into the ministry, and would often speak to him (see Exod. 3:2; Deut. 4:33; 5:4; 10:4). In fact, the voice from the fire was so gloriously terrifying that the people begged that the fire might be removed from among them.

> *For this is what you yourselves requested of the Lord your God when you were assembled at Mount Sinai. You said, "Don't let us hear the voice of the Lord our God anymore or see this blazing fire, for we will die"* (Deuteronomy 18:16).

And the cloud was with Moses when he learned of his own death.

> *And the Lord appeared to them in a pillar of cloud that stood at the entrance to the sacred tent. The Lord said to Moses, "You are about to die and join your ancestors. After you are gone, these people will begin to worship foreign gods, the gods of the land where they are going. They will abandon Me and break My covenant that I have made with them* (Deuteronomy 31:15-16).

The guidance of the Holy Spirit is so absolute and complete and so thorough that it followed Moses from the beginning of his ministry to his death.

The cloud and the fire are symbolic of the Holy Spirit.

Just as the cloud and the fire guided the people of Israel and Moses, so the Holy Spirit guides His Church. The fire and the cloud, those blessed signs of the Holy Spirit's presence, adorned the tabernacle. Today, they abide with you, the temple of the Holy Spirit. Spiritually speaking, the believer is guided in both the day and the night, in the darkness and the light.

The day represents our seasons of clarity. The night represents our seasons of uncertainty.

Sometimes, it is day, and we know what we ought to do. During the day, obstacles can be seen and avoided. There is safety and certainty. In seasons of light, we know what direction to take, and we walk confidently. Even when we are able to discern the path ahead, He is present to guide us, though we might not necessarily be desperate for that guidance. The Holy Spirit is the cloud by day that guides us.

Sometimes, it is night, and we struggle to find the way. In the night seasons, we are hesitant to move forward and uncertain about staying put. Not knowing whether to move or to wait, we find it difficult to maintain a clear focus. There in the night, the Holy Spirit guides us. When we don't know where to go, the Holy Spirit is the fire by night that burns amidst the darkness.

There are times when the fire and the cloud will move you forward. The fire and the cloud also sometimes halt, signifying that it's time to set up camp.

Now you might be asking the Lord, "Do I go forward, or do I remain here? Is there a new direction in which You are leading me?" Perhaps you feel stuck or concerned about moving outside the will of God. Just follow the fire, stay with the cloud.

So how do we experience the Spirit's faithful guidance in our lives? Well, let's look at how Moses interacted with God.

> *"If it is true that You look favorably on me, let me know Your ways*
> *so I may understand You more fully and continue to enjoy Your*
> *favor. And remember that this nation is Your very own people."*
> *The Lord replied, "I will personally go with you, Moses, and I will*
> *give you rest—everything will be fine for you." Then Moses said,*
> *"If You don't personally go with us, don't make us leave this place.*
> *How will anyone know that You look favorably on me—on me*
> *and on Your people—if You don't go with us? For Your presence*
> *among us sets Your people and me apart from all other people on*
> *the earth." The Lord replied to Moses, "I will indeed do what you*
> *have asked, for I look favorably on you, and I know you by name"*
> (Exodus 33:13-17).

Moses was a man who sought the direction and the presence of God. He didn't move unless God told Him to move. This does not mean that we must be inactive and useless. It simply means that we must not be presumptuous concerning the will of God. Avoid the extremes of laziness and presumption.

To receive the guidance of the Holy Spirit is a simple matter. Moses spent time with the Lord. He had a consistent prayer life. He consulted with the Lord and involved the Lord in his decision-making through prayer.

We often say that we depend on the guidance of God. We often say that we look to His instructions. But that's only talk. The real evidence of a desire to be guided by the Holy Spirit is your prayer life. We say that we want God's guidance, but do we pray? We say that we want direction, but do we pray?

Living without the guidance of the Holy Spirit is as deceptively simple as not praying. And living with the guidance of the Holy Spirit is as simple as praying. The clarity of the Holy Spirit's guidance is proportionate to the consistency of your seeking His direction.

Therefore, we need not worry. Rest in knowing that so long as you're seeking Him, looking at the fire, you cannot miss Him. If the children of Israel, who regularly rebelled and resisted, were able to receive the guidance of God, then you can receive the guidance of the Holy Spirit.

So long as we seek the guidance of the Holy Spirit in prayer, we will not be able to wander off too far. So long as we look for them, the cloud and the fire will be there for our spiritual reference. No matter the season, He will guide you. Whether you have clarity and just need the cloud by day or you are confused and are looking to see the fire by night, the Holy Spirit will guide you. Just look for His guidance.

THE OIL OF PROSPERITY—*Deuteronomy 33:24*

And of Asher he said, "Most blessed of sons be Asher; let him be the favorite of his brothers, and let him dip his foot in oil" (Deuteronomy 33:24 ESV).

The phrase *"dip his foot in oil"* can mean "become prosperous." In fact, the Hebrew meaning of the name Asher is "Blessed." Asher, who was able to dine on rich foods (see Gen. 49:20), is a symbolic example of the Holy Spirit's power to bring prosperity. The Holy Spirit has the power to attract resources and prosperity—the glory attracts finance! Think of the spectacular temple built by Solomon. Think of the riches of Israel. Think of the wealth of the Patriarchs. Even a disciple of Jesus, Joseph of Arimathea, was wealthy. The Holy Spirit is the oil of prosperity.

Chapter 7

THE HOLY SPIRIT IN JOSHUA

THE SPIRIT OF BREAKTHROUGH—*Joshua 6:3-5*

The Holy Spirit is the One who gives breakthrough.

My first blog had literally zero readers for more than one year. My first miracle service crowds filled less than 10 percent of the buildings in which I held them. My first weekly broadcasts averaged only twenty viewers per week. I stood at that number for more than a year. My first book sold less than 200 copies and was rejected by every publisher to whom I sent it. Even my preaching schedule was slow. If I preached just twice a month, then things were considered to be "really moving." For several years, my average ministry account balance was less than one hundred dollars. In other words, I needed a breakthrough in ministry.

My vision for ministry and my reality in ministry did not align with one another, but I kept obeying God. I learned to measure my success by obedience rather than by numbers. I learned to be faithful in the little things. And I would eventually learn about the power behind breakthrough.

I persisted in my service to the Lord. I can tell you in all honesty that I gave my best to Him. But despite my efforts, zeal, and knowledge, there was no breakthrough in my ministry for the first several years. After I had done all I knew to do, I told the Lord, "I can't do it. I don't have what it takes." When I came to the end of myself, I truly understood that I had no power on my own to accomplish the work of the ministry. You'd be surprised at how much self-reliance can hide itself within your own heart. It took some time, but I eventually realized how much I had depended upon my own efforts. I resolved to leave the breakthrough to God. I decided that I would, of course, be faithful to the work of the ministry and then just trust the Lord to do His part. I finally found the peace of giving my ministry pressures and burdens to the Lord.

And then came the breakthrough.

Out of nowhere, the ministry began to grow. The ratings and stats reflected that. The ministry bank account reflected that. We started to win more souls than ever before and reach more people than ever before. The events began to grow, and the ministry invitations began to pour in. But the breakthrough came in surrender. It was not my doing. I changed nothing but the posture of my heart, the placement of my reliance. I had just done what I had always done—until God breathed upon it. Ministry was a struggle until, suddenly, it wasn't.

No matter where we are in life or ministry, a breakthrough will take you to the next strata of success, influence, and responsibility. We see many breakthroughs in the Scripture.

In Genesis, God's people find favor with the Egyptians through Joseph. The Spirit of the Dreamer makes sure that Joseph is properly appointed. That was a breakthrough for God's people. However, Exodus records the enslavement of God's people. So, God speaks to Moses through the fire, and Moses is stirred to become a deliverer of God's people. Israel's exodus was a breakthrough. In Numbers, while preparing to enter the Promised Land, the Israelites begin to complain against Moses, except for Joshua and Caleb—they both have a different spirit in them. Sadly, in that generation, the people missed their breakthrough. Years later, in the Book of Deuteronomy, the children of Israel are again preparing to enter the Promised Land. This time, it's a new generation to be led by a new leader. That leader is Joshua. And it was through Joshua that breakthrough was again given to the people of Israel.

Moses dies. Joshua is appointed to lead. The Israelites look to conquer the land of Canaan, the Promised Land. Their first battle takes place at Jericho.

> *Now the gates of Jericho were tightly shut because the people were afraid of the Israelites. No one was allowed to go out or in. But the Lord said to Joshua, "I have given you Jericho, its king, and all its strong warriors"* (Joshua 6:1-2).

The walls of Jericho were large, robust structures that protected the city. Getting through the walls was an improbable task. And even if they had somehow succeeded in getting past the walls, the Israelites would have been too tired to finish the fight. To Israel, going beyond the walls seemed impossible.

Yet God had a plan—and a peculiar one at that.

> *You and your fighting men should march around the town once a day for six days. Seven priests will walk ahead of the Ark, each carrying a ram's horn. On the seventh day you are to march around the town seven times, with the priests blowing the horns. When you hear the priests give one long blast on the rams' horns, have all the people shout as loud as they can. Then the walls of the town will collapse, and the people can charge straight into the town* (Joshua 6:3-5).

When I read that, I thought, "Why wouldn't the Lord give them a more practical strategy? Why didn't He tell them how to get around the wall or sneak into the city? Of all the ways He could have instructed them, He chose a most peculiar way."

These were the instructions: March around the city once a day for six days. On the seventh day, march around seven times. Then blow the horns and shout. The walls will come down.

That just seemed so odd to me. There was no real warfare, no military strategy, and no battle technique. It was as simple as, "March around the city with the Ark while blowing horns and then shout." It was an odd strategy, but it worked.

> *The seven priests with the rams' horns marched in front of the Ark of the Lord, blowing their horns. Again the armed men marched both in front of the priests with the horns and behind the Ark of the Lord. All this time the priests were blowing their horns.... The seventh time around, as the priests sounded the long blast on their horns, Joshua commanded the people, "Shout! For the Lord has given you the town!" ...When the people heard the sound of the rams' horns, they shouted as loud as they could. Suddenly, the walls of Jericho collapsed, and the Israelites charged straight into the town and captured it* (Joshua 6:13,16,20).

The people obeyed the instructions of the Lord and, by faith, overtook the enemy's walls.

Contrast that with the actions of the generation that had gone before them. The previous generation had a rebellious spirit, but this generation, the very same that marched around the city of Jericho, had a spirit of faith.

It was by faith that the people of Israel marched around Jericho for seven days, and the walls came crashing down (Hebrews 11:30).

So what was it that brought down the walls of Jericho? What did God use to bring about this supernatural moment of breakthrough? Certainly, there was something to the faith of the Israelites. And yes, it was the power of God. But there's more to it than that. Think about what God had instructed them to do, specifically.

He instructed them to release their breath through the horns and their shouts. He instructed them to release the *Ruach*. It was the *Ruach* of God that brought down those walls—the very same that blew open the Red Sea.

At the blast of Your breath, the waters piled up! The surging waters stood straight like a wall; in the heart of the sea the deep waters became hard (Exodus 15:8).

The *Ruach* of God fortified the water to become like walls and weakened the walls to become like water.

It was not the shouts of men that collapsed the walls, nor was it the sound of the horns that removed the stubborn barrier to the Promised Land. It was the breath of God—the Holy Spirit—who cleared the way for God's people to claim what was promised to them.

The Holy Spirit is the Spirit of breakthrough.

Had the Israelites attempted to take down the walls in their own strength, they would have failed. Had they applied the plans of man to their predicament, they would not have succeeded. But because they obeyed the commands of God, because they released the breath, the walls crumbled to the ground.

How often have you and I attempted to find breakthrough in our own strength, and how many times have we failed in doing so? The commands of God are peculiar. At first, they are perceived as ineffective and even silly. I think the Lord does it that way on purpose.

You can exhaust all of your effort and emotion. You can try everything you know to do. But when the breakthrough finally comes, He wants you to know who brought it to pass. The famous Scripture shines upon this truth:

> *Then he answered and spake unto me, saying, This is the word of the Lord unto Zerubbabel, saying, Not by might, nor by power, but by My spirit, saith the Lord of hosts* (Zechariah 4:6 KJV).

Your breakthrough does not come in your struggle; it comes in your surrender. It won't be found in some brilliant strategy or aggressive action. Only when you do as God commands is the Holy Spirit able to bring down the walls that inhibit your progress.

In what do you need breakthrough? Your family? Your finances? Your ministry? Your business? Do you need breakthrough in your holiness, your evangelism, or your prayer life? Do you struggle with an addiction or a secret sin?

Just surrender to the Spirit of breakthrough. Recognize that only He can bring down the walls. Only the breath of the Spirit can carry you beyond the barriers of frustration.

THE SPIRIT OF DISCERNMENT—*Joshua 7:16-19*

The Holy Spirit protects us with discernment.

The ministry was seeing fruitfulness, and it was in the middle of this fruitfulness that my right-hand man fell away from the faith. It was discouraging—heartbreaking, honestly. Spiritually speaking, I felt like I had the breath knocked out of me.

Trying to keep things in order at the ministry and acting purely in emotion, I kept the man on the ministry team. I rationalized, "I can remove him from pulpit ministry, but he can still do the administrative tasks of the ministry. I don't want things to become unorganized."

I kept that individual on the team, and, within weeks, everything began to fail. The failure was just as surprising as the breakthrough that had previously come to our ministry. I had done only what I had always done—but now it was failing again. The invites slowed. The crowds dwindled. The financial flow began to crawl. Even the intensity of God's manifested presence in our services began to weaken. There truly was a spiritual problem.

Wondering what was happening, I approached the Lord in prayer. "What's going on here, Lord? I don't understand it!" And then the Holy Spirit scolded me, "Remove him from your team." His harsh words brought me to the realization that I was operating by the flesh, not by faith.

As soon as I complied with the direction of the Spirit, breakthrough returned to the ministry. It was quite the learning experience for me. What is given by the Spirit cannot be sustained by the flesh. Even those seemingly unspiritual positions on ministry teams can affect the spiritual dynamics of a ministry. Our affiliations matter. Joshua learned this in a much more drastic manner than I did.

Before conquering the city of Jericho, the Israelites were given simple instructions through Joshua from the Lord:

> *Jericho and everything in it must be completely destroyed as an offering to the Lord* (Joshua 6:17).

Unfortunately, not everyone in the camp obeyed that command. A man named Achan kept several valuables to himself instead of doing with them as he was commanded.

Israel spied upon the next city they were to conquer—the city of Ai. According to their intel, the battle was to be a relatively easy one to win. Having just experienced a miraculous victory at Jericho, Israel was emboldened and full of faith to conquer. However, they were met with a demoralizing defeat.

> *So approximately 3,000 warriors were sent, but they were soundly defeated. The men of Ai chased the Israelites from the town gate as far as the quarries, and they killed about thirty-six who were retreating down the slope. The Israelites were paralyzed with fear at this turn of events, and their courage melted away* (Joshua 7:4-5).

Perplexed and distraught, Joshua cried out to the Lord for clarity.

> *Then Joshua cried out, "Oh, Sovereign Lord, why did You bring us across the Jordan River if You are going to let the Amorites kill us? If only we had been content to stay on the other side! Lord, what can I say now that Israel has fled from its enemies?"* (Joshua 7:7-8)

It was then that the Lord revealed to Joshua that someone had broken His command. *"That is why the Israelites are running from their enemies in defeat,"* the Lord explained (Josh. 7:12).

The next morning, the perpetrator was revealed to Joshua. Through a process of elimination, Joshua singled out the tribe, then the clan, then the family, and then the man.

> *Early the next morning Joshua brought the tribes of Israel before the Lord, and the tribe of Judah was singled out. Then the clans of Judah came forward, and the clan of Zerah was singled out. Then the families of Zerah came forward, and the family of Zimri was singled out. Every member of Zimri's family was brought forward person by person, and Achan was singled out. Then Joshua said to Achan, "My son, give glory to the Lord, the God of Israel, by telling the truth. Make your confession and tell me what you have done. Don't hide it from me"* (Joshua 7:16-19).

Achan confessed to having taken several valuable items for himself. The items were uncovered, and Achan was executed—along with his family.

> *Then Joshua and all the Israelites took Achan, the silver, the robe, the bar of gold, his sons, daughters, cattle, donkeys, sheep, goats, tent, and everything he had, and they brought them to the valley of Achor. Then Joshua said to Achan, "Why have you brought trouble on us? The Lord will now bring trouble on you." And all the Israelites stoned Achan and his family and burned their bodies* (Joshua 7:24-25).

Israel once again began to win victories. The offender was revealed, and favor was restored.

So here's my question: How did Joshua know which tribe, clan, family, and individual to set aside?

The Scripture tells us that Joshua had the Holy Spirit within him:

> *The Lord replied, "Take Joshua son of Nun, who has the Spirit in him, and lay your hands on him"* (Numbers 27:18).

Yes, it was the leading of the Holy Spirit that pointed out Achan to Joshua.

The Holy Spirit speaks to you regarding those who are in the wrong. He will reveal to you what others try to keep hidden. He will reveal to you those who are bringing destruction to your life. And He will help you remove them from your life.

He will help you uncover unhealthy influences around you. Even when you cannot see the damage being done, the Holy Spirit can. Even when you cannot perceive the hidden motives of ill-intentioned hearts, the Holy Spirit can. He reveals the harm in the seemingly harmless and preserves the favor on your life by exposing it.

The Holy Spirit is the Spirit of discernment.

Chapter 8

THE HOLY SPIRIT IN
JUDGES

THE SPIRIT OF LEADERSHIP—*Judges 3:10*

The Holy Spirit is the One who empowers us for leadership.

God's people had entered the Promised Land, but there were still uncon-
quered people groups lingering throughout the Promised Land. The Bible
tells us that God intentionally allowed certain nations to remain in certain
regions so that He could test the faithfulness of Israel.

> *"I will no longer drive out the nations that Joshua left unconquered
> when he died. I did this to test Israel—to see whether or not they
> would follow the ways of the Lord as their ancestors did." That is
> why the Lord left those nations in place. He did not quickly drive
> them out or allow Joshua to conquer them all* (Judges 2:21-23).

The Lord also allowed those nations to stay so that the generations after
Joshua would remain militarily sharp.

> *He did this to teach warfare to generations of Israelites who had no
> experience in battle* (Judges 3:2).

Joshua and the chosen generation of Israelites, the very same who carried
the "different spirit" that pleased the Lord, eventually died. Remaining was
a generation that had yet to witness the work of the miracle-causing hand
of God. It was a generation that had heard of the power of God but had
never experienced the power for itself.

That generation, instead of passing the Lord's test by refusing to worship
the false gods of the pagan nations, debased themselves with the sin of idolatry. They began to worship the demonically inspired graven images of the

people they should have ruled and conquered. Repeating the sins of their ancestors, the Israelites displeased the Lord with their spiritual adultery.

The consequence of their idolatry was the loss of God's favor in battle. In fact, because of Israel's rebellion, the Lord went from fighting on their behalf to fighting against them.

> *Every time Israel went out to battle, the Lord fought against them, causing them to be defeated, just as He had warned. And the people were in great distress* (Judges 2:15).

Caught in a constant wavering, Israel would repeatedly repent of idolatry, only to descend into paganism again. This chaotic pattern continued for years. Each time God's people turned from worshiping the true God, He would allow their enemies to oppress them. And each time Israel came under oppression, God was faithful to hear their cries. Israel was a theocracy. They had no human royalty. So, to deliver His people, God used judges.

> *Whenever the Lord raised up a judge over Israel, He was with that judge and rescued the people from their enemies throughout the judge's lifetime. For the Lord took pity on His people, who were burdened by oppression and suffering* (Judges 2:18).

The first judge who God raised was Othniel, Caleb's nephew. Of Othniel, the Scripture says this:

> *The Spirit of the Lord came upon him, and he became Israel's judge. He went to war against King Cushan-rishathaim of Aram, and the Lord gave Othniel victory over him. So there was peace in the land for forty years. Then Othniel son of Kenaz died* (Judges 3:10-11).

It was the Holy Spirit who empowered the judges to lead God's people out of the oppression of their enemies and into victory ("The Spirit of the Lord came upon him…"). It was the Holy Spirit who gave them strategies for war, wisdom in judgment, and foresight. The Spirit moved through the judges to rescue Israel from the deception and darkness of idolatry. The Holy Spirit was with the judges of Israel.

- Deborah was prophetic (see Judg. 4:4).

- Gideon encountered the fire of God (see Judg. 6:21).

- Samson was stirred by the Holy Spirit (see Judg. 13:25).

Like the judges of Israel, God's chosen leaders are purposefully placed in key moments of history. Leaders are confrontational, bold, wise, and set upon a purpose.

You have the same Holy Spirit who dwelled within the judges of Israel. Today, even now, He empowers you to lead those whom God has willed under your influence. You're empowered to lead people away from distraction and into liberty.

The Holy Spirit is the Spirit of leadership.

THE FIRE FROM THE ROCK—*Judges 6:21*

Then the angel of the Lord touched the meat and bread with the tip of the staff in his hand, and fire flamed up from the rock and consumed all he had brought. And the angel of the Lord disappeared (Judges 6:21).

Jesus is the Rock (see Isa. 8:14; Rom. 9:33; 1 Peter 2:8) and the One who baptizes us in the Holy Spirit (see Matt. 3:11). The fire coming up from the rock is a prophetic picture of Jesus giving the Holy Spirit to His Church.

THE SPIRIT OF CONQUEST—*Judges 11:29*

At that time the Spirit of the Lord came upon Jephthah, and he went throughout the land of Gilead and Manasseh, including Mizpah in Gilead, and from there he led an army against the Ammonites (Judges 11:29).

When the Holy Spirit comes upon your life, He empowers you unto spiritual conquest. By the Spirit, you will come to possess all that God has ordained as yours. Wherever the enemy occupies will be made clear, as you take purposeful steps of faith. The days of frustration and exhaustive effort will come to an end when you allow the Holy Spirit to move ahead of you to unblock your path. The enemy cannot have your family, your finances, your business, your ministry, your mind, your emotions, your body, your peace, or your joy. The Holy Spirit can restore all and conquer all. No matter what you are facing today, expect to possess the land of promise.

THE FIRE OF HEAVEN—*Judges 13:20*

As the flames from the altar shot up toward the sky, the angel of the Lord ascended in the fire. When Manoah and his wife saw this, they fell with their faces to the ground (Judges 13:20).

The angel of the Lord ascended in the fire. That fire, the Holy Spirit, is the One who connects Heaven with earth.

THE SPIRIT OF SUPERNATURAL STRENGTH—*Judges 14:6*

The Holy Spirit is the One who gives us strength.

My team and I pulled our vehicles up to the building where my service was to begin in just an hour or so. People had come in vans from all over the region. As we pulled onto the property, I looked out of my window to study the crowd of people who had gathered. The crowd was larger than expected so chairs and speakers were being set up for an overflow section outside of the building.

People had come in crutches, wheelchairs, and braces of all kinds. Their needs were obvious and heart-breaking. It was then that I began to feel the pressure. I thought to myself, "If God doesn't move, I'm in trouble." I feared that the service would be a disappointment to the people who had come in such desperation and hunger. I feared that I would miss a divine instruction and fail to surrender effectively to the Holy Spirit.

Concerned, I hurried to a back room and locked myself into privacy. I then began to pray, worship, and cry out to the Lord. I wore myself out with pleadings and prayer requests. I did everything I could to ensure that God was going to use me as a vessel of His healing power.

Then I got out into the service.

It was everything I feared it would be and worse.

One by one, the people began to line up for prayer. But unlike the many other miracle services in which I had ministered, there was not a single healing that took place in that service. And I do literally mean that not a single healing occurred. Not only did the people have no faith for miracles (many of them were cynical), but I didn't sense the power of God like I normally do.

If someone came up in a wheelchair, they left the stage in that wheelchair. If someone came up with crutches, they left the stage using those crutches. I even recall a man with a severe back injury limping onto the stage, receiving prayer, and limping right back off the stage. He winced in pain as he moved back to his seat.

I began to ask the Lord internally, "Lord, what is going on here?"

I didn't imagine that it could get any worse. And then it did get worse.

A man came onto the stage. He said, "Pray for me."

I asked, "What do you need the Lord to do?"

"You tell me," he said.

Confused, I said, "Please, tell me what your sickness is."

He asked, "You don't know?"

I responded, "No, please tell me so we can pray."

In front of everyone, he told me, "If you can't tell me, then you're not blessed by Jesus."

He basically called me a fraud right in front of everyone. If there was any faith in that room at all, it was gone the moment he spoke those stifling words. I was more shocked than anything else by his statement. Persisting, I powered through that dead service. When it was finally over, I left the service and went to the Lord.

"Lord," I inquired, "what happened?"

It was then that the Holy Spirit gave me a revelation. He impressed this truth upon me: "You tried to do it in your own strength."

My little prayer session before the service was not one of faith or trust in the Lord. I had been so moved by the people's needs that I hastily attempted to make something happen. Your faith should not be in your own strength. Your faith should not be in your own gift. And as I learned, your faith should not even be in your own ability to pray. Your faith needs to be in the Holy Spirit's strength.

Samson, one of the judges of Israel, was given supernatural strength by the Holy Spirit.

> *At that moment the Spirit of the Lord came powerfully upon him, and he ripped the lion's jaws apart with his bare hands. He did it as easily as if it were a young goat. But he didn't tell his father or mother about it* (Judges 14:6).

I love that the Bible describes Samson's killing of the lion as being as easy as the killing of a young goat. What should be difficult becomes easy when the Holy Spirit empowers you to do it. This was true of Samson's overcoming of thirty men.

> *Then the Spirit of the Lord came powerfully upon him. He went down to the town of Ashkelon, killed thirty men, took their belongings, and gave their clothing to the men who had solved his riddle* (Judges 14:19).

It was also true of Samson's ripping of the ropes that bound him.

> *As Samson arrived at Lehi, the Philistines came shouting in triumph. But the Spirit of the Lord came powerfully upon Samson, and he snapped the ropes on his arms as if they were burnt strands of flax, and they fell from his wrists* (Judges 15:14).

When you operate under the strength of the Holy Spirit, nothing can tire you, destroy you, or bind you. The Holy Spirit can accomplish more through you in a single day than human effort and toil can accomplish in a thousand years. Far too many believers function in frustration and strain. They attempt to go through this life on their own strength. We only become spiritually weary when we attempt to give from ourselves instead of from the source. When you operate in the Spirit's strength, you are energized and swift. Don't live by your own strength. Do what cannot be done without His power.

The same Holy Spirit who gave Samson his physical strength gives you His inner strength.

The Holy Spirit is the Spirit of supernatural strength.

THE GENTLE SPIRIT—*Judges 16:20*

The Holy Spirit is gentle.

It was the Holy Spirit who gave Samson supernatural strength. Without the power of the Spirit, Samson became as weak as any man. The following verse is perhaps one of the most sobering you could ever read in all of Scripture:

> *Then she cried out, "Samson! The Philistines have come to capture you!" When he woke up, he thought, "I will do as before and shake*

myself free." But he didn't realize the Lord had left him (Judges 16:20).

The Lord was with Samson by the Holy Spirit, but Samson didn't realize that the Holy Spirit had departed from Him.

The Holy Spirit can be ignored and overlooked. What a frightening thought—that we can become so stubbornly self-reliant, so blatantly disobedient, that we do not recognize when the Holy Spirit is no longer in what we do. In fact, some become so dependent on human effort that, were the Holy Spirit to ever cease working in their life or ministry, they would never notice.

The Holy Spirit arrives as a rushing wind, but He leaves as a whispered breath. He has an announced arrival but a discreet departure. His coming draws attention; His leaving often goes unnoticed.

Don't disobey Him. Don't keep pushing aside His instructions. He won't force Himself on you or aggressively insist upon His ways. So don't overlook or ignore the gentle Spirit.

Chapter 9

THE HOLY SPIRIT IN
RUTH

THE KIND SPIRIT OF ADOPTION—*Ruth 2:21*

The Holy Spirit makes us a part of God's family.

As short as the Book of Ruth is, it is rich in symbolism, historic significance, and parallels. I do highly encourage you to study Jewish themes, genealogies, and culture in relation to the Book of Ruth. I found the study to be deeply illuminating.

Here, however, I'll be focusing only on selected portions from the story of Ruth.

The story of Ruth begins with a family tragedy. A father dies. Then his two sons die without ever having children. These three men leave behind three women. The father leaves behind his wife, Naomi. The two sons leave behind their wives, Ruth and Orpah—women from the land of Moab. Imagine that. The family suffered the tragic deaths of a father and two brothers.

So Naomi is left with her two daughters-in-law, Orpah and Ruth.

Naomi and her deceased husband were originally from Israel. Because of a famine, they had traveled to the land of Moab, where they found Orpah and Ruth. Eventually, Naomi decides that it's time to return home. While on her way to her homeland, Naomi is accompanied by Orpah and Ruth. It is while they are journeying to Israel that Naomi tries to dissuade her daughters-in-law from accompanying her.

> *But on the way, Naomi said to her two daughters-in-law, "Go back to your mothers' homes. And may the Lord reward you for*

*your kindness to your husbands and to me. May the Lord bless you
with the security of another marriage." Then she kissed them good-
bye, and they all broke down and wept* (Ruth 1:8-9).

Naomi insists that Ruth and Orpah can't possibly benefit from remaining
with her, especially because she can no longer have children. Naomi points
out the fact that even if she were, by some miracle, to have two more sons,
Orpah and Ruth would have to wait many years before marrying them.

Orpah is convinced and returns to her homeland, but Ruth is persistent
in her loyalty to Naomi. In fact, she even converts and commits to following the God of Israel.

*But Ruth replied, "Don't ask me to leave you and turn back. Wher-
ever you go, I will go; wherever you live, I will live. Your people
will be my people, and your God will be my God." …When Naomi
saw that Ruth was determined to go with her, she said nothing
more* (Ruth 1:16,18).

Ruth and Naomi arrive in Bethlehem. They are weary and poor. Ruth, a
Moabite, is unwelcome in Bethlehem. She's a foreigner and, in many ways,
doesn't belong there. However, according to the law, the poor and the foreigners were allowed to glean crops from the harvest fields.

*When you harvest the crops of your land, do not harvest the grain
along the edges of your fields, and do not pick up what the harvest-
ers drop. Leave it for the poor and the foreigners living among you.
I am the Lord your God* (Leviticus 23:22).

So Ruth finds herself harvesting in a field that belongs to a wealthy and
influential man named Boaz. Boaz takes notice of Ruth, makes her feel
welcome, and permits her to drink his well water when she is thirsty.

*…And when you are thirsty, help yourself to the water they have
drawn from the well* (Ruth 2:9).

Showing further kindness to Ruth, Boaz then instructs his young men
to allow Ruth to harvest right among the sheaves of the field, as opposed
to just along the edges of the field. He did above what the law required of
him. He even instructed his workers to purposely drop crops for Ruth to
pick up as she gleaned behind them.

Ruth, under the instruction of her mother-in-law Naomi, eventually
makes a very bold move and asks Boaz to marry her.

One day Naomi said to Ruth, "My daughter, it's time that I found a permanent home for you, so that you will be provided for. Boaz is a close relative of ours, and he's been very kind by letting you gather grain with his young women. Tonight he will be winnowing barley at the threshing floor" (Ruth 3:2).

I want to point out to you that Naomi says that Boaz is a close relative. In fact, he was related to Ruth's deceased father-in-law.

Around midnight Boaz suddenly woke up and turned over. He was surprised to find a woman lying at his feet! "Who are you?" he asked. "I am your servant Ruth," she replied. "Spread the corner of your covering over me, for you are my family redeemer" (Ruth 3:8-9).

Then Boaz says something very key, and I want you to note what he says:

"The Lord bless you, my daughter!" Boaz exclaimed. "You are showing even more family loyalty now than you did before, for you have not gone after a younger man, whether rich or poor" (Ruth 3:10).

At this point, it's important for me to share a Jewish term with you. That term is *yibbum*. *Yibbum* was an interesting sort of arranged marriage. The Book of Deuteronomy says this about it:

If two brothers are living together on the same property and one of them dies without a son, his widow may not be married to anyone from outside the family. Instead, her husband's brother should marry her and have intercourse with her to fulfill the duties of a brother-in-law. The first son she bears to him will be considered the son of the dead brother, so that his name will not be forgotten in Israel (Deuteronomy 25:5-6).

Because Ruth's former husband had passed away without having children, it was the responsibility of his brother to carry on his name. Tragically, as you'll recall, his brother also died. So somewhat of a moral obligation fell to the next closest male in the family to have a child with Ruth. Remember that Boaz was a close relative of Ruth's father-in-law. In asking Boaz to marry her, Ruth demonstrated her desire to continue the name of her deceased husband. That's why Boaz says, *"You are showing even more family loyalty now than you did before..."* (Ruth 3:10). Ruth could have gone to find another husband from another family, but she stood loyal to her husband's name.

Here's the catch: Ruth had some property that fell to her through the deaths of the men in her family. Whoever married Ruth had the right to the property. It had belonged to her father-in-law. Now Boaz was a relative of Naomi's husband. However, there was another man who was a more closely related relative and, therefore, the first in line to inherit the land and Ruth. If Boaz was to marry Ruth, he had to work out an agreement with that other man.

So Boaz makes an arrangement to buy the land and, along with it, the right to marry Ruth. Boaz becomes the kinsman-redeemer. He redeemed Ruth through the purchase of the property.

Boaz and Ruth are married, Naomi receives grandchildren, and a family name is redeemed. So Ruth, a foreigner who converted to Judaism, stood loyal to Naomi, gleaned in a field, found favor with Boaz (a relative), and married into the family of God. The son of Ruth and Boaz is Obed, the grandfather of King David.

This, ultimately, is a story of redemption and kindness.

What I want to highlight here are simply the parallels between Boaz and Jesus. Focusing on that parallel will help me show you what can be learned about the Holy Spirit in this relatively small book of the Bible.

Whenever you see a parallel of Christ in the Old Testament, look closely, for nearby you may find a parallel of the Holy Spirit. We see parallels of both Christ and the Holy Spirit in the Book of Ruth, and the message to you and me is one of acceptance. Looking back on it, we see the ways in which Boaz is a parallel of Christ.

Christ fulfilled the law for our benefit. Boaz fulfilled the law (of gleaning) for Ruth's benefit.

Christ went above the law and gave us His righteousness. Boaz went above the law and gave Ruth grain from among the sheaves.

Christ showed us unearned favor. Boaz showed Ruth unearned favor.

Christ redeemed us while we were sinners. Boaz redeemed Ruth while she was a Moabite.

Christ redeemed us with a price. Boaz redeemed Ruth with a price.

Christ redeemed us because of His love. Boaz redeemed Ruth because of his love.

By law, we, as sinners, could not be part of God's family without redemption. By law, Ruth, a Moabite, could not be part of Boaz's family without redemption.

We can even see salvation taking place in the story of Ruth. At the beginning of the story, Ruth commits to serving Naomi's God—the one true God. But at the threshing floor, we see that Ruth presents herself at Boaz's feet. I love the way the King James Version describes how she presents herself to Boaz:

> *Wash thyself therefore, and anoint thee, and put thy raiment upon thee, and get thee down to the floor: but make not thyself known unto the man, until he shall have done eating and drinking* (Ruth 3:3 KJV).

Consider the story's parallels to salvation. Ruth is washed, anointed, and clothed anew. All she can do is present herself to Boaz, but Boaz must do the redeeming work. The threshing floor is symbolic for the separation of the redeemed from the unredeemed, and the symbolism is powerful.

So where is the Holy Spirit in all of this?

Well, I could point you back to Ruth 3:3, where Ruth is anointed. Perhaps the Holy Spirit here is the oil of favor that wins the heart of Boaz. I could also point to the verse where Boaz offers Ruth water to refresh her (see Ruth 2:9). Because Boaz is a type of Christ, that could easily be a parallel of the giving of the Holy Spirit, for Jesus Himself promised to give us living water:

> *But those who drink the water I give will never be thirsty again. It becomes a fresh, bubbling spring within them, giving them eternal life* (John 4:14).

This living water is, of course, the Holy Spirit (see John 7:38-39).

Yet, while those parallels are powerful, there is a more profound truth concerning the Spirit hidden within the overall story. Again, simply and spiritually put: the Book of Ruth is about redemption.

There is redemption found within union. But this union between Boaz and Ruth is reflective of something bigger than their own marriage. And the clue to uncovering this mystery is found within a seemingly casual verse. While first telling Naomi of the kindness of Boaz, Ruth explains:

> *Then Ruth said, "What's more, Boaz even told me to come back and stay with his harvesters until the entire harvest is completed"* (Ruth 2:21).

What harvest?

Ruth was talking about the grain harvest, a harvest that lasted several weeks. At the conclusion of the grain harvest, the Jewish people celebrate what is known as Shavuot. Something very significant happened on a Shavuot that occurred generations prior to Ruth. It was the giving of the Torah at Mount Sinai.

The giving of the Torah at Mount Sinai was more than a legal event—it was a marriage between Jehovah and Israel. As Israel entered into this divine marriage, they became a redeemed people.

So the giving of the Torah took place on Shavuot. The story of the marriage of Boaz and Ruth centered around Shavuot. And generations later, another significant occurrence took place on Shavuot, except by another name.

The other name for Shavuot?

Pentecost.

At Pentecost, another union occurred: it was the union between the Holy Spirit and the Church. But this union didn't just occur between God and man—it occurred between all who would be baptized in the Spirit.

> *There is no longer Jew or Gentile, slave or free, male and female. For you are all one in Christ Jesus* (Galatians 3:28).

So it was at Pentecost that Israel and God were united. It was at Pentecost that Ruth, a Gentile, and Boaz, a Jew, were united. And it was at Pentecost that Jews and Gentiles were baptized into one Church. We were all baptized into one family, where we belong to God and each other.

The Holy Spirit is the One who works with Christ to redeem us into the family of God.

> *But you are not controlled by your sinful nature. You are controlled by the Spirit if you have the Spirit of God living in you. (And remember that those who do not have the Spirit of Christ living*

in them do not belong to Him at all.) *...For all who are led by the Spirit of God are children of God* (Romans 8:9,14).

Perhaps the Holy Spirit's most vital work is getting you to think and live according to your adopted state.

So you have not received a spirit that makes you fearful slaves. Instead, you received God's Spirit when He adopted you as His own children. Now we call Him, "Abba, Father" (Romans 8:15).

Ruth was just a foreigner in the field, but redemption made her a daughter of Israel. You and I were just unredeemed souls, but the Holy Spirit makes us children of God. The Holy Spirit pleads with you; He insists upon you speaking and acting according to your new identity.

He is the One who assures you of your belonging. The Dove of Heaven gives you refuge under His wings (see Ruth 2:12).

When your failures and troubles try to convince you to think like a foreigner, the Holy Spirit shouts them down and bids you to think as a child of God.

The Holy Spirit is the kind Spirit of adoption.

Chapter 10

THE HOLY SPIRIT IN
FIRST SAMUEL

THE APPOINTING SPIRIT—*1 Samuel 10:1; 16:1,13*

The Holy Spirit is the One who raises and tears down, who promotes and demotes.

Although it is named after the prophet, First Samuel is primarily about the kings Saul and David. Israel demands a king. Saul is appointed by God. Saul falls out of favor. David is anointed as king, and Saul is eventually replaced by David (this replacement happens in Second Samuel). There is, of course, much more to the saga than I've just described, but I want to focus in on an overall message in First Samuel. Let's look at two key portions of Scripture:

> *Then Samuel took a flask of olive oil and poured it over Saul's head. He kissed Saul and said, "I am doing this because the Lord has appointed you to be the ruler over Israel, His special possession"* (1 Samuel 10:1).

That verse records the appointing of Saul as king. Let's look at the second key Scripture:

> *Now the Lord said to Samuel, "You have mourned long enough for Saul. I have rejected him as king of Israel, so fill your flask with olive oil and go to Bethlehem. Find a man named Jesse who lives there, for I have selected one of his sons to be my king." ...So as David stood there among his brothers, Samuel took the flask of olive oil he had brought and anointed David with the oil. And the Spirit of the Lord came powerfully upon David from that day on. Then Samuel returned to Ramah* (1 Samuel 16:1,13).

The anointing oil is symbolic of the Holy Spirit. It was the Holy Spirit who empowered both King David and King Saul for rulership. Whomever God appoints to a position of authority He anoints with power. The Holy Spirit is the One who appoints us to positions, and, if need be, the Holy Spirit is the One who will remove us from positions. He raises and lowers, promotes and demotes.

Sadly, King Saul eventually began to walk in rebellion against God. Saul ignored God's voice and stubbornly persisted in rebellion. And when Saul began to disobey God, he was not just stripped of God's favor; he was stripped of the Holy Spirit as well.

> *Now the Spirit of the Lord had left Saul, and the Lord sent a torment-ing spirit that filled him with depression and fear* (1 Samuel 16:14).

I find very few verses in the Bible as terrifying as that one. Saul was stripped of the kingdom, and the kingdom was given to David. David too made his sinful errors, but he knew how to repent before the Lord. Travail-ing under the pains of guilt and possibly recounting what happened to Saul, David prays a prayer of sorrowful repentance:

> *Create in me a clean heart, O God. Renew a loyal spirit within me. Do not banish me from Your presence, and don't take Your Holy Spirit from me* (Psalm 51:10-11).

David valued his relationship with the Holy Spirit, and the Holy Spirit continued to favor David. You and I must recognize who has the power to anoint and appoint. Every position in ministry, every place of influence, every measure of authority is given to you by the Holy Spirit. And what He gives can also be taken away.

We do not and cannot appoint ourselves in places of power. And even if, by persistence of the flesh, you somehow manage to squeeze your way into a place of authority, realize that your footing is not solid. The only author-ity that is secure is the authority that the Holy Spirit appoints.

So obey His leading. Hear His voice. Yield to His commands, lest He be forced to demote you for the sake of your own soul. The Holy Spirit doesn't like pride; He loves humility. When you stay humble before the Holy Spirit, you stay empowered by the Holy Spirit. Don't take for granted the places of authority that He has given you.

The Holy Spirit is the appointing Spirit.

Chapter 11

THE HOLY SPIRIT IN
SECOND SAMUEL

THE SPIRIT WHO SPEAKS THROUGH YOU—*2 Samuel 23:2*

The Holy Spirit speaks through you.

The Church leaves social media highly criticized and underused. Really, social media and any Internet-based media platform can be used for the sake of either Heaven or hell. Whereas we once saw revival "in the streets," we are now poised to see revival spread across the stream. The "scroll down the feed" is the modern-day version of the "stroll down the street."

My ministry team and I see a divine opportunity to spread the Gospel further and more efficiently than ever before.

I often post encouraging messages, videos, and audio sermons on various media platforms. The results are encouraging. I can't even track how many messages my office receives about people being saved from sin, healed of sickness, delivered from addiction, or even baptized in the Holy Spirit while simply watching our ministry content online. In fact, one of the main reasons people like to consume our content is that many report feeling the power of the Holy Spirit while watching, listening, or even reading. The testimonies never stop streaming into our office.

I'm no fool. I don't believe I've had anything to do with the supernatural results except staying out of the way through surrender to the Holy Spirit. Such results cannot possibly come from just the content alone.

When does a message cease to be a message? When does a video cease to be just another video? When does a social media post cease to be another social media post?

When the Holy Spirit speaks through it.

One time, while posting about God's healing power (as I often do), I received a comment from someone asking to be healed of some ailment. Now, I know I don't have any healing power. Only God has healing power. All I do is point people to the one true Healer, Jesus. But there was faith in this person's request—I could sense it through my screen. Don't ask me how, but I'm telling you I could sense the faith in that comment.

I had never done anything like it before. I posted a bold response, as the Holy Spirit spoke through me. My response was something to the effect of, "Receive your healing now in the name of Jesus." The boldness wasn't necessarily in the words I typed. The boldness was in the faith behind those words.

Minutes later, the individual posted (and I'm paraphrasing), "I'm healed! The pain is gone!"

Think about that! Healing occurred through a social media comment. When your words become His Words, when your mouth becomes His mouth, there is power upon your very breath—there is power in the very pronunciation of whatever utterance the Holy Spirit has dictated.

This isn't about speaking special words or reciting certain sounds; this is about the faith and the power behind when the Holy Spirit speaks through you. When the Holy Spirit speaks through you, in that very moment, there is power to be received if there is faith present to receive it.

The Holy Spirit speaking through the believer is a distinguishing factor, and His voice is what made King David unique.

The Book of Second Samuel is primarily about the reign of King David. He is considered to have been one of the greatest kings of Israel. David's record is not perfectly clean, but God used Him. And while there are many factors that contribute to the greatness of David's reign, there is one factor, related to the Holy Spirit, that I want to focus in on here.

This is a short verse, a simple verse, but it reveals one of the keys to David's greatness.

> *The Spirit of the Lord spake by me, and His word was in my tongue* (2 Samuel 23:2 KJV).

King David, one of the greatest kings of Israel, allowed the Holy Spirit to speak through him. It's so wonderfully simple!

King David's royal decrees, his legal proclamations, his promises—many of them were inspired by the Holy Spirit. This is one of the things that set him apart. He didn't pretend to speak on behalf of the Holy Spirit. He didn't speak on behalf of his own imagination or emotions. He would actually speak as the Holy Spirit led him to speak.

The Holy Spirit spoke through King David, and He speaks through you and me. It is His voice in you that brings about greatness.

> *For it is not you who will be speaking—it will be the Spirit of your Father speaking through you* (Matthew 10:20).

If you are a believer, then you can hear the Holy Spirit. If you can hear the Holy Spirit, you can repeat what He says. If you can repeat what He says, then He can speak through you.

The Holy Spirit is the One who speaks through you.

Chapter 12

THE HOLY SPIRIT IN
FIRST KINGS

THE STILL SMALL VOICE—*1 Kings 19:12*

The Holy Spirit speaks softly.

Before the death of David, there is a power struggle for the kingdom of Israel. Although David's son Solomon is the rightful heir to his father's throne, David's other son Adonijah declares himself the king. So before David dies, he instructs the prophet Nathan to anoint Solomon as the rightful king. David's instructions to Solomon are simple:

> *As the time of King David's death approached, he gave this charge to his son Solomon: "I am going where everyone on earth must someday go. Take courage and be a man. Observe the requirements of the Lord your God, and follow all His ways. Keep the decrees, commands, regulations, and laws written in the Law of Moses so that you will be successful in all you do and wherever you go* (1 Kings 2:1-3).

Sometime after David imparts that wisdom to Solomon, David dies. The same wisdom would apply to future kings of Israel as well. It was simple, really: the king's obedience to God was the king's guarantee to a successful reign.

Still, human nature, the treacherous way of being, would complicate the matter. Solomon, despite his wisdom and wealth, would eventually depart from his obedience toward God. Solomon was the same man who was granted an unprecedented measure of wisdom by God. He was the same man who oversaw the construction of the great temple —the majestic structure that amazed royalty and laymen alike, the landmark that housed the Ark of the Covenant. Solomon was the writer of the Book of Proverbs, the Song of Solomon, and the Book of Ecclesiastes—three books of the Bible. Yet he too fell prey to his own flesh.

> *Now King Solomon loved many foreign women. Besides Pharaoh's daughter, he married women from Moab, Ammon, Edom, Sidon, and from among the Hittites. The Lord had clearly instructed the people of Israel, "You must not marry them, because they will turn your hearts to their gods." Yet Solomon insisted on loving them anyway. He had 700 wives of royal birth and 300 concubines. And in fact, they did turn his heart away from the Lord* (1 Kings 11:1-3).

From there, Israel rapidly descended under the leadership of several flawed kings. The kingdom of Israel split in two—northern and southern, ten tribes and two tribes, the kingdom of Israel and the kingdom of Judah.

The ten northern tribes followed a man named Jeroboam. The two southern tribes stood faithful to a man named Rehoboam. Both leaders failed to hold godly standards. Jeroboam led the people of Israel into idol worship and sin. His reign was so hostile to the holiness of God that God said this about him:

> *You have done more evil than all who lived before you. You have made other gods for yourself and have made Me furious with your gold calves* (1 Kings 14:9).

Jeroboam was severely punished. Meanwhile, Rehoboam led the southern kingdom of Judah into paganism.

King after king committed failure after failure. King Abijam disobeyed God. An exception, King Asa pleased God. King Nadab disobeyed God. King Baasha disobeyed God. King Elah disobeyed God. King Omri disobeyed God.

Then King Ahab came to power.

> *Ahab son of Omri began to rule over Israel in the thirty-eighth year of King Asa's reign in Judah. He reigned in Samaria twenty-two years. But Ahab son of Omri did what was evil in the Lord's sight, even more than any of the kings before him. And as though it were not enough to follow the example of Jeroboam, he married*

Jezebel, the daughter of King Ethbaal of the Sidonians, and he begin to bow down in worship of Baal (1 Kings 16:29-31).

To put an end to the corruption, to set a light amidst the darkness, God sends His prophet Elijah to King Ahab. Pronouncing the judgment of God against Israel, Elijah prophesies a drought on the land. The drought lasts for three years.

In the third year of the drought, Elijah is instructed to present himself before King Ahab. And when the prophet confronts the king, there is a spiritual showdown.

When Ahab saw him, he exclaimed, "So, is it really you, you trou-blemaker of Israel?" "I have made no trouble for Israel," Elijah replied. "You and your family are the troublemakers, for you have refused to obey the commands of the Lord and have worshiped the images of Baal instead. Now summon all Israel to join me at Mount Carmel, along with the 450 prophets of Baal and the 400 prophets of Asherah who are supported by Jezebel" (1 Kings 18:17-19).

King Ahab did as the prophet instructed. The challenge was simple: whoever could call down fire from Heaven was the servant of the true God. The false prophets exasperated and embarrassed themselves attempting to call down fire from Heaven. Yet Elijah was able to call down fire from Heaven with a simple prayer. The fire of Heaven roared down, consuming an altar that had been soaked with water.

I contend that Elijah soaked the altar to make the feat impossible without God.

When the people saw this display of power, the fire falling from Heaven, they sided with Elijah, and Elijah had all of the false prophets killed. After Elijah had called down fire from Heaven, he prophesied an end to the drought. First, he called down fire; then, he called down rain (both symbols of the Holy Spirit).

The fire and the rain that came from Heaven validated the man of God. In the same way, the Holy Spirit validates you, the message He speaks through you, and the work He does through you. The Holy Spirit distinguished Elijah, the true prophet of God, from the false prophets of Jezebel. What the pleadings and reasonings of man could not accomplish—the turning of a nation from the deception of idolatry—the Holy Spirit did through Elijah in a moment.

One simple display of the power of God and the curse of generations of disobedience was broken. The spell over the people had dissolved, and they saw the false prophets and false deities for what they truly were. In the face of generations of disobedience, the Holy Spirit raised the standard and made it clear that "this is My true servant Elijah, and he declares the message of the one true God." The Holy Spirit validates you and me. The Holy Spirit validated Elijah while humiliating the false prophets.

Naturally, this upset Jezebel, King Ahab's pagan wife, who then made threats against the life of Elijah. Ironically, Elijah fled in fear.

But Elijah wasn't just afraid; He was discouraged. Imagine what Elijah may have felt. He knew and loved the God who gave him life. He understood, like few ever could, the holiness of God. He cherished the commands of Jehovah, and he loved the nation of Israel. Yet he had witnessed so much evil in his day. Generations of kings had disobeyed God, along with generations of the people. No, Elijah wasn't just afraid for his life—he was burdened for a nation. He longed for there to be others who would stand with him.

It was during Elijah's moment of discouragement that the Holy Spirit spoke.

> *"Go out and stand before me on the mountain," the Lord told him. And as Elijah stood there, the Lord passed by, and a mighty windstorm hit the mountain. It was such a terrible blast that the rocks were torn loose, but the Lord was not in the wind. After the wind there was an earthquake, but the Lord was not in the earthquake. And after the earthquake there was a fire, but the Lord was not in the fire. And after the fire there was the sound of a gentle whisper. When Elijah heard it, he wrapped his face in his cloak and went out and stood at the entrance of the cave. And a voice said, "What are you doing here, Elijah?"* (1 Kings 19:11-13).

In that particular instance, the Holy Spirit wasn't to be found in the vehement wind, the blazing fire, or the tumultuous earthquake. He was to be found in the gentle voice. The King James Version describes the voice in a more poetic fashion:

And after the earthquake a fire; but the Lord was not in the fire: and after the fire a still small voice (1 Kings 19:12).

The Holy Spirit spoke to Elijah in a still small voice. One of the most profound things the Holy Spirit has revealed to me about Himself is that He speaks with a gentle voice. He does not force Himself on anyone, not even the believer. He is gentle, elegant, and regal.

Looking at First Kings as a whole, you can begin to see that the Holy Spirit was ignored time and time again. To confront the evil that had overtaken a nation, God needed a prophet who was able to hear that still small voice.

What would have happened had Solomon remained sensitive to the still small voice? He had riches. He had God's favor. He had unrivaled wisdom from God. But even he was susceptible to ignoring the voice of the Holy Spirit.

Most of the kings of Israel—men of power and influence, men who commanded armies—in all of their strength were too spiritually weak to hear the still small voice. What trouble might Israel have avoided? What miracles would they have seen? What stories of greatness and blessing would have been recorded in the books of the kings had Israel's leadership remained attentive to the voice of the Holy Spirit?

Would the kingdom of Israel have split? Would Jezebel have ever gained power? Would the people have ever wandered so often into paganism had the kings heard the gentle prompting of the Holy Spirit?

Think of the wasted destinies. Think of the heartache. Think of the bloodshed and the suffering. Much of it, if not all of it, could have been avoided if only the kings had been able, like the prophet Elijah, to hear the still small voice.

How many times had the Holy Spirit been ignored? Surely the kings repressed His convicting power. Certainly they resisted Him in many moments, in many ways. The entire Book of First Kings teaches us that the Holy Spirit will speak gently and leave one to their decisions if they decide to stifle His still small voice.

Dear reader, the Holy Spirit speaks in a whisper, and in order to hear that whisper, you must be listening attentively. So often we find ourselves trapped in avoidable troubles and distracted by the concerns of living. The price to pay for resisting the Holy Spirit's guiding nudge is a destructive mixture of confusion, apathy, frustration, and sin. Ignoring His softly whispered instructions, we go out of our way to step on the grounds of temptation. Disobedience doesn't keep the Holy Spirit from speaking; it keeps us from hearing.

The longer you ignore the Holy Spirit, the easier it becomes to ignore Him. The longer you resist the Holy Spirit's call, the harder it becomes to respond to that same call.

We must cherish, above all earthly pleasures, the sweet voice of the Holy Spirit. In every moment, you must be ready to hear the Holy Spirit speak to your heart.

The Holy Spirit speaks with a still small voice.

Chapter 13

THE HOLY SPIRIT IN
SECOND KINGS

THE PERVASIVE OIL—*2 Kings 4:1-7*

The Holy Spirit will fill only what is made available to Him.

The problems with the rulership found in First Kings continue to trouble Israel in Second Kings, in which the patterns of disobedience and the lure of idolatry prove to be consistent.

In both First and Second Kings, we see a pattern: Israel obeys God, and God blesses them. Israel disobeys God, and God leaves them vulnerable to the oppression and attacks of their surrounding enemies. The national tragedy of First Kings is the splitting of Israel into two kingdoms. And in Second Kings, the consequences of that split are fully realized. And in that realization, we are reminded of this wise saying of Jesus:

And if a kingdom be divided against itself, that kingdom cannot stand (Mark 3:24 KJV).

Because Israel and its kings continue to be enticed by idolatry, another national tragedy occurs. The northern and southern kingdoms of Israel are destroyed. The north (Israel) is taken by the Assyrians. The south (Judah) is taken by the Babylonians.

Now if we look back on all the reigns of the kings, we see an overall deprivation of righteousness. After Solomon, none of the kings of Israel are counted as pleasing to the Lord, and only a handful of the kings of Judah do what is right before Him.

Now, while studying the reigns of the kings listed in First and Second Kings, I found something quite interesting. After the reign of Solomon, none of the kings who ruled the northern kingdom of Israel were counted as righteous rulers. Only one came close. His name was Jehu. The Scripture says this about Jehu:

> *Nonetheless the Lord said to Jehu, "You have done well in follow-ing My instructions to destroy the family of Ahab. Therefore, your descendants will be kings of Israel down to the fourth generation"* (2 Kings 10:30).

That the Scripture records the Lord telling Jehu that he did "well" makes Jehu unique among the kings of Israel. But do you know what else makes him unique? The Bible records him being anointed for kingship:

> *So Jehu left the others and went into the house. Then the young prophet poured the oil over Jehu's head and said, "This is what the Lord, the God of Israel, says: I anoint you king over the Lord's people, Israel"* (2 Kings 9:6).

After Solomon, we see no other king of Israel being anointed in First Kings or Second Kings. The only king who did well was the king who was anointed.

Now, this does not necessarily mean that the other kings didn't go through the ceremonial anointing. This just means that the Scripture emphasizes the anointing of King Jehu. He was truly anointed by God.

Jehu destroyed the family of King Ahab, had Jezebel cast down, smashed and burned the pagan pillars, and desecrated the temple of Baal. That's what the anointing does; that's what the Holy Spirit does—He destroys the kingdom of hell.

> *In this way, Jehu destroyed every trace of Baal worship from Israel* (2 Kings 10:28).

But there was a problem. As zealous as Jehu was to fulfill the commands of God and as anointed as he was to do so, Jehu compromised. He obeyed the Lord in some areas but not in all.

> *But Jehu did not obey the Law of the Lord, the God of Israel, with all his heart. He refused to turn from the sins that Jeroboam had led Israel to commit* (2 Kings 10:31).

That oil of the Holy Spirit did not fill every part of his heart. The Holy Spirit will only go as far as you allow. It is the nature of the Holy Spirit to fill what is empty, to empower what is weak, and to bless what is surrendered. The Holy Spirit has a pervasive nature. In Second Kings, we find another example of this aspect of the Holy Spirit's nature.

A poor widow approaches the prophet Elisha. She is broken and desperate because a creditor, whom she cannot pay, is threatening to enslave her sons to reconcile her debt. She pleads with the prophet to do something. Elisha asks the woman what she has in her house. She replies by telling him that she has a flask of oil. So the prophet instructs her:

> *Borrow as many empty jars as you can from your friends and neighbors. Then go into your house with your sons and shut the door behind you. Pour olive oil from your flask into the jars, setting each one aside when it is filled* (2 Kings 4:3-4).

As the widow poured the oil from her flask into the empty jars, there was a supernatural multiplication of that oil. She and her sons kept collecting and filling jars. The oil kept flowing until there was nowhere else for it to flow.

> *Soon every container was full to the brim! "Bring me another jar,"* she said to one of her sons. "There aren't any more!" he told her. *And then the olive oil stopped flowing* (2 Kings 4:6).

The Holy Spirit will move as far as you allow Him to move in your life. King Jehu had an anointing from God, but he did not allow that oil to touch every aspect of his life. The Scripture says, *"But Jehu did not obey the Law of the Lord, the God of Israel, with all his heart..."* (2 Kings 10:31). The widow and her sons experienced a supernatural flow of oil, but it stopped as soon as there was nowhere else for it to go.

The Holy Spirit's gentle nature is again revealed in Second Kings, as it was in First Kings concerning His voice. He is a gentleman. Often, He awaits our invitation to act in our lives.

People often ask me, "Brother David, how can I get more of the Holy Spirit?" The truth is that you can't get any more of the Holy Spirit than you already have right now. The Holy Spirit is an eternal Being, and that which is eternal cannot be divided into portions. When you were born again, the Holy Spirit came to reside in you in fullness. All the Holy Spirit was, is, or ever shall be lives within you. When the Holy Spirit comes, He comes in fullness. You can't get any more of His power, His presence, or His essence. He simply is.

It's not a matter of how much you have of the Holy Spirit but rather how much the Holy Spirit has of you.

Will you be like Jehu, who only surrendered some of his heart even though he had the anointing, the Holy Spirit?

Will you stop giving the Holy Spirit jars to fill?

You don't have to force the Holy Spirit to act; He wants to act. He's just waiting for something to fill, someone to use. The Holy Spirit is not invasive; He's pervasive. He will not force Himself upon you, but He will be quick and faithful to fill what is yielded to Him.

THE HEAVENLY WIND—*2 Kings 2:11*

As they were walking along and talking, suddenly a chariot of fire appeared, drawn by horses of fire. It drove between the two men, separating them, and Elijah was carried by a whirlwind into heaven (2 Kings 2:11).[1]

The whirlwind carried Elijah into Heaven. The Holy Spirit is the Wind that sweeps us up and carries us into the depths of God's presence. He carries us to spiritual heights we could not reach on our own.

---

1 See also Second Kings 2:1.

Chapter 14

THE HOLY SPIRIT IN FIRST CHRONICLES

A KINDRED SPIRIT—*1 Chronicles 12:18*

The Holy Spirit facilitates divine connections.

The history of Israel and Judah are again recorded in First and Second Chronicles. The same themes from First and Second Kings reappear—the destructive nature of idolatry, the faithfulness of God, the power of the choices we make, and so forth.

There is one instance that stands out to me in First Chronicles, one that gives us insight into yet another characteristic of the Holy Spirit.

David is being pursued by King Saul, whom David has already been anointed to replace. The situation is tense. Driven by jealousy and tormented by the demonic, Saul is out for the life of David. David, honoring the anointing upon the life of Saul, refuses to retaliate.

David and his men, defectors from Saul's authority, were hiding from Saul in the town of Ziklag. The Scripture tells us that David was well protected by skilled archers (among other kinds of warriors):

All of them were expert archers, and they could shoot arrows or sling stones with their left hand as well as their right. They were all relatives of Saul from the tribe of Benjamin (1 Chronicles 12:2).

The archers would have protected David from any approaching enemies, and those skilled with the spear and shield would have killed any enemies who came close to David.

Some brave and experienced warriors from the tribe of Gad also defected to David while he was at the stronghold in the wilderness.

They were expert with both shield and spear, as fierce as lions and as swift as deer on the mountains (1 Chronicles 12:8).

The warriors who defended the future king had formed a hedge around him; David was insulated, covered. Only those whom David chose to allow near him would be able to come close.

David is approached by more men from the tribes of Benjamin and Judah. He knows not whether they are there to join his ranks or to take his life. And how could he have known? For all David knew, these men who approached him could have been spies sent by Saul to perform an assassination. So David speaks out:

David went out to meet them and said, "If you have come in peace to help me, we are friends. But if you have come to betray me to my enemies when I am innocent, then may the God of our ancestors see it and punish you" (1 Chronicles 12:17).

There was tension about the air, as the men at Ziklag studied the approaching men. Were those men enemies or new comrades?

Often, we find ourselves studying those who cross our paths. How are you to know who God is sending your way, who the enemy is sending your way, or who is just passing by?

Then the Spirit came upon Amasai, the leader of the Thirty, and he said, "We are yours, David! We are on your side, son of Jesse. Peace and prosperity be with you, and success to all who help you, for your God is the one who helps you." So David let them join him, and he made them officers over his troops (1 Chronicles 12:18).

The Holy Spirit will protect your inner circle by closely connecting you with people of a kindred spirit.

It's amazing how easily you can identify other Christians. We run into each other all the time. I don't know how many times I've said to a total stranger, "You're a Christian, aren't you?" Each time, they become excited and say, "Yes! How did you know?"

What is it within them that makes them identifiable?

I know them by the Spirit. We know each other by the Spirit. David didn't know whether or not the men from the tribes of Benjamin and Judah were friends or assassins until the Spirit of the Lord moved upon them. Once they began to prophesy, they were easily identifiable.

Allow the Holy Spirit to help you identify those who are of a kindred spirit. And I'm not just writing about identifying other believers; I'm writing about divine connections. Follow that inner leading within you when forming relationships in ministry, in business, and in life. Let the Holy Spirit bring to you people who are a perfect fit. Divine connections are a work of the Holy Spirit.

The Holy Spirit is the kindred Spirit.

Chapter 15

THE HOLY SPIRIT IN SECOND CHRONICLES

THE FORTIFYING SPIRIT—*2 Chronicles 15:1-4*

The Holy Spirit reveals our compromises.

Second Chronicles continues where First Chronicles leaves off. It documents the reign of King Solomon, the building of the tabernacle, and the reigns of other kings.

In Second Chronicles 14, we see that King Asa pleased the Lord by ridding Judah of idol worship. Because of the obedience of King Asa, God gave Israel rest from their enemies and allowed them to fortify their land.

> *During those peaceful years, he was able to build up the fortified
> towns throughout Judah. No one tried to make war against him
> at this time, for the Lord was giving him rest from his enemies*
> (2 Chronicles 14:6).

Suddenly, the peace of Judah was disrupted when there was an attack from an Ethiopian army. Asa cried out to the Lord for victory, and victory was granted. However, there were some things that Asa needed to set in order.

Why had the peace been disrupted in the first place? Why was the enemy suddenly bold enough to attack? The Holy Spirit gave Asa the answer through a man named Azariah:

> *Then the Spirit of God came upon Azariah son of Oded, and he
> went out to meet King Asa as he was returning from the battle.
> "Listen to me, Asa!" he shouted. "Listen, all you people of Judah
> and Benjamin! The Lord will stay with you as long as you stay*

with Him! Whenever you seek Him, you will find Him. But if you abandon Him, He will abandon you. For a long time Israel was without the true God, without a priest to teach them, and without the Law to instruct them. But whenever they were in trouble and turned to the Lord, the God of Israel, and sought Him out, they found Him" (2 Chronicles 15:1-4).

Why was the Holy Spirit speaking this message of warning to King Asa? King Asa's response reveals the problem:

When Asa heard this message from Azariah the prophet, he took courage and removed all the detestable idols from the land of Judah and Benjamin and in the towns he had captured in the hill country of Ephraim. And he repaired the altar of the Lord, which stood in front of the entry room of the Lord's Temple (2 Chronicles 15:8).

There had been some setbacks in the righteousness of the land. Although Asa had issued decrees that combatted idolatry in Judah and Benjamin, there was a slow and secret return to idolatry among God's people. This subtle internal spiritual death released the scent of decay, which attracted foes like vultures. Because internal righteousness was compromised, external enemies were emboldened. Yet God sent a messenger to correct the errors, patch the leaks, and reroute the wandering.

And how often it is that we wander. Like a weary body that fades away into sleep without your awareness or permission, so the spiritual state of a man will regress without one's knowledge. By nature we wander, lose focus, and move adrift. Our distraction is unwelcome, yet subtle. If we do not remain alert, we too will leave ourselves vulnerable to our enemies, especially the most destructive enemy—the flesh.

Thankfully, we have the Holy Spirit. Just as He fortified the spiritual weaknesses of King Asa through Azariah, so He fortifies you today. We may not always be alert, but He is.

Have you ever suddenly received a fresh wind of spiritual enthusiasm? You're going about your week as usual, when suddenly you are given a strong desire to pray and you feel a pull toward the matters of the Spirit. You didn't necessarily do anything to incite this renewed passion for the things of God; it just came upon you. That's the work of the Holy Spirit. This is why it is so important that you yield to the leading of the Holy

Spirit. He's trying to fortify your weaknesses. He's trying to stop the leaks in your spiritual reservoir. He sees the small compromises in prayer, devotion to the Word, and righteous living. He sees when you get too comfortable. And He moves in to help you renew the promises you made to the Lord.

Be like King Asa and repair the altar of God in your life. Return to spiritual vigilance. Obey the leading of the Holy Spirit, who desires to reinvigorate your spiritual senses.

The Holy Spirit is the fortifying Spirit.

Chapter 16

THE HOLY SPIRIT IN
EZRA

THE CONVICTING SPIRIT—*Ezra 10:1*

The Holy Spirit is the One who convicts.

I had just finished presenting what most would consider to be a typical evangelistic invitation. All across the room, heads were bowed and eyes were closed. Adding to the typical call to repentance, I stoically instructed, "I don't want anyone looking around the room right now. This moment is just between you and God."

The music played while I pleaded, but after the passing of several awkward minutes, not a single person responded to my heartfelt invitation. I was tempted to dismiss the matter and transition to another portion of the service. However, before I made the switch, the Holy Spirit gently nudged me in a different direction.

In my spirit, I sensed His desire for the people to begin praying in the spirit—praying in tongues.

Following the leading of the Holy Spirit, I instructed the people to begin praying in tongues. They lifted their hands and began to do so.

About two minutes had passed, and we were all continuing to pray in tongues.

It was right around this time that a man about my age came walking down the aisle and toward the stage upon which I stood. He was visibly shaken. With tears streaming down his face and his mouth shaking with prayers, he walked right up to the platform, fell to his knees, and began to weep.

At this point, I calmed the crowd and stepped down to converse with the man. I said, "Hey there, look up at me for a second. I'd like to talk with you." When he looked up at me, his eyes were still filled with tears, and his face was red from sobbing.

I asked him, "Can you tell me why you're crying?" I put the microphone to his mouth and waited for his response. What he said touched my heart.

"Because," he explained, "I've been trying to find God for so long. And tonight, He found me."

The church began to cheer and worship the Lord. And right there, in front of us all, that man gave his heart to Jesus and was born again.

What couldn't be accomplished by human effort was accomplished by the work of the Holy Spirit. That happened several years ago, but the lesson I learned in that service has been cemented into the foundation of my faith and ministry.

Dear reader, I had, at that point, been in ministry for a few years and had grown accustomed to an almost systematic approach to evangelism. Thankfully, I have a friendship with the Holy Spirit that guided me to embrace a more effective flow of ministry.

> *And my speech and my preaching was not with enticing words of man's wisdom, but in demonstration of the Spirit and of power* (1 Corinthians 2:4).

I believe that the Holy Spirit is Heaven's greatest evangelist. When it comes to preaching the Gospel and evangelizing the lost, we must be careful to not rely upon techniques, systems, or programs.

Now when I write that we must never rely upon systems and programs, I am certain that you, dear reader, will enthusiastically affirm such a truth.

But ministry can become so familiar to us that we enter a place of human effort, often without realizing it. In fact, almost everyone who is relying on human effort for ministry and spirituality is doing so without knowing it.

After all, who really decides, "I think I'll do it my way instead"?

No, most believers wouldn't dare to so blatantly reject or stifle the work of the Holy Spirit. So, if one does stop depending on the Spirit, he usually does so unknowingly. I would even go as far as to say that most believers would become offended at the suggestion that they have moved away from the Spirit's method of ministry approach. But many have. None of us would do so willingly, so we must humbly and honestly open ourselves up to the question, "Have I begun to rely upon my efforts instead of His?"

In that church service, all of my practiced presentation and expended effort couldn't present Christ in a way that compelled the lost to surrender in humble repentance at His feet.

I may have worn the title of "evangelist." Furthermore, I may have even led several hundreds to Christ at that point in my ministry.

Who cares? That didn't matter.

What mattered was my surrender to His leading. What always matters is obedience to His gentle, guiding voice. He is, after all, Heaven's greatest evangelist. No one can present the glory of the Person of Christ like He can. No one can convict a soul of sin as the Spirit does. In matters of ministry, He is masterful.

Every time I preach the Gospel, I am amazed at how people respond to it with such intensity. Without the power and presence of the Holy Spirit, my salvation messages would simply be speeches. Having preached to many people, I have come to see the difference between when someone is being drawn by the Holy Spirit and when they are not.

In the Book of Ezra, God's people are allowed to return to Jerusalem to rebuild the temple. In the first six chapters of Ezra, the work on the temple begins, is disrupted, and then is finally completed. Consider the mercy of God. After all that we have read concerning the waywardness of God's people, God was still willing to show mercy in allowing His people to return to the land He promised them—and even rebuild the temple!

Several years after the temple was rebuilt, Ezra arrived in Jerusalem from Babylon. The Bible tells us that God's hand was on Ezra:

> *...for the gracious hand of his God was on him. This was because Ezra had determined to study and obey the Law of the Lord and to teach those decrees and regulations to the people of Israel* (Ezra 7:9-10).

Although Israel had yet again been shown the wonderful mercy of God, they yielded to their ancient temptations. Ezra records the sad state of God's people:

> *When these things had been done, the Jewish leaders came to me and said, "Many of the people of Israel, and even some of the*

priests and Levites, have not kept themselves separate from the
other peoples living in the land. They have taken up the detestable
practices of the Canaanites, Hittites, Perizzites, Jebusites, Ammo-
nites, Moabites, Egyptians, and Amorites" (Ezra 9:1).

Even some of the leaders of Israel were participating in active rebellion
against God's commands. It was then that Ezra released a passionate prayer
unto God:

O my God, I am utterly ashamed; I blush to lift up my face to You.
For our sins are piled higher than our heads, and our guilt has
reached to the heavens (Ezra 9:6).

Ezra prayed with a holy boldness, and his prayer contained truths that
pierced the hearts of its hearers. He uttered many convicting phrases (see
Ezra 9:6-15). Indicting the people of God, Ezra contrasted the constant sinfulness of man with the faithful mercy of God. His words made it clear that
the people of Israel were overdue for and deserving of the wrath of God.

But something powerful happened while Ezra prayed. The people
were convicted.

While Ezra prayed and made this confession, weeping and lying
face down on the ground in front of the Temple of God, a very
large crowd of people from Israel—men, women, and children—
gathered and wept bitterly with him (Ezra 10:1).

The convicting power of the Holy Spirit had so potently rested upon the
prayer of Ezra that it caused the people to feel the weight of sin upon their
consciences. Within three days, all of the people had gathered in repentance, and they were trembling with the fear of God.

…They were trembling both because of the seriousness of the matter
and because it was raining (Ezra 10:9).

When Ezra made a distinct call to repentance, the people responded
with humility and acknowledged their sins.

Then the whole assembly raised their voices and answered, "Yes,
you are right; we must do as you say!" (Ezra 10:12)

Ezra was a man who was well versed in the Word of God. But when it
came to causing the people to repent, there was nothing that he could do
but preach and pray. Ezra could live and teach the Word, but he couldn't

force people to repent. Only the Holy Spirit could move the hearts of the people toward repentance. However, Ezra did know and live the Word. When you live and teach it, the Holy Spirit will back it. He needs someone to work through, someone who both lives and declares it. If it is declared but not lived, it lacks power. If it is lived but not declared, no one will hear it.

> *And when He comes, He will convict the world of its sin, and of God's righteousness, and of the coming judgment* (John 16:8).

Want to win souls? Be graced by the Holy Spirit, Heaven's greatest evangelist.

The Holy Spirit is the One who brings the conviction.

Chapter 17

THE HOLY SPIRIT IN
NEHEMIAH

THE COMFORTER—*Hebrew Meaning of "Nehemiah"*

The Holy Spirit brings comfort.

Exiles were returning to Jerusalem. The temple had been rebuilt. However, the walls of Jerusalem were in disrepair. With people beginning to return to Jerusalem and the potential of enemy threats, the rebuilding of the walls was becoming a pressing need. Nehemiah, a cup-bearer to the king of Persia, was especially burdened by the vulnerability of Jerusalem. After praying for favor with the king of Persia and pleading for God's mercy (see Neh. 1), Nehemiah makes a bold request:

> *The king asked, "Well, how can I help you?" With a prayer to the God of heaven, I replied, "If it please the king, and if you are pleased with me, your servant, send me to Judah to rebuild the city where my ancestors are buried"* (Nehemiah 2:4-5).

Nehemiah was granted the permission and the resources necessary to rebuild the walls. Despite enemy opposition and with admirable persistence, Nehemiah succeeds in rebuilding the walls. He then leads the people in national repentance (for they had yet again disobeyed God's laws), and he institutes helpful reforms.

In addition to overseeing the building of the wall, Nehemiah cared for the least among the people. He cared for the oppressed, the helpless, the enslaved, and the poor (see Neh. 5:1-19). He fed the hungry, redeemed slaves, and stood up for the weak. Through his work, which was not motivated by material gain, you can see his compassion.

Without walls, the people were vulnerable and afraid. They lived under the constant fear of being attacked. The walls brought certainty and protection, security and comfort. Does that not sound like the work of the Holy Spirit? After all, Jesus said this of the Holy Spirit:

> *And I will pray the Father, and He shall give you another Comforter, that He may abide with you for ever* (John 14:16 KJV).

And you'll love this: Nehemiah's name means "Yah comforts" or "the Lord comforts." Nehemiah, the comforter who sought to restore the peace of Jerusalem through the rebuilding of the walls, is a shadow of the Holy Spirit.

The Holy Spirit cares for the broken and the down-and-out. Just as the building of the walls soothed the fears of God's people, so the Holy Spirit comforts you when you're afraid. Just as Nehemiah worked to lift the burdens of the oppressed, so the Holy Spirit will lift you from yours.

The Holy Spirit doesn't just comfort our fears; He comforts our hurts. The burned rubble of the walls was a symbol of the past failures of Israel. They had disobeyed and destroyed their own interests. But Nehemiah rebuilt from the rubble.

The chaos and shame of your past, the wrestling with what could have or may have been, brings discomfort. But the Holy Spirit is your Comforter. The Holy Spirit restores and comforts. The Holy Spirit comforts you by soothing the pain of the past. He assures you by surrounding you to protect you from the enemy.

THE GOOD SPIRIT—*Nehemiah 9:20*

> *You sent Your good Spirit to instruct them, and You did not stop giving them manna from heaven or water for their thirst* (Nehemiah 9:20).

There is nothing defiled about the nature of the Holy Spirit. He is divine. He is pure. He is not just good; He is goodness itself. His every action and aspect arises from the intrinsic goodness of God.

Chapter 18

THE HOLY SPIRIT IN
ESTHER

THE VOICE OF DESTINY—*Esther 4:13-14*

The Holy Spirit speaks at key moments and through key people.

The Jews were living in exile in Persia, where King Xerxes was searching for a new queen. King Xerxes sent representatives throughout the empire to search for beautiful women who became candidates, one of whom Xerxes would choose as his queen.

Esther, a Jewish woman, was among the women selected. Esther kept her nationality a secret just as her cousin Mordecai instructed. Along with the other women, she underwent a lengthy preparation.

> *Before each young woman was taken to the king's bed, she was given the prescribed twelve months of beauty treatments—six months with oil of myrrh, followed by six months with special perfumes and ointments* (Esther 2:12).

Esther won the favor of King Xerxes. She was made the queen, and her cousin Mordecai became a palace official.

Sometime later, a man named Haman was given a promotion by King Xerxes and became the most powerful official in the empire.

Refusing to follow custom, Mordecai didn't bow when Haman would pass by. That upset Haman's ego. Haman discovered Mordecai's Jewish nationality and devised a horrendous plan of revenge. Driven by a vengeful anger, Haman suggested to King Xerxes that the Jewish people be destroyed. What an ego! Think of how petty Haman was to incite a genocide all because one man refused to bow as he walked by. That must have been demonic. Haman's reasoning to the king was that the Jews were separate from the empire in customs and laws and thus were too dangerous to keep alive.

Convinced, King Xerxes permitted Haman to carry on with the genocide. Haman was given the power and the resources to murder all the Jews who lived in the empire. At that point, Esther's nationality was still kept a secret from King Xerxes.

In a message to Esther, Mordecai asked the queen to then reveal her nationality to King Xerxes, put her life at risk, and request that King Xerxes cancel the order to kill the Jewish people.

> *Mordecai sent this reply to Esther: "Don't think for a moment that because you're in the palace you will escape when all other Jews are killed. If you keep quiet at a time like this, deliverance and relief for the Jews will arise from some other place, but you and your relatives will die. Who knows if perhaps you were made queen for just such a time as this?"* (Esther 4:13-14).

Esther selflessly and courageously did as Mordecai instructed her to do. She approached King Xerxes and Esther found favor. King Xerxes said this to her:

> *Now go ahead and send a message to the Jews in the king's name, telling them whatever you want, and seal it with the king's signet ring. But remember that whatever has already been written in the king's name and sealed with his signet ring can never be revoked* (Esther 8:8).

An entire nation was spared from death because of the perfectly timed boldness of one woman. Had Esther chosen inaction, the consequences would have been deathly tragic. Furthermore, had Esther not heard the words of Mordecai, the Jewish people may have been wiped from existence.

The Holy Spirit's influence in the Book of Esther is undeniable.

Like Ruth, Esther was anointed with oil before making a key request. I think of how the Holy Spirit must have given favor to Esther when she approached King Xerxes.

I also see that the salvation of a nation was sealed by the king's ring, just as our salvation is sealed by our King's Holy Spirit.

In Him, you also, after listening to the message of truth, the gospel of your salvation—having also believed, you were sealed in Him with the Holy Spirit of promise, who is given as a pledge of our inheritance, with a view to the redemption of God's own possession, to the praise of His glory (Ephesians 1:13-14 NASB).[1]

Yet in the Book of Esther, where I see the Holy Spirit most clearly at work is in the prophetic words of Mordecai. Consider the weightiness of the moment. Esther's actions would lead to the salvation of not just the Jews, but of all, for eternal salvation would eventually come through the Jews.

As I asked in the introduction of my book, was it not promised to us that the Holy Spirit would speak through us at pivotal moments?

For the Holy Spirit will teach you at that time what needs to be said (Luke 12:12).

For it is not you who will be speaking—it will be the Spirit of your Father speaking through you (Matthew 10:20).

Knowing that the Holy Spirit is the One who speaks through human vessels at divine moments, we can clearly see the Holy Spirit at work through Mordecai when he spoke those consequential and prophetic words.

The Book of Esther is often said to be about the sovereignty of God. I believe that to be true. I also believe that it's about the power of our choices in response to His leading. God positioned Esther, but Esther chose to act. The Holy Spirit spoke, but Esther chose to obey. The timely voice of the Holy Spirit harmonizes the sovereignty of God with the will of man.

The Holy Spirit will also speak to you at pivotal moments, through key people.

---

1   See also Second Corinthians 1:22.

Chapter 19

THE HOLY SPIRIT IN
JOB

THE LIFE-GIVING SPIRIT—*Job 33:4*

The Holy Spirit sustains all life.

I was ministering in Northern California at one of my ministry miracle services. In the front row sat a Hindu family that had been invited by one of their family members who had converted to Christianity. Hearing that there were miracles taking place, the family came to receive the healing touch of God.

The father was in a wheelchair, and it was his son, the Christian, who had brought him. They didn't understand most of what I preached. They didn't even really understand English. But when the power of God started to flow, they became very attentive.

After praying with several others who needed healing, I finally went to pray for the Hindu family. The man in the wheelchair was healed and began to walk. The people there began to praise God for the miracle, and the Hindu family received Christ.

I've often seen the Lord heal nonbelievers. For some reason, that surprises Christians, but let me take this even further. The goodness of God touches all. God doesn't just heal the nonbeliever; He sustains the very life of the nonbeliever.

You see, every living being is sustained by the power of the Holy Spirit. He has power over everything and love for all.

In the Book of Job, the Holy Spirit is revealed as the breath of life and the Creator of man:

> *For the Spirit of God has made me, and the breath of the Almighty gives me life* (Job 33:4).

The Book of Job records the testing of a man who lost everything—his family, his health, his riches. It causes us to reflect upon the tired question, "Why does God allow tragedy and evil?" But this revelation about the Holy Spirit doesn't have to do with the overall narrative of Job—it is simply a hidden treasure of wisdom about the Holy Spirit. I suppose that if one were to desire a more thematic "tie-in," one could say this: Who are we to question the living God? Our very breath with which we question His wisdom is sustained by His Holy Spirit.

The Holy Spirit doesn't just empower the believer; He sustains the life of the sinner. The very breath with which many curse and mock the Holy Spirit is given by the Holy Spirit. All of creation, every life, every breath is graced by the Holy Spirit.[1]

Every living being on this earth is sustained by the breath of life that was breathed in the beginning (see Gen. 2:7).

He does not dwell in every person as He dwells in the believer, but His work, the sustaining of life itself, touches all. The Holy Spirit is truly merciful and powerful. He truly is the life-giving Spirit.

---

1 See also Job 27:3; Genesis 2:7; Genesis 6:17; Genesis 7:15,22; Isaiah 42:5; Ecclesiastes 3:19; Daniel 5:23; and Psalm 104:29-30.

Chapter 20

THE HOLY SPIRIT IN
PSALMS

THE SPIRIT OF WORSHIP—*Psalm 51:11*

The Holy Spirit inspires worship.

Worship is simply an expression of love, adoration, admiration, praise, or awe for the glory, nature, and Person of God. Worship is giving God glory as He reveals His Glory to you—it is an eternal cycle of awe and revelation. We see something in God that invokes a response of adoration. That adoration leads to God showing us more of Himself. But it begins with a revelation of God. Otherwise, how can one adore what doesn't even cross into his awareness?

In the beginning of my walk with the Lord, when I was in my early teens, I struggled with finding a "flow" in my worship. I found myself frustrated with what seemed to be a lack of connection with God. There was something very distracted about my approach. I wasn't searching for a feeling or an emotion; I was searching for a genuine connection with God as I worshiped Him—still, that connection eluded me.

I would jump and shout, plead and cry. Yet there remained a very systematic dryness to my worship. I knew how to sing songs to the Lord. I knew how to speak His praises. Yet while trying to worship the Lord, my mind would be bombarded with the responsibilities of life, the shame of yesterday, and the worries of the future. My emotions were in the way. My scattered thoughts were in the way. My insecurities were in the way. My uncertainty about what God thought of me was in the way. I was too preoccupied with self.

That all changed in one night. On that night, the Holy spirit showed me how to truly worship.

I attended a youth service in Orange, California. To be honest with you, I don't really remember what the preacher talked about. I don't remember the videos, the theme, or even where I sat during the service. The service was good; it went as youth services usually go. But there was nothing especially memorable about it. I had yet to receive anything that one could consider life altering. Still, within my heart, I knew there was more. Something was about to happen, and I just knew it.

The preacher finished his sermon, and the worship team joined him on stage. It was then that he challenged everyone in attendance: "I want everyone in this place to feel free to worship God tonight." I was happy to hear it. "Just close your eyes, lift your hands, and focus on the Lord."

And then the pastor did something unique, something I had never seen anyone ever do during a worship service. He explained, "You know, sometimes we're too distracted by everything around us. We're too distracted by how we look, who is doing what, and whatever else is happening. Here's what I'm gonna do. I want all the lights off. Just forget about everything around you. When the room becomes dark, just focus on the Lord and sing."

And then they turned off the lights. At first I thought it was a strange thing to do, and the religious part of my mind thought it was silly. But in that moment, when all the lights were off, I had nothing to look at and nobody to consider except the Lord. I lifted my hands and forgot about my surroundings. The sound of the anointed music filled the room. In the dark, I became keenly aware of the vibrations of the music. They seemed to carry a power on them as they surged through the worshiping crowd.

The sound of the worship music drowned out the noise of my inner conflict, and the darkness of the room left me with nothing to notice. My mind was left with one focus: the King of Glory. For the first time, I felt overwhelmed as I worshiped the Lord.

As I worshiped, tears began to flow down my face, and I felt a heavy pressing sensation come over me. There were times when I had pressed into God, but in that service, I could feel Him pressing back into me. Such a weight came upon me. And as my tears began to flow, they acted as the trickling waters that ultimately break a dam. My gentle tears soon turned into deep, uncontrollable sobbing. I had to catch my breath. The weight of the Holy Spirit's presence literally took my breath away.

Oh, and the love I felt! I wasn't just thinking, "God loves me" or hearing someone say, "God loves you." God Himself was leaning on me, embracing me, and allowing me to sense the unfathomable depth of His immense love. I knew God loved me, but too often had I allowed the enemy and the flesh to make me feel unloved and unlovable. In that moment, I felt like I was in Heaven. There was such a sweetness, such a warmth to the embrace of God's love. I could feel God's love beaming through me, wrapping around me, and moving all about the room.

That moment wasn't made by a man. It was surrendered by man, but it was made by the Holy Spirit.

The preacher said, "On the count of three, I'm going to turn on the lights. Don't worry about who's looking at you. Don't worry about who is or isn't worshiping. Don't get distracted. Just keep worshiping."

When the lights went on, I just continued to sob and worship. Hardly able to sing, with my mouth shaking, I simply stood there and adored the Lord. The band began to play that song "Who Is This King of Glory?" And when we began to sing, "His name is Jesus, precious Jesus," the glorious ecstasy that I was experiencing only intensified. I shook and sobbed so hard that my knees began to weaken.

Believe me when I tell you that, from that moment on, there was no longer a frustration in my worship.

So what happened?

Well, before that moment, I had tried to worship the Lord in my own effort. I sang in my own effort. I thought about the Lord in my own effort. I tried to connect with God in my own effort. But when I stopped thinking about myself and stopped focusing on every thought that rushed through my mind, I was finally able to see where the Holy Spirit was pointing. He was pointing at Jesus all along.

All true worship begins with revelation, and all true revelation comes by the Spirit. This is why you cannot worship God without the help of the Holy Spirit.

For God is Spirit, so those who worship Him must worship in spirit and in truth (John 4:24).

The Book of Psalms exudes Spirit-inspired adoration of God. All throughout the book, there is worship and praise. The Holy Spirit inspired every bit of that. In Psalms, David praises and worships the many facets of God's power, nature, and character. Look at the heart of David being put on display. You can see his heart of worship through his writings.

I will bless the Lord at all times: His praise shall continually be in my mouth. My soul shall make her boast in the Lord: the humble shall hear thereof, and be glad. O magnify the Lord with me, and let us exalt His name together (Psalm 34:1-3 KJV).

David loved to praise and worship the Lord. His love for God overflowed and was poured out in worship. His worship didn't have to be forced. It just sprung up from deep within him. Containing rich revelation, the psalms of David were actually inspired by the Holy Spirit. Yes, King David was filled with the Holy Spirit, and he cherished that precious presence on his life.

Do not banish me from Your presence, and don't take Your Holy Spirit from me (Psalm 51:11).

The Psalms are prophetic, inspired, and glorifying of the Lord. It was the Holy Spirit in David who moved him to write such beautiful descriptions of the splendor of God. It was the Holy Spirit who inspired poetic stanzas of worship in the heart of David. And it is the Holy Spirit who leads you into the adoration of the Father and the Son. He accents the majesty of our great God, reveals the nature of the Lord, and uncovers the mysteries of His eternal Being. The Holy Spirit reveals the unsearchable riches found within the depths of the Almighty.

This jubilance, this whole-minded obsession for the Person of God, is of the Holy Spirit. Don't struggle—surrender. Don't become frustrated—relax. Allow the Holy Spirit to reveal Jesus to you, and then allow Him to inspire you with what He revealed. You can sing in the flesh, but you can't see in the flesh. You must be still to allow His working.

Be still, and know that I am God!... (Psalm 46:10).

Be still and know. Stillness precedes revelation, and revelation is the foundation of worship. You can't look at yourself and receive revelation. You can't look at your past, your problems, or your worries, and receive revelation. You have to look at what the Holy Spirit reveals to you. If He hasn't revealed anything to you lately, then read the Word until He gives you some fresh revelation from the Word—some revelation of Jesus that ignites the fires of passionate worship. The Holy Spirit is speaking to you, even in this very moment, and He wants to inspire worship within you. The day of frustration halting your worship is over. Just allow your inner chaos to be calmed as you focus on something about the Lord.

Learn to relax and refocus. Allow the Holy Spirit, like the wind, to bring movement to your worship. Just as He inspired it in David, so He will inspire it in you.

The Holy Spirit is the Spirit of worship.

THE OIL OF HONOR—*Psalm 23:5*

You prepare a feast for me in the presence of my enemies. You honor me by anointing my head with oil. My cup overflows with blessings (Psalm 23:5).

To anoint with oil is to show honor. Living a life influenced and guided by the Holy Spirit will bring honor. A Spirit-led life is an honorable one.

THE OIL OF JOY—*Psalm 45:7*

You love justice and hate evil. Therefore God, your God, has anointed you, pouring out the oil of joy on you more than on anyone else (Psalm 45:7).

Upon whoever welcomes Him, the Holy Spirit pours joy. Whoever is graced by His presence walks free from heavy burdens. Truly spiritual people are joyful people, not angry people. The Holy Spirit is the oil of joy.

THE OIL OF FAVOR—*Psalm 84:9*

O God, look with favor upon the king, our shield! Show favor to the one You have anointed (Psalm 84:9).

The writer of Psalm 84:9 asked the Lord to grant favor because of the anointing. The Holy Spirit's presence in your life will attract favor. Opportunities, unavailable to anyone else, become available to friends of the Holy Spirit. Friends of the Holy Spirit cannot be stopped, because they are favored by God. The Holy Spirit is the oil of favor.

Chapter 21

THE HOLY SPIRIT IN PROVERBS

THE SPIRIT OF WISDOM—*Proverbs 1:20-23*

The Holy Spirit gives us wisdom.

Controversy has followed me ever since I began in the ministry. Oral Roberts said that the healing ministry attracts three things: "crowds, controversy, and criticism." I add to that by saying the healing ministry also attracts "conversions," because it brings souls into the Kingdom of God.

So I've had my share of criticism. People tell me I'm a fraud, a scam artist, and a false prophet. I'm accused of being greedy, manipulative, and uncaring toward the sick. I've even been threatened—I mean that people have made death threats against me. And social media makes it worse! Hardly a day goes by that I don't receive some kind of hateful correspondence—many times from Christians. If I'm being transparent with you, I must admit that those criticisms used to get to me. They would penetrate my heart and weigh on my mind.

When I first began in ministry, I was emotionally stirred by the criticisms. My ego was disturbed. I would even engage in online social media comment debates. Side note: trust me when I tell you that online arguments hardly ever make anyone look poised or level-headed.

I would be bated into arguments, and no matter how specifically I tried to address a criticism, the conversations would stem into four or five other criticisms. Criticism, I learned, multiplies when you address it. For several years, I was very moved by my critics.

Then one day, the Holy Spirit gently spoke to me: "Don't live for compliments or criticism. Live for Christ."

That impartation of wisdom completely changed my approach in ministry and life. It liberated me. I've learned that you can transcend the noise of criticism simply by not responding to it. Knowledge told me how to fight the criticisms, but wisdom told me I didn't have to. Intellect justified my defensiveness, but wisdom told me I didn't need to defend myself.

How I responded to my critics was just one area in which the Holy Spirit's wisdom changed me. Time and time again, the Holy Spirit gives me wisdom that betters my life and ministry. The Holy Spirit's wisdom saves me time, minimizes my losses, mends my relationships, grows my ministry, improves my preaching, increases my finances, and so forth. The benefits of the Holy Spirit's wisdom are countless.

The Holy Spirit wants to impart wisdom into you as well. He has been giving wisdom to men and women for ages.

In the same way that the Holy Spirit inspired the psalmist to write worshipful masterpieces about the glory of God, so the Holy Spirit also inspired the son of David to impart wisdom. Solomon, the author of the Book of Proverbs, describes wisdom as a person:

> *Wisdom shouts in the streets. She cries out in the public square. She calls to the crowds along the main street, to those gathered in front of the city gate: "How long, you simpletons, will you insist on being simpleminded? How long will you mockers relish your mocking? How long will you fools hate knowledge? Come and listen to my counsel. I'll share my heart with you and make you wise* (Proverbs 1:20-23).

Although Solomon's personification of wisdom is presented in the female gender, we know that it is ultimately the Holy Spirit who is the Giver of wisdom.

> *Now Joshua son of Nun was full of the spirit of wisdom, for Moses had laid his hands on him. So the people of Israel obeyed him, doing just as the Lord had commanded Moses* (Deuteronomy 34:9).

And the Spirit of the Lord will rest on him—the Spirit of wisdom and understanding, the Spirit of counsel and might, the Spirit of knowledge and the fear of the Lord (Isaiah 11:2).

No doubt, it was the Holy Spirit who enabled Solomon to write with divine wisdom. Solomon needed the Spirit's wisdom, and we sure do also need the wisdom of the Holy Spirit. For those questions and situations that are not specifically addressed in the Scripture, the Holy Spirit gives you wisdom. You don't have to handle your difficult situations in the flesh. You don't have to live in confusion and constant apprehension.

No matter the difficulties that you face, no matter how complicated or touchy the matter, the Holy Spirit will give you the wisdom to make it through. The very same kind of wisdom, which was given unto the writer of Proverbs, is available to you, right now.

For me, the Holy Spirit comes through on countless issues. He has helped me deal with difficult people, navigate complex problems, and attain the seemingly unattainable. He will do the same for you.

The Holy Spirit is the Spirit of wisdom.

Chapter 22

THE HOLY SPIRIT IN ECCLESIASTES

THE SPIRIT OF PURPOSE—*Ecclesiastes 3:11*

The Holy Spirit pulls us toward purpose.

The world needs more philanthropy, more feeding projects, more orphanages, more social justice reforms, more charities, and yes, to some degree, more environmental initiatives. But think about this: after all is lived and experienced, when the earth is no more, when even history itself is forgotten, what good will all that have been if it didn't result in something eternal? What good are projects if they aren't ultimately focused on the saving of the everlasting soul? What good is anything at all if it doesn't, in some way, affect someone's eternity?

Without eternity, without Heaven and hell, without God, it's all really the same. Without eternity, if everything finishes in darkness, there is no purpose for anything or anyone at all. Solomon, the wisest man who ever lived, concluded something very similar.

Solomon, the writer of Ecclesiastes, was searching for the meaning of life; he was longing for purpose. As a man of immense power and wealth, he was uniquely positioned to try everything the world could offer. Ecclesiastes records King Solomon's findings in his life "experiment," his pursuit of true purpose.

The opening of Ecclesiastes is cynical. Solomon, "the Teacher," asserts that everything is ultimately meaningless, that not a single soul really reaps anything for their toil, and that there's nothing new under the sun—history merely repeats itself.

Solomon searched for purpose in wisdom, worldly pleasures, and even hard work. His conclusion in his search for meaning is always the same:

But as I looked at everything I had worked so hard to accomplish, it was all so meaningless—like chasing the wind. There was nothing really worthwhile anywhere (Ecclesiastes 2:11).

Solomon reasons that if both the foolish and the wise eventually go to the same grave, what purpose is there in anything? The Teacher's desperate attempt to find meaning brings about nothing but disappointment. Agitated further by the injustices and tragedies in the world, Solomon seems convinced that everything is, ultimately and truly, utterly meaningless.

Still, he admits something profound:

Yet God has made everything beautiful for its own time. He has planted eternity in the human heart, but even so, people cannot see the whole scope of God's work from beginning to end (Ecclesiastes 3:11).

Solomon is telling us that God has placed, within each and every person, an intrinsic awareness of eternity and a longing for purpose. Within every heart, there is a knowing of the something more, the world beyond our own. There is a pull into purpose, a call into the meaningful. God has set *"eternity in the human heart"* (Eccles. 3:11).

Eternity within our hearts is the Holy Spirit. He is the gentle whisper in the human spirit that says, "There's something more." The Holy Spirit points to the never-ending hereafter. He intentionally and persistently provokes us unto purposeful action.

So what does the Holy Spirit tell us concerning the purpose of life and the things that are truly of eternal consequence? The writer of Ecclesiastes tells us.

Overcoming his disappointment and cynicism, having exhausted all attempts to find purpose in the earth, Solomon makes a powerful conclusion:

That's the whole story. Here now is my final conclusion: Fear God and obey His commands, for this is everyone's duty (Ecclesiastes 12:13).

"…Fear God and obey His commands…" (Eccles. 12:13). But why? If all is meaningless, why does Solomon conclude that we should obey God's commands? What sets that apart from everything else? Why is purpose found in obeying God's commands?

Meaning is found in God's commands because meaning is only found in the eternal.

> *For then the dust will return to the earth, and the spirit will return to God who gave it* (Ecclesiastes 12:7).

God has set eternity in our hearts, the Holy Spirit, as an inner pull toward actual purpose. He is the one who reminds us to think and live in consideration of the eternal. All that counts is what we do for eternity, and only what is done in spirit can count for eternity. The Holy Spirit wants us to focus on finding our purpose in God's commands because God's commands ultimately lead us to God's purposes.

You know that inner drive to be more? That comes from the Holy Spirit. He is drawing all people to a greater purpose—to serve the Lord. He helps us to stay focused on the eternal, not just the earthly. He challenges us to exchange the corruptible for the incorruptible. He pricks the heart. He nudges you to fulfill the call of God for eternity's sake.

What eternal consequences await your present obedience to His leading? We all too often focus on the purposeless—that is, the things that don't matter in eternity.

For example, I'm saddened that my generation is more concerned with the causes and humanitarian efforts of this earth than they are with the preaching of the Gospel. I'm for charity, social justice, and the support of worthy causes. But we should be more focused on eternity and souls than on those efforts.

Use humanitarian work as a tool for the Gospel? Yes. Be a church concerned with justice for the oppressed? Of course. Help the needy, the weak, and the depressed? Absolutely. But what good does it do to feed a man today who is going to hell tomorrow? What value is there in sheltering the wanderer who slips into eternity without Christ?

Why gather riches if we don't use those riches to impact eternity? Why live a life of pleasure without purpose? What good is the here and now if not for the eternal? Allow the Holy Spirit to inspire you to live in the light of eternity, to focus on what truly matters.

Do good. Enjoy life. Be wise. Work, eat, and live. But pay attention to eternity in your heart. Pay attention to the Holy Spirit, who causes you to see beyond this world. It is in the eternal that we find purpose.

The Holy Spirit is the Spirit of purpose.

Chapter 23

THE HOLY SPIRIT IN
THE SONG OF SOLOMON

THE HIDDEN DOVE—*Song of Solomon 2:14*

The Holy Spirit has a hiding nature.

The Song of Solomon is a poetic conversation between lovers, but it doubles as a parallel for Christ's love for the Church. The young man represents Christ, and the young woman represents the Church.

The Holy Spirit appears a few times in the Song of Solomon. He's the unquenchable fire of God's love for us:

Place me like a seal over your heart, like a seal on your arm. For love is as strong as death, its jealousy as enduring as the grave. Love flashes like fire, the brightest kind of flame. Many waters cannot quench love, nor can rivers drown it (Song of Solomon 8:6-7).

He's the sweet and alluring wind that draws the two lovers together:

Awake, north wind! Rise up, south wind! Blow on my garden and spread its fragrance all around. Come into your garden, my love; taste its finest fruits (Song of Solomon 4:16).

In Song of Solomon 2:14, the young man tells the young woman:

My dove is hiding behind the rocks, behind an outcrop on the cliff. Let me see your face; let me hear your voice. For your voice is pleasant, and your face is lovely (Song of Solomon 2:14).

The young man calls the young woman his "dove". While this reference isn't necessarily a directly symbolic reference to the Holy Spirit, it reveals something about the nature of doves and, thus, something about the nature of the Holy Spirit.

From that portion of Scripture, we learn that doves hide. Thus, the Holy Spirit has a hiding nature.

Doves nest in the hidden places alongside cliffs and rocks.

> *You people of Moab, flee from your towns and live in the caves. Hide like doves that nest in the clefts of the rocks* (Jeremiah 48:28).

In the Books of Psalms, the Israelites were said to have found treasures in plunder. Among the treasures they found were doves.

> *Even those who lived among the sheepfolds found treasures—doves with wings of silver and feathers of gold* (Psalm 68:13).

The Holy Spirit never leaves you, but He sometimes hides. It's in His nature to hide.

> *Verily Thou art a God that hidest Thyself, O God of Israel, the Saviour* (Isaiah 45:15 KJV).

Why does the Holy Spirit hide? Simply because He wants to be sought.

The Holy Spirit hides to draw you.

> *And ye shall seek Me, and find Me, when ye shall search for Me with all your heart* (Jeremiah 29:13 KJV).

He doesn't hide to hurt you or to tease you. He hides to draw you deeper. When the Holy Spirit hides, our desperation grows. That desperation pushes us to go further into the depths of His presence. When the Holy Spirit hides, He is not leaving you; He is leading you. When God seems to withdraw from you and you sense a longing in your heart to be nearer to Him, recognize what's happening. The Holy Spirit is calling you into deeper waters. He hides simply so that we'll seek Him.

The Holy Spirit hides also to test you.

> *However, when ambassadors arrived from Babylon to ask about the remarkable events that had taken place in the land, God withdrew from Hezekiah in order to test him and to see what was really in his heart* (2 Chronicles 32:31).

> *The Lord looks down from heaven on the entire human race; He looks to see if anyone is truly wise, if anyone seeks God* (Psalm 14:2).

In those seasons where you sense a supposed distance between you and the Lord, you can either leave it at that or seek the Lord. God is watching to see how you'll respond. When we cannot see Him at work in our circumstances, when His voice seems to be silent, we should seek Him. He is watching where you place your reliance, your trust, and your faith.

The Holy Spirit hides also to purify you.

> *Sow to yourselves in righteousness, reap in mercy; break up your fallow ground: for it is time to seek the Lord, till He come and rain righteousness upon you* (Hosea 10:12 KJV).

When we seek the Lord, righteousness is rained down upon us. The Holy Spirit withdraws, the dove hides, because it is in our seeking that we are purified and processed. It is the seeking of the Holy Spirit's presence that purifies you. It is the seeking that weakens the flesh. This is why your flesh begins to squirm when you seek the face of God in prayer—the flesh knows when it is dying. In the process of seeking we become people who are purified. We become people who can handle the weightier matters of the Spirit.

The Holy Spirit hides to draw you, to test you, and to purify you.

The Holy Spirit is the hidden Dove.

Chapter 24

THE HOLY SPIRIT IN ISAIAH

THE GENERATIONAL SPIRIT—*Isaiah 44:3*

The Holy Spirit works generationally.

For I will pour out water on the thirsty land and streams on the dry ground; I will pour out My Spirit on your offspring and My blessing on your descendants (Isaiah 44:3).

The Holy Spirit is poured out upon generations. Flowing from one people to another, the Holy Spirit's power sets His agenda throughout the eras of history. We think in terms of lifetimes, but the Holy Spirit thinks in terms of generations.

If we will humbly submit to the Holy Spirit's generationally centered plan, each of us can receive of Him and give into the next generation.

I think of how the Holy Spirit has worked in my life. I'm a fourth-generation Christian, third-generation minister. The decisions of my grandparents, though they could not see the future, led to your reading this very sentence—they led to your reading this very book. My family decided to serve the Lord years ago, but we are still seeing the fruit of that decision today.

My life has also been touched by the Holy Spirit through the life of Benny Hinn. Pastor Benny's life was touched by Kathryn Kuhlman's. Kathryn Kuhlman's life was touched by other servants of the Lord. The Holy Spirit works generationally.

You see, it's not about any one individual. It's about Jesus. The Holy Spirit's generational agenda is all about lifting the name of Jesus. We are privileged to have such a small part in His grand plan. All names will eventually be forgotten. Only one name will be worshiped forever—Jesus.

Behind us, we all have a spiritual heritage, a succession of Holy Spirit inspiration. We all have spiritual parents, and we all should have spiritual children. So be intentional about finding your place in spiritual generations. Who really knows how the Holy Spirit will use your life to impact the future generations?

When you allow the Holy Spirit to work in your life, you are participating in His plan that spans generations. He is the generational Spirit.

THE SPIRIT UPON JESUS—*Isaiah 61:1*

The Holy Spirit was the One who empowered Jesus.

In the Book of Isaiah, we see that the Holy Spirit was the One who rested upon Jesus.

> *Then a shoot will spring from the stem of Jesse, and a branch from his roots will bear fruit. The Spirit of the Lord will rest on Him, the spirit of wisdom and understanding, the spirit of counsel and strength, the spirit of knowledge and the fear of the Lord* (Isaiah 11:1-2 NASB).

Everything Jesus accomplished was by the Holy Spirit. The Holy Spirit was the One who empowered Jesus for ministry.

> *The Spirit of the Sovereign Lord is upon me, for the Lord has anointed me to bring good news to the poor. He has sent me to comfort the brokenhearted and to proclaim that captives will be released and prisoners will be freed* (Isaiah 61:1).

Jesus laid claim to the fulfillment of that prophetic word in the Gospel of Luke (see Luke 4:18).

Now I'm going to say something that you may not like or that you may find shocking. But it's the truth. Were it not for the power of the Holy Spirit, Jesus would not have been able to perform a single miracle.

While many become appalled at the revelation of that truth, they should instead become encouraged. You see, believers are in the limiting habit of dismissing the miraculous and embracing small thinking. With phrases like, "Well, that was Jesus" or "He was the Son of God," we relieve ourselves of the responsibility of doing what Jesus did.

It may seem humble to say, "I can't do what Jesus did," but it's actually quite a prideful statement. To say so would be like saying, "The Holy Spirit was powerful enough to perform miracles through Jesus, but He's not powerful enough to perform the miraculous through me."

And Jesus did, indeed, depend on the Holy Spirit. After all, Jesus stripped Himself of His divine nature:

> *Though He was God, He did not think of equality with God as something to cling to. Instead, He gave up His divine privileges; He took the humble position of a slave and was born as a human being. When He appeared in human form, He humbled Himself in obedience to God and died a criminal's death on a cross* (Philippians 2:6-8).

Had Jesus been divine in nature, He would not have been able to die. Jesus was truly God and truly man. He was divine in identity, but He was man in nature. So, everything supernatural that Jesus did was done by the power of the Holy Spirit.

Jesus cast out demons by the Holy Spirit.

> *But if I am casting out demons by the Spirit of God, then the Kingdom of God has arrived among you* (Matthew 12:28).

Jesus healed the sick by the power of the Holy Spirit.

> *How God anointed Jesus of Nazareth with the Holy Ghost and with power: who went about doing good, and healing all that were oppressed of the devil; for God was with Him* (Acts 10:38 KJV).

Jesus preached by the power of the Holy Spirit.

> *The Spirit of the Sovereign Lord is upon Me, for the Lord has anointed Me to bring good news to the poor. He has sent Me to comfort the brokenhearted and to proclaim that captives will be released and prisoners will be freed* (Isaiah 61:1).

Jesus was even resurrected by the Holy Spirit.

> *And He was shown to be the Son of God when He was raised from the dead by the power of the Holy Spirit. He is Jesus Christ our Lord* (Romans 1:4).

The Spirit of God, who raised Jesus from the dead, lives in you... (Romans 8:11).

While Jesus was here on earth, He offered prayers and pleadings, with a loud cry and tears, to the one who could rescue Him from death. And God heard His prayers because of His deep reverence for God (Hebrews 5:7).

Ponder the fact that Jesus depended on the Holy Spirit for the resurrection. Jesus, who had never before experienced death, braved the underworld, fully trusting that the Holy Spirit would bring Him back to life. Now if that's not faith in the Holy Spirit, I don't know what is. Jesus trusted the Holy Spirit to do His part of the plan—to resurrect. Jesus laid it all in the care of the Holy Spirit.

If Jesus relied on the Holy Spirit, how much more should we? If Jesus needed the Holy Spirit, how much more do we?

The Holy Spirit still has the power to heal the sick, drive out demons, and anoint the preaching of the Good News. And He will perform all those things through you. In fact, He will even resurrect you when your body is no more. That's not a fringe belief or an extreme doctrine; that is a clear promise of Scripture.

It is the same way with the resurrection of the dead. Our earthly bodies are planted in the ground when we die, but they will be raised to live forever (1 Corinthians 15:42).

The Holy Spirit is the same Spirit who rested upon Christ, and He now rests upon you—He enables you to do what Jesus did.

Chapter 25

THE HOLY SPIRIT IN
JEREMIAH

THE FIRE IN YOUR BONES—*Jeremiah 20:9*

The Holy Spirit stirs a passion for God's Word.

By the time Jeremiah began to prophesy to Judah, God had already made up His mind. God's verdict: Judah was to succumb to the strength of Babylon. Jeremiah contended that the people of Judah should repent of their sins, embrace God's punishment, and set themselves up for restoration in the future—after the discipline was over, of course.

Jeremiah was not well received. So he told himself that he would no longer preach what the Holy Spirit had spoken to him. However, the words that Jeremiah heard from Heaven could not be contained.

> *But if I say I'll never mention the Lord or speak in His name, His word burns in my heart like a fire. It's like a fire in my bones! I am worn out trying to hold it in! I can't do it!* (Jeremiah 20:9)

Jeremiah felt a fiery compulsion to speak what God had spoken. Describing what was like fire in his bones, Jeremiah told of how the message burned throughout every part of his inner man.

So who was moving Jeremiah to such a state of zeal? We know that it was the Holy Spirit speaking through Jeremiah because of what Second Peter 1:21 says.

> *…No, those prophets were moved by the Holy Spirit, and they spoke from God* (2 Peter 1:21).

Additionally, we know that it was the Holy Spirit speaking through Jeremiah because of what the Book of Hebrews says concerning Jeremiah's prophetic ministry. Take a look at one of the prophetic declarations of the prophet Jeremiah.

"But this is the new covenant I will make with the people of Israel on that day," says the Lord. "I will put My instructions deep within them, and I will write them on their hearts. I will be their God, and they will be My people" (Jeremiah 31:33).

Now look at what the book of Hebrews tells us about that declaration.

And the Holy Spirit also testifies that this is so. For He says, "This is the new covenant I will make with My people on that day, says the Lord: I will put My laws in their hearts, and I will write them on their minds" (Hebrews 10:15-16).

Hebrews tells us that Jeremiah was speaking by the Holy Spirit.

The Holy Spirit was the fire in Jeremiah's bones. The Holy Spirit stirs passion for the Word.

There was a time when, to me, reading the Bible felt more like a discipline than a pleasure. I would read chapters of the Bible only to realize that I had paid no attention to what I had just read. More motivated by duty than by hunger, I moved through dozens of chapters of the Bible a day without any real substance.

The Pharisees knew the Scripture, but they didn't know Jesus. Atheists read the Bible, but there is no change in their hearts. Religious people memorize the Scriptures, but they continue to be the same people they were when they first began to read them. Cult leaders preach from the Bible, but they walk in deception. People read the Bible out of obligation, out of a sense of duty, and as a part of a system. But not all who read the Word can see the depths of Christ in the Word. Not all who read the Word love the Word or are changed by the Word.

I've sat in services where anointed teachers of the Word were sharing valuable secrets of Scripture, all while some were falling asleep or staring blankly at their phones. Jesus talks about those who are unable to truly receive the Word as it is meant to be received:

Hear ye therefore the parable of the sower. When any one heareth the word of the kingdom, and understandeth it not, then cometh the wicked one, and catcheth away that which was sown in his heart. This is he which received seed by the way side (Matthew 13:18-19).

It wasn't until I came to know the Holy Spirit on a personal level that I began to receive a passion for the Word of God. Without the Holy Spirit, the truth of the Word cannot be received in the deepest part of your heart. Once I began to acknowledge the presence of the Holy Spirit, reading the Word became exciting and lively.

Not only does the Holy Spirit impart a great reverence for the Word; He also imparts a great passion for the Word. Sometimes, I become so filled with God's Word that I have to talk about it with my friends and family. Once I become stirred, no matter the topic of conversation, I will find a way to steer the conversation toward the Scripture and the revelation of the Holy Spirit.

Jeremiah, who at one point tried to keep silent about God's Word, found that he could not contain himself. He was hated, persecuted, mocked, and disliked, but the Holy Spirit moved the prophet to speak out despite the confrontation. That's what the Holy Spirit wants to do for you. He wants to so stir your spirit that you love and declare the Word of God without reservation or a sense of self. He spreads a passion for the Word and truth all throughout the inner man. One sure way to know if you have received the baptism of the Holy Spirit is if you have received a zeal for the truth of God's Word.

The Holy Spirit is the One who ignites the Word. The Holy Spirit and the Word become like a fire in your bones, a stirring of the inner man.[1]

---

1   See also Jeremiah 23:29.

Chapter 26

THE HOLY SPIRIT IN
LAMENTATIONS

THE ONE WHO GRIEVES OVER SIN—*Lamentations 2:11*

The Holy Spirit can be grieved, and He grieves over sin.

The destruction of Jerusalem and the Babylonian oppression of God's people were both tragic realities that caused Jeremiah, the weeping prophet, to grieve. A lamentation is a funeral song, and the Book of Lamentations is a book of grief. In the Book of Lamentations, the Holy Spirit grieves over the sins of His people through the prophet Jeremiah.

> *I have cried until the tears no longer come; my heart is broken. My spirit is poured out in agony as I see the desperate plight of my people. Little children and tiny babies are fainting and dying in the streets* (Lamentations 2:11).

> *Lord, remember what has happened to us. See how we have been disgraced! Our inheritance has been turned over to strangers, our homes to foreigners. We are orphaned and fatherless. Our mothers are widowed. We have to pay for water to drink, and even firewood is expensive. Those who pursue us are at our heels; we are exhausted but are given no rest. We submitted to Egypt and Assyria to get enough food to survive. Our ancestors sinned, but they have died—and we are suffering the punishment they deserved!* (Lamentations 5:1-7).

What grief sin brings! What destruction it invites. Sin degrades the people of God; it strips them of dignity. Sin brings darkness and sorrow. The consequences, when they finally arrive, are more than men can bear. This is why God hates sin—not for the sake of hating what gives us temporary pleasure; He hates what sin does to us. In violating the holy nature of God, we violate our own nature. We violate ourselves, for we are born of the life-giving Spirit. Both sin and its outcomes grieve the Holy Spirit.

And do not bring sorrow to God's Holy Spirit by the way you live. Remember, He has identified you as His own, guaranteeing that you will be saved on the day of redemption (Ephesians 4:30).

Isaiah the prophet speaks of a dove in mourning:

Delirious, I chattered like a swallow or a crane, and then I moaned like a mourning dove. My eyes grew tired of looking to heaven for help. I am in trouble, Lord. Help me! (Isaiah 38:14).

The Holy Spirit is that mourning dove.

The Holy Spirit has feelings—He can be grieved. The Holy Spirit has desires—He can be disappointed. The Holy Spirit has a heart—He can be hurt.

How many times have you ignored His gentle pleadings to pursue what you ought not pursue? How many times have you placed your hand over His mouth to keep Him from speaking? Pretending that the Holy Spirit is not right there with us, we indulge in the filth of the flesh, all while He stands nearby to witness our disobedience.

He can see further than we can see. He understands more than we understand. What does He see in the spiritual realm when men debase themselves before Him? What does He know about sin that we do not? What darkness surrounds the one who indulges in the unholy? What damage is done to the soul that we cannot see? The Holy Spirit sees it all.

We crush Him when we sin. We hurt Him when we stray. When we ignore Him, when we reject Him, when we are embarrassed by Him—that's when we hurt Him. The gentle dove of Heaven, faithful to abide with us, mourns when we wander into the darkness of iniquity. Because of His faithful love, He refuses to leave us. What we put Him through!

Weeping before thousands, Kathryn Kuhlman once said, "Please, don't grieve the Holy Spirit. Don't you understand? He's all I've got!"

The Holy Spirit is a personal being. Please, dear reader, don't grieve Him. Don't cause Him to lament. Let us become people who consider the feelings of the precious and gentle Holy Spirit. Let us grieve not the Holy Spirit.

The Holy Spirit is the One who grieves over sin.

Chapter 27

THE HOLY SPIRIT IN
EZEKIEL

LIFE OF HEAVENLY BEINGS—*Ezekiel 1:20-21*

Wherever the spirit was about to go, they would go in that direction. And the wheels rose close beside them; for the spirit of the living beings was in the wheels. Whenever those went, these went; and whenever those stood still, these stood still. And whenever those rose from the earth, the wheels rose close beside them; for the spirit of the living beings was in the wheels (Ezekiel 1:20-21 NASB).

The Spirit gave life, movement, and direction to the living beings. Even heavenly beings are sustained by the life of the Spirit.

THE FIERY BEING—*Ezekiel 8:1-4*

It came about in the sixth year, on the fifth day of the sixth month, as I was sitting in my house with the elders of Judah sitting before me, that the hand of the Lord God fell on me there. Then I looked, and behold, a likeness as the appearance of a man; fro5m His loins and downward there was the appearance of fire, and from His loins and upward the appearance of brightness, like the appearance of glowing metal. He stretched out the form of a hand and caught me by a lock of my head; and the Spirit lifted me up between earth and heaven and brought me in the visions of God to Jerusalem, to the entrance of the north gate of the inner court, where the seat of the idol of jealousy, which provokes to jealousy, was located. And behold, the glory of the God of Israel was there, like the appearance which I saw in the plain (Ezekiel 8:1-4 NASB).

I'm very intrigued by the heavenly visions of Ezekiel the prophet, but the vision that he had of the fiery being *really* has my attention. The fiery being had the likeness of a man, consisted of what appeared to be fire, and glowed like hot metal. Notice also that Ezekiel says the fiery being grabbed him with the *"form of a hand"* (Ezek. 8:3). It wasn't an actual hand of flesh. Picture that—a flame of fire taking on the shape of a hand. Ezekiel's descriptions don't seem to be describing an angel or even the Lord Jesus.

What does Ezekiel call this fiery being who grabbed him by the lock of his head?

> *"He stretched out the form of a hand and caught me by a lock of my head; and the Spirit lifted me up between earth and heaven..."* (Ezek. 8:3).

He called this being the "Spirit." Ezekiel's vision may very well have been of the Holy Spirit Himself.

THE GIVER OF SPIRITUAL VISIONS—*Ezekiel 11:24*

> *Afterward the Spirit of God carried me back again to Babylonia, to the people in exile there. And so ended the vision of my visit to Jerusalem* (Ezekiel 11:24).

The seeing of heavenly visions is not restricted to being an Old Testament phenomenon because the Holy Spirit is not restricted to Old Testament times. There are many New Testament examples of God's servants seeing visions (see Acts 9:10; Acts 16:9-10; the Book of Revelation, etc.). The Holy Spirit is still very much interested in speaking through visions. The closer one becomes to the Spirit, the more common these visions typically become.

THE SPIRIT OF ONENESS—*Ezekiel 36:25-27*

The Holy Spirit cultivates union with God.

As a captive in Babylon, Ezekiel prophesied, among other things, the restoration of Israel. Speaking of that restoration, Ezekiel said this:

Then I will sprinkle clean water on you, and you will be clean.
Your filth will be washed away, and you will no longer worship
idols. And I will give you a new heart, and I will put a new spirit
in you. I will take out your stony, stubborn heart and give you a
tender, responsive heart. And I will put My Spirit in you so that
you will follow My decrees and be careful to obey My regulations
(Ezekiel 36:25-27).

God promised to give His people a new heart and spirit. Notice that the
first "spirit" isn't capitalized. He's promising to make the spirit of man new.
However, the second "Spirit" is capitalized. There, He is talking about the
Holy Spirit.

God makes your spirit new by making it one with His Holy Spirit. When
it comes to spiritual matters, oneness is newness. Basically, and amazingly,
God promises to mingle His Spirit with your spirit. This is oneness.

I pray that they will all be one, just as You and I are one—as You
are in Me, Father, and I am in You. And may they be in Us so
that the world will believe You sent Me (John 17:21).

This makes me think of Enoch. Enoch walked so closely with God that
he simply ceased to be.

And Enoch walked with God: and he was not; for God took him
(Genesis 5:24 KJV).

You can enter such a depth in God that, as Pastor Benny Hinn puts it,
"your presence becomes His presence."

The deeper you go in the Spirit, the less you look like yourself. The
Holy Spirit fellowships with your spirit and makes you one with God. This
oneness progressively overtakes you—day by day, moment by moment,
surrender by surrender. In the Spirit, we are already one with Him. The
more we surrender to Him, the more of that oneness we will see manifested
in our lives.

Union with God is found in fellowship with the Holy Spirit. That union
will make you heavenly. It will change you. People will sense it while being
around you.

I myself have experienced glimpses of glory in oneness with God. And
it has manifested itself in both the strange and the practical. Practically,
I notice that oneness with the Spirit makes it easier to exercise patience,

harder to doubt, effortless to be kind, and more. On the supernatural side, people have reported seeing my face glow while I preach. Some have even reported seeing angels hovering around me. Oneness with the Spirit makes you a heavenly atmosphere, a center of divine activity. It's not us; it's who is around us—the Holy Spirit. There's not something special about me; there's *someone* special about me. And He is one with you too.

Put to death the old self and become alive in the newness of oneness with God. Let the Holy Spirit purge self and merge you with God.

The Holy Spirit is the Spirit of oneness.

Chapter 28

THE HOLY SPIRIT IN DANIEL

THE EXCELLENT SPIRIT—*Daniel 5:12*

The Holy Spirit inspires excellence.

My philosophy in ministry is one of simplicity.

Simplicity is the key to effectiveness. It's better to do a few things with excellence than many things with mediocrity. In order to be effective, one must first become specific.

As it goes with my ministry, I really only have two major outreaches: media and events. Our events are focused on evangelizing the lost. Our media is focused on equipping the believer. All of our resources and energy are poured into doing those two things.

Even when it comes to the message of our ministry, we keep it simple. For the most part, I stay focused on just a few themes: salvation, the Holy Spirit, healing, and prayer. Of course, I cover other topics. But the focus of the ministry is ultimately very specific.

Why do I do it that way? For the sake of excellence. One cannot operate in excellence if one cannot find their specific flow. Find your "sweet spot" and stay there. I learned to pursue excellence from the Holy Spirit.

You see, the Holy Spirit inspires excellence.

Daniel had a spirit of excellence.

Forasmuch as an excellent spirit, and knowledge, and understanding, interpreting of dreams, and shewing of hard sentences, and dissolving of doubts, were found in the same Daniel, whom the king named Belteshazzar: now let Daniel be called, and he will shew the interpretation (Daniel 5:12 KJV).

The excellence in Daniel's spirit came from the Holy Spirit. Daniel carried himself with excellence, and that excellence elevated him.

Think of how the Holy Spirit operates. He's orderly and organized. He's consistent and passionate. He's punctual and effective. He's focused and intentional. He speaks with eloquence, creates with detail, and builds with sustainability. And those who are Spirit-filled have access to His excellent manner.

Excellence is not a financial status or a level of resource; it is a spirit. Excellence is the culture of Heaven.

Pastors, does your church building reflect the Holy Spirit's excellence? The issue is not the financial standing. The issue is not the size, style, price, or quality of the church building. The issue is the culture. I've been to impoverished churches that were well kept and to wealthy churches that were poorly kept. My point is not about income or style. My point is about excellence. Excellence is not having the best of everything but doing the best with everything that you have. Does your service start on time? Is the flow of the service organized and clearly communicated to the workers? Is your building clean?

Ministers and teachers, are your sermons prepared with diligent study? All too often I hear fellow ministers complain to me about how long they've had to serve the Lord with no breakthrough in ministry. They say, "I've been faithful for so long, and still nothing has happened." But many fail to realize that faithfulness isn't just consistency; it's consistency with excellence. If you just keep being consistent without being excellent, you're busy, not productive. And there's a difference.

Are you digging into the Word of God for yourself or are you taking sermons from online? Worship leaders, are you regularly practicing the craft of your music? Believer, are you organized? Are your finances in order? Do you keep your commitments? Are you focused? Passionate? Thoughtful? Intentional?

Take notes from the Holy Spirit. Let's walk in excellence. I've noticed that the Holy Spirit moves more freely in excellent atmospheres. Excellence is a mark of the Spirit-filled.

Let us aspire to the standards of the Holy Spirit. He is cultured of Heaven's best.

The Holy Spirit is the excellent Spirit.

Chapter 29

THE HOLY SPIRIT IN
HOSEA

THE PATIENT SPIRIT—*Hosea 2:14*

The Holy Spirit is patient with us in failure.

To illustrate God's frustrations with Israel, Hosea the prophet was instructed to marry an unfaithful woman by the name of Gomer. Despite her adulterous wandering, Hosea pursued Gomer and eventually loved her into restoration.

Through the messages and life of Hosea the prophet, the Holy Spirit reveals to us His faithful nature, His willingness to abide with us in spite of ourselves. The Holy Spirit was the One speaking *through* Hosea.

> *But then I will win her back once again. I will lead her into the desert and speak tenderly to her there* (Hosea 2:14).

How does God pursue us? By His patient Holy Spirit. God's nature is the Spirit's nature and vice versa. The Holy Spirit doesn't just pursue us until salvation; He continually pursues us until perfection.

In an effort to restore, the Holy Spirit has always been faithful to the sinful ones.

In Genesis 6, we find that the sins of men began to anguish the heart of God. God's creation, His beloved masterpiece, turned to rebellion. The creation that God had so lovingly and attentively formed began to descend deeper into the darkness of sin.

> *And God saw that the wickedness of man was great in the earth, and that every imagination of the thoughts of his heart was only evil continually. And it repented the Lord that He had made man*

on the earth, and it grieved Him at His heart (Genesis 6:5-6 KJV).

Being a patient and loving Creator, God did not immediately pour wrath upon the earth. For some time, God waited.

And the Lord said, My spirit shall not always strive with man, for that he also is flesh: yet his days shall be an hundred and twenty years (Genesis 6:3 KJV).

Now I want you to really consider the weightiness of the words spoken by the Father. Really think about what He said. The Scripture records the fact that it is the Spirit of God who strives with man. The Holy Spirit has been striving with the human race since Genesis, and Hosea illustrates, with his life, just how gracious the Holy Spirit is with us.

He is the One who patiently tolerates our humanity. Although He does not condone or accept sin, the Holy Spirit works with us to rid us of sin, and He waits for us to repent. The Holy Spirit patiently pursues the heart of every man and woman.

Aren't you thankful for His patience? He is kind, loving, gentle, and understanding.

I recall a time that I was approached by an exhausted-looking man who asked me a question. I could tell by his demeanor that this question had been weighing upon his worry-cluttered mind. I think that Christians worry too much, especially for people who believe that they are unconditionally loved by a supremely powerful Being.

The man was fretting. His speech was broken. His eyes were tired. His posture was defeated. I'll never forget what he asked me. In fact, I am asked the question often by many different believers. He said in an unsure voice, "Brother David, does the Holy Spirit ever leave the believer?" Discerning that the man's question was rooted in condemnation, I answered his question with a question of my own, "Sir, what do you think would make Him leave you?"

"Well," he quietly confessed, "I am struggling with sin. I am trying to stop, but I just don't know how to stop." The Holy Spirit inspired me to reply, "My brother, if the Holy Spirit left us every time we sinned, there would be no hope of repentance."

You see, dear reader, the Holy Spirit does not leave us when we sin. He is not an overly sensitive Being. Sure, His heart grieves when we disobey, which is why we should live in holiness. But that does not mean that He abandons us to ourselves. He does not leave you to struggle alone. Without His help, you wouldn't even desire to live in holiness anyway.

The very fact that you desire to do better, that you desire to make things right before God, is proof that He remains with you. Since He is the One who strives with us, He is the only One that can stir us to repentance. He is the *Holy* Spirit. Holiness is His work in you.

He strives. He endures. He judges.

The Book of Hosea shows us, beyond any doubt, that the merciful Holy Spirit doesn't leave you in the darkness. Think of how you were before you came to Christ. Do you believe that you came to Christ all on your own? Of course you didn't. Dead men don't seek. It was the Holy Spirit who sought you. He pursued you. While you were in your sin, the Holy Spirit relentlessly called you forth because He loves you. He cried, "Come out of the darkness and into the marvelous light!"

Even the believer—no, *especially* the believer—is continually pursued by the Holy Spirit. Yes, this is a beautiful truth.

He is the One who patiently strives with the fallen nature of man.

Chapter 30

THE HOLY SPIRIT IN
JOEL

THE PROMISE OF THE FATHER—*Joel 2:28-31*

The Holy Spirit is a gift from the Father and should not be rejected.

In the Book of Joel, yet again God is dealing with the sins of His people. The book opens with a prophetic picture of locusts swarming in a rage of destructive chaos. Devastating the agriculture of Israel, the locusts are a symbol of the justified wrath of God.

What is interesting to me are some of descriptions of destruction that are found in the Book of Joel. Remember, the Holy Spirit is associated with wine, oil, and Pentecost (the marking of the end of the wheat harvest).

> *For there is no grain or wine to offer at the Temple of the Lord. So the priests are in mourning. The ministers of the Lord are weeping. The fields are ruined, the land is stripped bare. The grain is destroyed, the grapes have shriveled, and the olive oil is gone* (Joel 1:9-10).

The grain is destroyed. The grapes for wine have shriveled. The oil is gone. This is a prophetic description of a lack of the presence of the Holy Spirit. The Holy Spirit needed to be poured out afresh, as He does today. Joel was describing the state of Israel's crops, but he was also describing a need for heavenly rain.

The locusts, whether they literally ravaged Israel's agriculture or not, also prophetically represented the coming judgment of God. Joel's words have a double meaning. They are a message to ancient Israel as well as an end-times prophecy. Joel's prophetic words reach far into the future to tell of the day of the outpouring of the Holy Spirit.

Then, after doing all those things, I will pour out My Spirit upon all people. Your sons and daughters will prophesy. Your old men will dream dreams, and your young men will see visions. In those days I will pour out My Spirit even on servants—men and women alike. And I will cause wonders in the heavens and on the earth— blood and fire and columns of smoke. The sun will become dark, and the moon will turn blood red before that great and terrible day of the Lord arrives. And everyone who calls on the name of the Lord will be saved... (Joel 2:28-32).

The prophetic promise of a fresh outpouring of the Holy Spirit was later fulfilled in the Book of Acts.

But this is what was spoken by the prophet Joel: "And it shall come to pass in the last days, says God, That I will pour out of My Spirit on all flesh; your sons and your daughters shall prophesy, your young men shall see visions, your old men shall dream dreams" (Acts 2:16-17 NKJV).

Joel prophesied the coming of the Holy Spirit during a time of agricultural disaster. The Holy Spirit came during a time of agricultural abundance (Pentecost/the grain harvest).

The Holy Spirit is the promise of the Father—He is a gift. He is given to us by a loving God. A gift from Heaven, the Spirit should be welcomed in our lives, our ministries, our churches, and our hearts. We must not reject this gift, promised long ago in the Book of Joel. We must love Him, embrace Him, and never—not for even a moment—be ashamed of His work.

Looking at the state of some of the Church today, I would say that we are living in a day where there is hardly any oil—it's difficult to find. So few are open to the Holy Spirit. Many churches don't even mention the Holy Spirit anymore. Oh, how we need the rain of Heaven again. It's time that we the Church, with open arms and in one unified voice, again declare, "Welcome, Holy Spirit."

The Holy Spirit is the promise of the Father.[1]

---

1 See also Acts 1:4-5.

Chapter 31

THE HOLY SPIRIT IN
AMOS

THE CONSUMING FIRE—*Amos 5:4-6*

The Holy Spirit consumes our false perceptions of God.

The Book of Amos can be summarized in one word: judgment. A shepherd from Judah, Amos was God's chosen instrument to deliver a scathing rebuke. Amos withholds nothing as he pronounces the fiery verdicts of God.

Listing charge after charge, Amos announces that God promises to send fire from Heaven to consume the wickedness that has permeated the land. The sins of Israel and Judah are many. Violence, injustice, perversion—the list is extensive. The Lord's message through Amos was clear: the fire of judgment was coming.

> *Now this is what the Lord says to the family of Israel: "Come back to Me and live! Don't worship at the pagan altars at Bethel; don't go to the shrines at Gilgal or Beersheba. For the people of Gilgal will be dragged off into exile, and the people of Bethel will be reduced to nothing." Come back to the Lord and live! Otherwise, He will roar through Israel like a fire, devouring you completely. Your gods in Bethel won't be able to quench the flames* (Amos 5:4-6).

Idolatry, as we can see through their history, is one of Israel's most prominent sins. I dare even say that idolatry was their root sin. Just look closely at the indictments brought against the people of Israel and Judah; then consider the many false gods they worshiped. There is an obvious correlation between how they worshipped and how they behaved.

Not all their false gods are mentioned in the Book of Amos. But, for example, the Israelites worshiped the false god Molech unto whom they sacrificed their children in fire (see Lev. 18:21). How could people who throw their own children into a pagan fire have any value for human life? That callousness toward human life pronounced itself in many ways, so no wonder they mercilessly sold people for financial gain.

> *This is what the Lord says: "The people of Israel have sinned again and again, and I will not let them go unpunished! They sell honorable people for silver and poor people for a pair of sandals"* (Amos 2:6).

God's people bowed to Baal and Ashtaroth, false gods who were worshiped through perverse sex acts (see Judg. 2:13). Is it any wonder then that God's people became sexually perverse?

> *They trample helpless people in the dust and shove the oppressed out of the way. Both father and son sleep with the same woman, corrupting My holy name* (Amos 2:7).

In every ritual they performed in honor of a false god, the Israelites lost something of themselves. For every perverse view they developed a perverse way of life. The twisting of the human soul, the darkening of the mind and conscience, is why the Lord's anger so furiously burned against the sin of idolatry. To purge His people from the evils of idolatry, the Lord would send a cleansing fire, His vengeance on the demonic deception that ruined lives.

Now there are many references in the Bible that equate fire with destruction, judgment, and punishment. I don't need to list them all to make my point, so here are a few for your reference: Genesis 19:24; Leviticus 10:2; Numbers 16:35; Deuteronomy 4:24; 7:5,25; 9:3; 12:3; Second Kings 1:10; 19:18; Psalm 50:3; 68:2; 79:5; 89:46; 97:3; Isaiah 4:4; 5:24; 66:15-16; Ezekiel 28:18; Nahum 1:6; Second Thessalonians 1:8-9; Second Peter 3:7; Jude 1:7; Revelation 14:10; 21:8.

Looking at those many references of the Scripture, you'll begin to see a distinct pattern form. The fire, which is a symbol of God's Holy Spirit, speaks of God's wrath, anger, and jealousy.

There were many sins that Israel and Judah constantly committed, but in the context of God's fire of judgment, idolatry seems to reappear more than the others.

> *This is what the Lord says: "The people of Judah have sinned again and again, and I will not let them go unpunished! They have rejected the instruction of the Lord, refusing to obey His decrees. They have been led astray by the same lies that deceived their ancestors. So I will send down fire on Judah, and all the fortresses of Jerusalem will be destroyed"* (Amos 2:4-5).

Idolatry was a persistent, generational issue. God's response to idolatry was fire.

> *I took your sin—the calf you had made—and I melted it down in the fire and ground it into fine dust. Then I threw the dust into the stream that flows down the mountain* (Deuteronomy 9:21).

> *The Philistines had abandoned their gods there, so David gave orders to burn them* (1 Chronicles 14:12).

> *And have cast their gods into the fire: for they were no gods, but the work of men's hands, wood and stone: therefore they have destroyed them* (Isaiah 37:19 KJV).

False perceptions about Christ are burned away by the Holy Spirit. He is the fire that consumes the idolatrous rubble. He blazes a clear view in front of you, and He removes the blockages that keep you from seeing Jesus as He is.

The Holy Spirit is the One who reveals the Father and the Son. The image of Jesus, the only one that is worthy of our adoration and praise, is vivified and intensified through the work of the Holy Spirit. I often pray, "Holy Spirit, show me what Jesus is really like." It is the desire of the Holy Spirit that you see Jesus clearly, without any perversion or disruption in your perception.

The Holy Spirit's uncompromising protectiveness for the Lordship of Christ is partly why Paul the apostle told the Corinthian church that the Holy Spirit would be the key to discerning the true work of the Lord.

> *So I want you to know that no one speaking by the Spirit of God will curse Jesus, and no one can say Jesus is Lord, except by the Holy Spirit* (1 Corinthians 12:3).

The Holy Spirit keeps us from idolatry, and idolatry is simply a false perception of the true God.

Many have built and embraced false perceptions of God. And idolatry is, fundamentally, a false or perverted view of God. So if our unfounded perceptions of God are the materials with which we craft our idols, then the Holy Spirit is the fire that consumes such perceptions.

Every false perception of God results in a belief that manifests in your emotions, thoughts, and actions. If your perception of God is lacking in mercy, grace, and love, you begin to worship an angry God and your lifestyle becomes religiously burdensome. If your perception of God is lacking in holiness, judgment, and righteousness, you begin to worship a sin-accepting God and your lifestyle becomes sinful. When we add or take away from our perception of the fullness of God, we are at risk of forming for ourselves the idols we long to worship. Manipulating the truth to our own liking, we are prone to perceiving what we wish was true of God. But the images we form lack power. Idols cannot set you free. Idols cannot love you. Idols cannot answer your prayers.

The idols of the nations are merely things of silver and gold, shaped by human hands. They have mouths but cannot speak, and eyes but cannot see. They have ears but cannot hear, and noses but cannot smell. And those who make idols are just like them, as are all who trust in them (Psalm 135:15-18).

You become like that which you worship. If you perceive God as angry or judgmental, you'll become an angry and judgmental person. If you perceive God as unholy, you become unholy. If you perceive God as a means to acquire wealth, you'll become greedy. What you believe about God affects everything about you.

This is why we need the Holy Spirit, the consuming fire who destroys the images of idols.

The Holy Spirit wants to consume your every false idea about God. If the Holy Spirit is the One who reveals truth, then He is also the One who destroys lies. Idolatry is any false perception or image of God.

For you have not come to a mountain that can be touched and to a blazing fire, and to darkness and gloom and whirlwind.... Therefore, since we receive a kingdom which cannot be shaken, let us show gratitude, by which we may offer to God an acceptable service with reverence and awe; for our God is a consuming fire (Hebrews 12:18,28-29 NASB).

A consuming fire, the Holy Spirit will destroy any image that is not the image of Jesus; He will consume whatever is not of God. The Holy Spirit brings clarity to your perception of God. He reveals Jesus as He truly is. Fire doesn't consume fire or anything pure. As the Holy Spirit scorches away the chaff of our powerless idols, He leaves only Jesus.

Chapter 32

THE HOLY SPIRIT IN
OBADIAH

THE VINDICATING FIRE—*Obadiah 1:18*

The Holy Spirit vindicates the righteous.

After Jerusalem had fallen under the power of the Babylonians, the Edomites, who should have come to Israel's aid, took advantage of the weakness of God's people by participating in their demise. The Edomites, relatives of Israel, betrayed the Israelites, and Obadiah prophesied the vengeance of the Lord against them.

> *Because of the violence you did to your close relatives in Israel, you will be filled with shame and destroyed forever* (Obadiah 1:1).

The Book of Obadiah focuses in part on the vindication of God's people. Those who had betrayed the Israelites were promised punishment. Israel would become as a fire.

> *The people of Israel will be a raging fire, and Edom a field of dry stubble. The descendants of Joseph will be a flame roaring across the field, devouring everything. There will be no survivors in Edom. I, the Lord, have spoken!* (Obadiah 1:18).

Even though Israel was described as a fire, it was ultimately the Lord who was enacting vengeance.

> *The Lord says to Edom, "I will cut you down to size among the nations; you will be greatly despised"* (Obadiah 1:2).

I was speaking to a pastor one day, and he began to tell me of how certain people had cheated him financially. I wasn't given the full story, but I knew enough about the situation to be vicariously offended.

I asked the pastor, "How do you feel when people steal from you?" He responded, "Nobody can steal from me. That's just not possible." Perplexed, I used silence to nudge the pastor to explain further. He said, "David, when people take from me, I just tell God, 'I'm sowing it.' Then it becomes a seed instead of a loss." Those words inspired me, and they reminded me that vengeance is ultimately in the Lord's hands, as we learn from Obadiah.

Obadiah was speaking of the vengeance of the Lord, and he described the children of Israel as a fire that would devour their enemies. Because the Holy Spirit was with them, the Israelites took on His fiery nature.

The Holy Spirit is the vindicating fire. He is kind, yes. He is gentle, of course. But He is also an inferno who presses against those who come against the Lord and the Lord's children.

For example, when Saul was pursuing David, the Holy Spirit Himself took care of David's pursuers.

> *Word came to Saul: "David is in Naioth at Ramah"; so he sent men to capture him. But when they saw a group of prophets prophesying, with Samuel standing there as their leader, the Spirit of God came on Saul's men, and they also prophesied. Saul was told about it, and he sent more men, and they prophesied too. Saul sent men a third time, and they also prophesied. Finally, he himself left for Ramah and went to the great cistern at Seku. And he asked, "Where are Samuel and David?" "Over in Naioth at Ramah," they said. So Saul went to Naioth at Ramah. But the Spirit of God came even on him, and he walked along prophesying until he came to Naioth* (1 Samuel 19:19-23 NIV).

In almost a playful way, the Holy Spirit disrupted David's enemies. David refused to harm Saul, so the Holy Spirit backed David. When you refuse to take matters into your own hands, the Holy Spirit is also the disrupter of your enemies.

Often, I am approached by people who tell me that at one point they couldn't stand me. They'll tell me things like, "I hated you" or "I didn't like you at all." But then they also describe the heavy conviction they experienced while harboring hateful feelings toward me in their hearts. The Holy Spirit convicts those who hate me.

People have betrayed me. People have lied to me and about me. People have cheated me. But it's not my job to seek justice. I leave that to the Holy Spirit. He vindicates His own.

Whatever trap is set for you, the Spirit will spring it against the one who set it. Whoever goes against you goes against the fire. There is a furious side to the Holy Spirit too, especially when it comes to protecting His own.

Think also of Ananias and Sapphira. They sold their property and brought the money to the apostles. Even though they kept a portion of the money for themselves (which was not wrong for them to do), they lied to the apostles and claimed that they were giving all the money.

> *Then Peter said, "Ananias, why have you let satan fill your heart? You lied to the Holy Spirit, and you kept some of the money for yourself. The property was yours to sell or not sell, as you wished. And after selling it, the money was also yours to give away. How could you do a thing like this? You weren't lying to us but to God!" As soon as Ananias heard these words, he fell to the floor and died. Everyone who heard about it was terrified* (Acts 5:3-5).

Ananias and Sapphira spoke to Peter but lied to the Holy Spirit. How is this so? You see, Peter and the Holy Spirit were one. So even though Ananias and Sapphira spoke the lie to Peter, the Holy Spirit took it personally. When people lie to the Spirit-filled, they are lying to the Spirit. When people lie to you, they are lying to the Holy Spirit. When people wrong you, they are wronging the Holy Spirit.

Peter didn't have to lift a hand for revenge; the Holy Spirit took care of those who rose against Peter. You don't have to lift a hand of revenge either, because the Holy Spirit will vindicate you.

Refuse to take revenge into your own hands and let the Holy Spirit handle it, He will become a vindicating fire in you.

Chapter 33

THE HOLY SPIRIT IN
JONAH

THE PROTECTOR OF THE CALL—*Jonah 1:4*

The Holy Spirit keeps you in the will of God.

All sincere believers are concerned about fulfilling the will of God. Not wanting to step outside of the purpose and safety of God's plan, we strive for the will of God to be accomplished. Many even fret over this, believing that the will of God is a fragile thing. It was the will of God that brought everything into existence, and it is the will of God that holds all things together. How can God's will, therefore, be fragile? The call of God on your life is fulfilled because of the faithfulness of the Holy Spirit, not your willpower. The Holy Spirit is your peace of mind, your assurance that you will not miss the will of God.

Jonah is an encouraging example of just how faithful the Lord is to us. Jonah was a prophet called by God to preach to the inhabitants of Nineveh, an ungodly and violent people. Jonah wasn't trying to fulfill the call of God; he was trying to run from it. So instead of sailing to Nineveh, Jonah boarded a ship to Tarshish. But something disrupted the plans of Jonah, something that would eventually set him back on course toward the call of God.

What was it that disrupted Jonah's plans?

> *But the Lord hurled a powerful wind over the sea, causing a violent storm that threatened to break the ship apart* (Jonah 1:4).

To set Jonah back on spiritual course, the Lord sent a *powerful wind.* Wind, a symbol of the Holy Spirit, was used by God to redirect Jonah. But it wasn't just a wind—it was a powerful wind. Jonah couldn't fight against it. Jonah couldn't run from it. The wind stopped Jonah from moving in the direction he desired while also threatening to destroy his boat, the only means he had to flee from God's call. Jonah couldn't miss God's call because of a powerful wind, and the call of God on your life is protected by the Holy Spirit. Perhaps the will of God isn't as easy to miss as we might have imagined.

As the storm intensified, the sailors aboard the ship cast lots to see who among them had offended "the gods."

> *Then the crew cast lots to see which of them had offended the gods and caused the terrible storm. When they did this, the lots identified Jonah as the culprit* (Jonah 1:7).

After he was identified as the cause of the storm, Jonah instructed the men to throw him overboard. Jonah was tossed from the ship, and the storm ceased. It was then that a "great fish" was sent by the Lord to swallow Jonah. After three days and three nights, Jonah was regurgitated onto the shore, where he received the command of God.

> *Then the Lord spoke to Jonah a second time: "Get up and go to the great city of Nineveh, and deliver the message I have given you"* (Jonah 3:1-2).

Jonah finally obeyed the Lord in preaching to the people of Nineveh, and there was a city-wide revival. The people repented, and God spared the city. Disgruntled, Jonah was not happy about Ninevah's repentance, so the Lord disciplined him.

> *And as the sun grew hot, God arranged for a scorching east wind to blow on Jonah. The sun beat down on his head until he grew faint and wished to die. "Death is certainly better than living like this!" he exclaimed* (Jonah 4:8).

There again we see the Wind with Jonah.

The Wind was near Jonah in his rebellious journey to flee the call of God, and the Wind remained with him to discipline him for his inappropriate attitude.

When I look at the life of Jonah, I see no reason to live in fear of missing the call of God. If ever you stray off course, God will send a wind, the Holy Spirit. He guides you and protects the call of God on your life. Although we may stray from time to time, the Holy Spirit won't allow you to miss the will of God. Think of how the Holy Spirit corrected the course of Paul the apostle.

> *Next Paul and Silas traveled through the area of Phrygia and Galatia, because the Holy Spirit had prevented them from preaching the word in the province of Asia at that time. Then coming to the borders of Mysia, they headed north for the province of Bithynia, but again the Spirit of Jesus did not allow them to go there* (Acts 16:6-7).

Some believers are so worried about missing the will of God that they remain motionless; their gifts lay dormant. The clarity comes as you go. The will of God is revealed as you obey. And if ever you are tempted to live in fear, remember the faithfulness of God to Jonah. If God fulfilled His will through Jonah, who sought to run from the call, how can you doubt that He will fulfill His call through you, who is pursuing the call?

The Holy Spirit won't let you miss it. He'll speak to you. He'll strengthen you. He'll protect you.

The Holy Spirit is that corrective wind, the Protector of your call.

Chapter 34

THE HOLY SPIRIT IN
MICAH

THE UNCHANGING SPIRIT—*Micah 2:7*

The Holy Spirit does not change.

Micah, like most of the prophets in Scripture, was used by God to warn of coming judgment and offer mercy in exchange for repentance. The prophet Micah makes it clear that there are consequences to sin and that the Holy Spirit does not change His mind to meet our preferences.

> *O thou that art named the house of Jacob, is the spirit of the Lord straitened? are these His doings? do not my words do good to him that walketh uprightly?* (Micah 2:7 KJV)

The Holy Spirit will not bend to our whims. As gentle and comforting as He is, He can also be confrontational at times. He does not speak loudly, but He does speak consistently. In His mercy, He keeps speaking to the believer until the moment of obedient surrender. In His love, He will weigh upon you. King David described this persistent confrontation of the Holy Spirit as a "heavy hand":

> *For day and night Thy hand was heavy upon me: my moisture is turned into the drought of summer* (Psalm 32:4 KJV).

Once the Holy Spirit has made His instructions clear, the response to His instructions rests on you. How many times do we try to bargain with Him, to reason with Him? How many times have we said, "Can't we do it this way?" or "Why do I have to do it like that?" We try to justify our own ways and approaches. We try to repress what He wants us to confess. We try to keep what He says to release. But He persists. He loves us too much not to persist.

Is the Spirit of the Lord straitened? Can He be persuaded? Can you convince the Holy Spirit to do it your way? Certainly not. Micah, who was filled with the Holy Spirit, remained boldly committed to the message he was to deliver:

> *But as for me, I am filled with power—with the Spirit of the Lord. I am filled with justice and strength to boldly declare Israel's sin and rebellion* (Micah 3:8).

The Holy Spirit doesn't take "no" for an answer, at least not from those who belong to Him. You can't convince Him to do it your way. Believe me, He's stronger than you, more patient than you, and more committed than you. You might as well just do it His way.

He is the unchanging Spirit.

Chapter 35

THE HOLY SPIRIT IN
NAHUM

THE SPIRIT OF WARNING—*Nahum 1:6*

The Holy Spirit warns the stubborn.

The Book of Nahum records God's warnings of judgment against the city of Nineveh, the capital of Assyria. The Assyrians were merciless and oppressive in their treatment of the Israelites. Because of their cruelty toward God's holy nation, the Assyrians were caught in the vengeful glare of God's fiery eyes. The Holy Spirit through Nahum made threats against Nineveh:

> *Who can stand before His fierce anger? Who can survive His burning fury? His rage blazes forth like fire, and the mountains crumble to dust in His presence* (Nahum 1:6).

As angry as the Holy Spirit was, we know, after reading the Book of Jonah, wherein Ninevah was spared, that God was willing to retract His judgment were He to see repentance and brokenness. Ninevah was offered the chance to repent in the Book of Jonah, and God doesn't change. So Nahum was warning Ninevah because God was offering them a chance to repent. Otherwise, why warn them at all? That's how God works with man's behavior. The Bible clearly states that's how God works in the Book of Jeremiah. The prophet Jeremiah communicates this "prophetic clause" in the "contract" between God and man:

> *If I announce that a certain nation or kingdom is to be uprooted, torn down, and destroyed, but then that nation renounces its evil ways, I will not destroy it as I had planned. And if I announce*

that I will plant and build up a certain nation or kingdom, but then that nation turns to evil and refuses to obey Me, I will not bless it as I said I would (Jeremiah 18:7-10).

After we sin, the Holy Spirit convicts us. If we compromise, the Holy Spirit fortifies us. But as we maintain an unrepentant posture of the heart, the Holy Spirit harshly warns us. His conviction is for our sinful mistakes. His fortification is for our unnoticed compromise. But His warning is for our consistent and stubborn refusal to obey.

Just as the Holy Spirit warned Ninevah through Nahum, so the Holy Spirit warns you. This is the uncomfortable truth: the Holy Spirit makes threats. He does so because He loves you. You see, God does punish people, but He does so to bring forth repentance. Desire will place a man in sin, but pride will keep him there. In order to break that pride, God brings forth chastisement. God would rather save your soul than your reputation, your ministry, or your material possessions.

Growing up as a pastor's kid, I witnessed the rise and fall of many great men and women of God. I've seen men walk in integrity and dignity. And I've seen men fall into adulterous affairs, money scandals, and bizarre heresies. Hardly anything is more sobering to a minister of the Gospel than to watch another minister of the Gospel go through a scandal of some sort.

But while looking at the "why" behind every embarrassing fall, I've come to see a pattern. Those who fall into scandal and sin don't fall in an instant. It takes months, and sometimes even years, for a man or woman of God to fall. Secret sinful habits dominate the private life before public disqualifying acts are committed. Those who are publicly exposed all have one thing in common: pride.

They stubbornly refuse to repent despite many warnings and close calls. I dare even say that God wouldn't have exposed the sins of many of the fallen had they just repented in time.

The Holy Spirit is patient with us, yes. The Holy Spirit convicts us when we do wrong, yes. But when a believer begins to tread down a dangerous and deliberately sinful path, the Spirit begins to burn against that believer's mind and conscience.

Nineveh was given a warning because God was giving them a chance to repent. God does not give warnings where there is no opportunity for repentance. When He warns of His judgment, the Holy Spirit is enacting a form of His own tough love. He is telling us that God is about to punish wrongdoing.

It's important that you understand that I'm not writing here about your struggle with sin. I'm writing about the sinful things in your life that you're not even attempting to overcome, the things you've allowed in your life, the things you try to compartmentalize or justify. God wants to rescue you from your stubbornness, but He will avoid punishment if He can. That is why the Holy Spirit speaks so harshly sometimes: He's trying to get you to be broken by choice before you're broken by the wrath of God.

Those fallen preachers I'm writing about are just examples of this. They are publicly exposed and humiliated as a punishment from their Father who loves them. But many could have found restoration in the safety of repentance rather than in the chaos of the public eye.

The Holy Spirit warns those who persist in unrighteousness. He wrestles with the one who thinks he can control his hidden sins. Listen to His warnings and avoid the punishment. Come clean before God, and receive His mercy. Listen to the voice of the Holy Spirit.

For the Holy Spirit is the Spirit of warning.

Chapter 36

THE HOLY SPIRIT IN
HABAKKUK

THE SPIRIT OF INDIGNATION—*Habakkuk 1:13*

The Holy Spirit is offended by sin.

The prophet Habakkuk was searching for answers. He wanted to know why God would seemingly allow sin to go unpunished. Through his mournful questioning, you can sense the indignation of the prophet:

> *Thou art of purer eyes than to behold evil, and canst not look on iniquity: wherefore lookest Thou upon them that deal treacherously, and holdest Thy tongue when the wicked devoureth the man that is more righteous than he?* (Habakkuk 1:13 KJV)

Habakkuk was offended at the sight of sin. He was disturbed by what he saw.

That same indignation that the Holy Spirit inspired in Habakkuk was the very same He enflamed in the heart of the Master when He forcefully removed the thieves from the temple:

> *And they come to Jerusalem: and Jesus went into the temple, and began to cast out them that sold and bought in the temple, and overthrew the tables of the moneychangers, and the seats of them that sold doves; And would not suffer that any man should carry any vessel through the temple. And He taught, saying unto them, Is it not written, My house shall be called of all nations the house of prayer? but ye have made it a den of thieves* (Mark 11:15-17 KJV).

The Holy Spirit is that fire of indignation that so burns in the heart of God.

Behold, the name of the Lord cometh from far, burning with His anger, and the burden thereof is heavy: His lips are full of indignation, and His tongue as a devouring fire (Isaiah 30:27 KJV).

King David burned with holy offense at the wickedness of those around him.

I said to myself, "I will watch what I do and not sin in what I say. I will hold my tongue when the ungodly are around me." But as I stood there in silence—not even speaking of good things—the turmoil within me grew worse. The more I thought about it, the hotter I got, igniting a fire of words. (Psalm 39:1-3)

The Holy Spirit causes us to love what God loves and hate what He hates. There arises in the heart of the one who is Spirit-filled a holy uproar, a fiery disdain for that which contradicts the nature or the will of God.

Rescue others by snatching them from the flames of judgment. Show mercy to still others, but do so with great caution, hating the sins that contaminate their lives (Jude 1:23).

Then the Spirit of God came powerfully upon Saul, and he became very angry (1 Samuel 11:6).

The more surrendered you are to the Holy Spirit, the less tolerance you have for sin and injustice. Of course, I am not writing about a self-righteous piety or a condescending disposition. I am writing of a holy hatred for the destructiveness of sin itself. He inspires an offense for sin. Who cares if people accuse you of being religious? What does it matter if they think you are too strict? Be gentle with others while being aggressive with the sin in your own life. Allow the Holy Spirit to align your likes and dislikes with the nature of God.

The Holy Spirit is the Spirit of indignation.

Chapter 37

THE HOLY SPIRIT IN ZEPHANIAH

THE SPIRIT OF HOPE—*Zephaniah 3:14-15*

The Holy Spirit stirs our hope to believe for a brighter future.

Zephaniah prophesied judgment against God's people. As you probably have noticed by now, the judgment of God is a recurring theme in the books of the prophets. Although Zephaniah prophesied about God's judgment, he also spoke of the coming mercy of God.

> *Sing, O daughter of Zion; shout, O Israel; be glad and rejoice with all the heart, O daughter of Jerusalem. The Lord hath taken away thy judgments, He hath cast out thine enemy: the king of Israel, even the Lord, is in the midst of thee: thou shalt not see evil any more (Zephaniah 3:14-15 KJV).*

Through Zephaniah, the Holy Spirit spoke of a coming restoration, a reason to hope in the future. The Holy Spirit has a heart to give His people hope.

No matter what has been lost, whether by the random circumstances of life, the deception of the enemy, the selfish choices of others, the foolish decisions of your own, or even the judgments of God, the Holy Spirit keeps hope alive.

For the grieving, the depressed, the fearful, the lonely, and the aimless—there's hope. The Holy Spirit gives freedom from the past, joy for the moment, and faith for the future. He is that deep knowing within the troubled heart, that assurance that "all is well." He stirs faith and expectation for the greater things ahead. He is that voice that declares, "It can be restored" and "The future is bright."

Perhaps you're in a hopeless place. Perhaps you're there because of your own sin. Whether it was your own doing or life's circumstances that caused you to feel the weight of hopelessness, know that the Holy Spirit is fighting for you. He's encouraging and strengthening you.

I love what the prophet Kim Clement said: "You're somewhere in the future, and you look much better than you look right now." That is the heart of faith, hope, and expectation.

When demonic whispers deceive you into embracing less than what God has in store for you, the Holy Spirit stirs your faith to imagine something greater. The Holy Spirit lets you see into the future and glimpse the greater things ahead. Don't look back; look within, for the Spirit of hope lives within you. He's drawing your attention toward the future.

The Holy Spirit is the Spirit of hope.

Chapter 38

THE HOLY SPIRIT IN
HAGGAI

THE ENEMY OF FEAR—*Haggai 2:5*

The Holy Spirit makes you bold and fearless.

When I was a teenager, my friends and I would often do open-air preaching. I would preach on college campuses, at high schools, in parks—you name it. I recall reasoning with college students (and professors), getting cussed at by people who found the gift of the word of knowledge to be too invasive, and even getting a knife pulled on me while I preached to a man who was in the act of stealing a car.

But one memory of street preaching stands out to me more than the others. I recall that one of my friends had begun to fall away from the faith and had planned a wild party. My Spirit-filled friends and I decided that we would go to the party together and preach as the Holy Spirit led.

When we arrived, we heard loud music coming from a crowded house. Drunken teens were stumbling throughout the property. The atmosphere was demonic, but I had also brought an atmosphere of my own.

As soon as I arrived, I was met with hostility by one of the makeshift "bouncers" they had screening people. He recognized me and questioned why I was there. I told him that I was there to see my friend and preach to people.

After some disagreement, I said, "Look. I am looking all around, and I see many underage drinkers. You can either let me in or I can call the cops and shut the whole thing down." Some might say that's obnoxious, rude, or unloving. Sadly, some believers might say that's "judgmental" or "something that can 'turn people off' to the Gospel." To be honest with you, I don't really care what people think. I'll do anything to reach souls. And if we truly believe that people are perishing, how can we not act?

We made it into the party, and I recognized a few of the drunken people—some of them were leaders from the churches I had ministered at before. When they saw me, their eyes widened and they turned their heads in the opposite direction. Some of them even left the party.

With my friend's reluctant permission, I began to preach the Gospel. I told them that they needed to repent and that God was able to set them free from sin.

People threw cans of beer at me, mocked me. I even heard someone yell, "Tell Diga to shut up and leave!" But I didn't leave. I kept preaching. Some threatened to beat me up. A few demons even manifested as some of the teenagers began to scream and growl. After only a matter of minutes, I finished preaching and thanked everyone for listening. As I left, some came up to me and cussed me out. Some so-called Christians told me, "This isn't the time or the place." And some of the partygoers, beer in hand, said things like, "I really respect that. It's like you really believe what you're saying."

For my altar call, I challenged the people and said, "If you want to leave this life and follow Jesus, follow me out of this party. Come out of the darkness and step into the light." Many told me that they wanted to follow me out but that it was difficult. They just couldn't bring themselves to leave.

But there was one boy about my age who approached me. He was shaken by what he had seen and heard. He followed me outside the house and told me that he wanted to turn from that life and toward Christ. He left that party with me and my friends and was in church that following Sunday.

The Holy Spirit makes you bold.

The prophet Haggai was stirred by the Spirit to challenge the people of God to finish the building of the temple. He confronted the governor Zerubbabel and the high priest Jeshua about neglecting God's house.

> *Then came the word of the Lord by Haggai the prophet, saying, Is it time for you, O ye, to dwell in your cieled houses, and this house lie waste?* (Haggai 1:3-4 KJV).

Energizing them to fulfill what the Lord had commanded them to do, the prophet Haggai gives them this prophetic encouragement:

According to the word that I covenanted with you when ye came out of Egypt, so My spirit remaineth among you: fear ye not (Haggai 2:5 KJV).

Haggai's message here is simple: Because the Holy Spirit is with you, there is no reason to fear.

Should we fear death? No, for the Holy Spirit who lives in you is the same who raised Christ from the dead. Should we fear the demonic? Of course not. The Spirit of God is greater than any spirit of any kind. Is there reason to be afraid of what men can do to you? Not at all. For the Spirit who dwells in you is the One who gives them their breath and sustains their very lives.

The Holy Spirit is the enemy of fear. What was it that enabled the early martyrs to lay down their lives and face the tortuous opposition of Gospel-hating governments? What power stills the inner beings of those who spill their blood for the sake of Christ? This force, this holy and unrelenting boldness, is the trailblazer for the Gospel. Even those who identify as introverted can experience this power to speak and act out audaciously. He will quicken your speech and plant your footing. He will make you a lovingly persuasive and boldly unapologetic upset to the systemized sins of society. He will make you unafraid to dismantle the worldly philosophies and deceptions of our time. Fear not. The Holy Spirit is with you.

The Holy Spirit is the enemy of fear.

Chapter 39

THE HOLY SPIRIT IN ZECHARIAH

A WALL OF PROTECTION—*Zechariah 2:5*

Then I, Myself, will be a protective wall of fire around Jerusalem, says the Lord. And I will be the glory inside the city! (Zechariah 2:5).

The wall of protection being described is not a thing, the wall is a Person—He said "I, Myself, will be a protective wall." And not just a wall but a wall of fire. We, of course, know who that living flame is. The Holy Spirit is our fire wall of protection. Inhabiting our very bodies, He keeps a vigilant watch and prevents our enemies from doing us harm. He is your protector.

THE SPIRIT OF GRACE—*Zechariah 12:10*

The Holy Spirit gives us grace.

Many believers are uncomfortable with the word *grace* because of how much it is abused today. But, in fact, the Holy Spirit is called the Spirit of grace.

In the Book of Zechariah, the Holy Spirit is referred to as the Spirit of grace, and Zechariah prophesies the crucifixion of Jesus. The Spirit of grace and the crucifixion are mentioned together because it is the Spirit of grace who draws our attention to the cross. Salvation and grace go hand in hand. The Spirit of grace and supplication comes upon God's people and causes them to look upon Jesus and mourn.

And I will pour upon the house of David, and upon the inhabitants of Jerusalem, the spirit of grace and of supplications: and they shall look upon Me whom they have pierced, and they shall mourn for Him, as one mourneth for his only son, and shall be in bitterness for Him, as one that is in bitterness for his firstborn (Zechariah 12:10 KJV).[1]

What comes after this mourning? A cleansing fountain is opened.

On that day a fountain will be opened for the dynasty of David and for the people of Jerusalem, a fountain to cleanse them from all their sins and impurity (Zechariah 13:1).

Before we can receive from the fountain of salvation, we must be drawn to the fountain of salvation. The Spirit of grace draws us to that fountain. Nothing about salvation can be experienced without grace. You can't know of salvation, desire salvation, or live in the benefits of salvation without grace.

Many have said that grace is "unmerited favor." I believe that's true, but it's also more than that. What comes with God's unmerited favor? What undeserved blessings does He bestow upon us? Forgiveness? Yes. Mercy? Yes.

But what else?

Grace is the Holy Spirit within you. The grace of God is the empowering presence of the Holy Spirit. Grace is God, by His Spirit, doing for us what we cannot do for ourselves. Grace is God, by His Spirit, giving to us what we don't deserve. Grace is God, by His Spirit, empowering us to do what we could not do without Him. Without the Holy Spirit of grace, not only could you not be saved; you wouldn't even desire salvation.

Think of all the Spirit of grace empowers us to do and be.

Grace empowered Paul the apostle to carry out his ministry.

But whatever I am now, it is all because God poured out His special favor on me—and not without results. For I have worked harder than any of the other apostles; yet it was not I but God who was working through me by His grace (1 Corinthians 15:10).

---

1   See also Hebrews 10:29.

Grace enables us to resist evil desires.

> *But He gives us even more grace to stand against such evil desires. As the Scriptures say, "God opposes the proud but favors the humble"* (James 4:6).

Grace teaches us to deny ungodliness.

> *For the grace of God that bringeth salvation hath appeared to all men, teaching us that, denying ungodliness and worldly lusts, we should live soberly, righteously, and godly, in this present world* (Titus 2:11-12 KJV).

It is by grace that we serve God acceptably.

> *Wherefore we receiving a kingdom which cannot be moved, let us have grace, whereby we may serve God acceptably with reverence and godly fear* (Hebrews 12:28 KJV).[1]

Grace is all we need to overcome the weakness of the flesh.

> *Three different times I begged the Lord to take it away. Each time He said, "My grace is all you need. My power works best in weakness." So now I am glad to boast about my weaknesses, so that the power of Christ can work through me* (2 Corinthians 12:8-9).

Grace and holiness are not opposites that need to be balanced. Grace is the power to live in holiness.

> *Teach me to do Your will, for You are my God. May Your gracious Spirit lead me forward on a firm footing* (Psalm 143:10).

The Holy Spirit within you helps you fight to resist the temptations around you.

> *So I say, let the Holy Spirit guide your lives. Then you won't be doing what your sinful nature craves. The sinful nature wants to do evil, which is just the opposite of what the Spirit wants. And the Spirit gives us desires that are the opposite of what the sinful nature desires. These two forces are constantly fighting each other, so you are not free to carry out your good intentions. But when you are*

---

1 See also Philippians 2:13.

directed by the Spirit, you are not under obligation to the law of Moses (Galatians 5:16-18).

You are not left alone to fight the battle against the flesh. I love the way that King David cried out to God for help against His own flesh:

Take control of what I say, O Lord, and guard my lips. Don't let me drift toward evil or take part in acts of wickedness. Don't let me share in the delicacies of those who do wrong (Psalm 141:3-4).

Rescue me from my rebellion. Do not let fools mock me (Psalm 39:8).

When you understand the true nature of grace, you avoid the extremes of legalism and liberalism. Legalism says that your salvation depends on your works. The Scripture clearly refutes legalism:

God saved you by His grace when you believed. And you can't take credit for this; it is a gift from God (Ephesians 2:8).

And liberalism tells us that we can live however we want without consequences. The Scripture clearly refutes liberalism too:

I say this because some ungodly people have wormed their way into your churches, saying that God's marvelous grace allows us to live immoral lives. The condemnation of such people was recorded long ago, for they have denied our only Master and Lord, Jesus Christ (Jude 1:4).

Grace is the balance. Grace is God working in us to accomplish His own will. Grace is freedom from sin.

Sin is no longer your master, for you no longer live under the requirements of the law. Instead, you live under the freedom of God's grace (Romans 6:14).

We don't walk in holiness to receive salvation; we walk in holiness as a result of salvation.

But how have we received this grace? How are we empowered? We are empowered by the Holy Spirit within us.

The Spirit of grace lives within you. He enables you to live in holiness. He enables you to be free of sin's dominance. The Holy Spirit weakens your flesh and strengthens your desire to do God's will.

So I say, let the Holy Spirit guide your lives. Then you won't be doing what your sinful nature craves (Galatians 5:16).

The key then to overcoming the flesh is not willpower, discipline, or self-loathing. The key to overcoming the flesh is surrendering to the Spirit of grace. Recognize that it's not your power; it's His.

When temptation pulls on the desires of your flesh, call upon the Holy Spirit. Stop what you're doing, look upward, and say, "Help me, Holy Spirit. I'm in trouble. Spirit of grace, give me the power to resist this." And don't stop calling upon Him until the ungodly desire wanes. You don't have to fight the flesh on your own. You're not powerless to live the will of God. You can live your life to the glory of God because you have grace within you. The same Spirit who showed you salvation and drew you to salvation is the same Spirit who will help you to live in salvation. And He will empower you to do much more.

He is the Spirit of grace.

Chapter 40

THE HOLY SPIRIT IN MALACHI

THE REFINER'S FIRE—*Malachi 3:1-2*

The Holy Spirit refines our character.

Malachi addressed the apathy of God's people and warned them about God's displeasure with half-heartedness. While addressing this apathy, Malachi prophesies the coming of John the Baptist and the Lord:

> *Behold, I will send My messenger, and he shall prepare the way before Me: and the Lord, whom ye seek, shall suddenly come to his temple, even the messenger of the covenant, whom ye delight in: behold, He shall come, saith the Lord of hosts. But who may abide the day of His coming? and who shall stand when He appeareth? for He is like a refiner's fire, and like fullers' soap* (Malachi 3:1-2 KJV).

The fire that Malachi describes is a purifying fire, one that refines and perfects precious metals. The Messiah was to bring this fire and purify His people with it. The fire that the Messiah was to bring was the fire of the Holy Spirit.

> *I baptize with water those who repent of their sins and turn to God. But someone is coming soon who is greater than I am—so much greater that I'm not worthy even to be His slave and carry His sandals. He will baptize you with the Holy Spirit and with fire* (Matthew 3:11).

The Holy Spirit is the refiner's fire.

The more time we spend with the Holy Spirit, the more refined we become. He burns away the flaws of the flesh and rids us of our unhealthy habits. The Holy Spirit, above most other things, desires to conform your character to the character of Christ. Each moment you spend with the Holy Spirit is a moment in the refiner's fire. For every second you spend with Him, you are being transformed.

He purifies your conscience. He purifies your motives. He purifies your mind, your actions, and your speech.

Fire burns. Fire brings discomfort. But fire ultimately purifies. Let the Holy Spirit consume you and refine you to be more like Jesus. Allow Him to refine you

The Holy Spirit is the refiner's fire.

Chapter 41

THE HOLY SPIRIT IN
MATTHEW

THE SPIRIT OF THE INCARNATION—*Matthew 1:18*

The Holy Spirit was the power behind the Incarnation.

If it weren't for the power of the Holy Spirit, the Word would have never been made flesh. The Holy Spirit took God—all that He is or ever shall be, infinite and all powerful, all knowing and ever present—and seeded Him into the vulnerability of Mary's womb. In Him did the vastness of the cosmos dwell, yet He limited Himself to the confines of a seed. The infinite became physical; the invisible, tangible.

> *Now the birth of Jesus Christ was on this wise: When as His mother Mary was espoused to Joseph, before they came together, she was found with child of the Holy Ghost* (Matthew 1:18 KJV).

The Holy Spirit opened the possibility, that tiny unthinkable door, and allowed the Creator to step into creation. His work was so perfect, His power so great, that not a single divine attribute was missed. The Holy Spirit didn't cause some of the Word to be made flesh; He caused all of the Word to be made flesh. The completeness of the Holy Spirit's masterful work is why the Scripture can say:

> *For in Him dwelleth all the fulness of the Godhead bodily* (Colossians 2:9 KJV).

> *Jesus saith unto him, Have I been so long time with you, and yet hast thou not known Me, Philip? he that hath seen Me hath seen the Father; and how sayest thou then, Shew us the Father?* (John 14:9 KJV).

The Word became flesh that flesh might become the Word. The spiritual became carnal that the carnal might become spiritual. This extraordinary feat was accomplished by the Holy Spirit.

The Holy Spirit is the Spirit of the Incarnation.

THE SPIRIT OF THE FATHER—*Matthew 10:20*

> *For it is not you who will be speaking—it will be the Spirit of your Father speaking through you* (Matthew 10:20).

The Holy Spirit is referred to as the Spirit of the Father. Just as we know Jesus by the Holy Spirit, so we also know the Father by the Holy Spirit. They are all united in one Spirit, the Holy Spirit. Your heavenly Father desires to be close to you. That is why He gave you the gift of His Holy Spirit. The Father is near to you by the Holy Spirit. Deep calls unto deep. The depths of the Father connect with the depths of you. By the Spirit, you know the Father and the Father knows you.

THE SPIRIT OF DELIVERANCE—*Matthew 12:28*

The Holy Spirit liberates people from demons.

I was ministering at a church in the Midwest. I preached the Word and made an altar call. A group of people lined up to receive prayer. Walking beside me as I prayed over the people was a church leader who was listening in to the prophetic words I was speaking.

I moved down the prayer line and eventually found myself standing in front of a teenage girl. She was quiet, modestly dressed, and standing there with her eyes closed. I placed my hand on top of her head and began to pray in tongues. She jolted back as soon as I placed my hand on her head—as if struck by a bolt of electricity. It was then that I noticed her becoming uncomfortable. She fidgeted and glanced around the room.

I knew that look. I had seen it many times before. Realizing what was happening, I turned to the church leader next to me and boldly uttered, "This girl has a demon in her." With a puzzled facial expression forming on her face, the church leader told me, "No, that can't be. This girl serves here in the ministry." A holy indignation came over me, and I insisted, "I don't care who she is. This girl has a demon in her."

While the church leader and I politely refuted one another, the girl I was praying over began to laugh. It was mockery. She let out an antagonistic chuckle. Turning toward the demon-possessed girl, I made eye contact with her and commanded the demonic spirit to "Leave this girl now." The girl crumpled to the floor and was delivered, instantly.

That's the way Jesus did it—instantly.

Demons still exist, and the Holy Spirit still has the power to expel them.

Jesus didn't spend hours arguing with demonic spirits. He didn't interview them or try to find the root cause of their influence. He simply exercised His authority over them and commanded them to leave. Except for the man with a legion of demons (who asked while they were on their way out if they could go into a herd of pigs), Jesus delivered demon-possessed people instantly.

You may say, "Yes, but I can't cast out demons like Jesus did." Why not? You have the same Holy Spirit who dwelled in Jesus, and it was the Holy Spirit who enabled Jesus to cast out demons.

> But if I cast out devils by the Spirit of God, then the kingdom of God is come unto you (Matthew 12:28 KJV).

The Holy Spirit within you is your power to drive out demons. The Bible tells us that His presence alone brings about freedom:

> Now the Lord is that Spirit: and where the Spirit of the Lord is, there is liberty (2 Corinthians 3:17 KJV).

The Bible doesn't say, "Where the Spirit of the Lord is, there is eventually liberty." It says that where the Spirit of the Lord is there *is* liberty—present tense, instantaneous. Casting out demons doesn't require rituals, memorized prayers, or "holy" trinkets. That's just fighting the demonic with superstition. And there is no power in superstition.

It truly is as simple as having the power of the Holy Spirit. He is the One who brings deliverance. Demonic powers are darkness, and the Holy Spirit is light. Darkness simply cannot be where light is.

The Holy Spirit is the Spirit of deliverance.

Chapter 42

THE HOLY SPIRIT IN
MARK

THE BELOVED SPIRIT—*Mark 3:29*

The Holy Spirit is equal to the Father and the Son.

I've heard believers make remarks such as, "We shouldn't focus so much on the Holy Spirit; we should focus on Jesus." Some are a little more subtle, making claims like "God emphasizes Jesus, not the Holy Spirit." And I understand the heart behind what these well-meaning believers are attempting to communicate. Of course our focus needs to be Jesus. Of course the Holy Spirit emphasizes Jesus. Of course the Holy Spirit's work is to reveal Jesus. That's fundamental. But beyond that, I want you to really think about how the Church treats the Holy Spirit in general.

We claim to believe that the Father, the Son, and the Holy Spirit are all equal. Yet so many cringe when I say things like, "I love the Holy Spirit" or "I worship the Holy Spirit." That discomfort is quite revealing. Do you really believe that each member of the Trinity is equal? Then let's take the phrase "We shouldn't focus so much on the Holy Spirit; we should focus on Jesus" and reverse it.

How odd does this sound? "We shouldn't focus so much on Jesus; we should focus on the Holy Spirit." That doesn't sound right, does it? Then why do we say such things about the Holy Spirit, who is an equal member of the Trinity?

I love talking about the Holy Spirit. In emphasizing the Holy Spirit so often and in so many instances, I am not attempting to skew the focus in a way that unevenly accentuates the Holy Spirit. Rather, I am trying to compensate for what I believe is a lack of honor and acknowledgement of the Holy Spirit.

I want to demonstrate to you just how much the Father and the Son love the Holy Spirit—how much they honor Him. In my book *Carriers of the Glory*, I dedicated a section to the topic of the blasphemy of the Holy Spirit—what it is and why it's unforgivable. I won't go into detail on that topic, as I have already done so in my other book.

Instead, what I do want to point out to you is the reverence that the Father and the Son have for the Holy Spirit.

> *Verily I say unto you, All sins shall be forgiven unto the sons of men, and blasphemies wherewith soever they shall blaspheme: But he that shall blaspheme against the Holy Ghost hath never forgiveness, but is in danger of eternal damnation* (Mark 3:28-29 KJV).

Here again the gentle nature of the Holy Spirit is revealed. The Father will forgive blasphemies against the Son, but not against the Holy Spirit. The Father and Son are protective of the Holy Spirit. Why? Because He is honored among them equally. They love Him. He is precious to them.

The Holy Spirit is the beloved Spirit.

Chapter 43

THE HOLY SPIRIT IN LUKE

THE OMNI SPIRIT—*Luke 1:35*

The Holy Spirit is omnipotent, omniscient, and omnipresent.

The Holy Spirit is all-powerful. His power is one and the same as the power of the "Most High." The Holy Spirit is omnipotent.

> *The angel replied, "The Holy Spirit will come upon you, and the power of the Most High will overshadow you. So the baby to be born will be holy, and He will be called the Son of God"* (Luke 1:35).

The Holy Spirit is all-knowing. He searches and knows the mind and depths of the Father. The Holy Spirit is omniscient.

> *But God hath revealed them unto us by His Spirit: for the Spirit searcheth all things, yea, the deep things of God* (1 Corinthians 2:10 KJV).

The Holy Spirit is everywhere at all times. There is nowhere that anyone can go to escape His presence. The Holy Spirit is omnipresent.

> *I can never escape from Your Spirit! I can never get away from Your presence! (Psalm 139:7).*

The Holy Spirit is omnipotent, omniscient, and omnipresent.

THE THRESHING WIND—*Luke 3:16-17*

The Holy Spirit separates the holy from the unholy.

John the Baptist prepared the way of the Lord by announcing His coming. He preached repentance and opposed the religious hypocrites of his day. He describes Jesus in an insightful manner:

> *John answered, saying unto them all, I indeed baptize you with water; but one mightier than I cometh, the latchet of whose shoes I am not worthy to unloose: He shall baptize you with the Holy Ghost and with fire: whose fan is in His hand, and He will throughly purge His floor, and will gather the wheat into His garner; but the chaff He will burn with fire unquenchable* (Luke 3:16-17 KJV).

The word *fan* means *winnowing fork*. A winnowing fork was used to separate wheat from chaff. Chaff is a term used to describe the unwanted extras that mixed in with the wheat. The separating of the wheat from the chaff was called threshing. During threshing, the winnowing fork would be used to toss the wheat and the chaff into the air. The wind would carry away the chaff, and the wheat would fall to the threshing floor. The wheat would be collected, and the chaff would be burned with fire.

The threshing floor was a place of separation, where the useful was divided from the useless. Spiritually speaking, it is a place where God separates the godly from the ungodly—not just ungodly people from godly people, but also godly people from their ungodly ways and attributes.

> *The two necessary elements for threshing are wind and fire, both blatant symbols of the Holy Spirit. John himself identified the Holy Spirit's involvement in the threshing when he said, "He shall baptize you with the Holy Ghost and with fire: whose fan is in His hand, and He will thoroughly purge His floor…"* (Luke 3:17).

The Holy Spirit is the threshing wind and the threshing fire. He sifts us and separates us from whatever is not useful in our lives. He pulled worldliness from you, and He blew away unhealthy influences. Then He burned the chaff, forever separating you from what made you spiritually useless.

The Holy Spirit is the wind and the fire of the threshing floor.

Chapter 44

THE HOLY SPIRIT IN
JOHN

THE SPIRIT OF SALVATION—*John 3:3-8*

The Holy Spirit allows you to be born again.

> *Jesus replied, "I tell you the truth, unless you are born again, you cannot see the Kingdom of God." "What do you mean?" exclaimed Nicodemus. "How can an old man go back into his mother's womb and be born again?" Jesus replied, "I assure you, no one can enter the Kingdom of God without being born of water and the Spirit. Humans can reproduce only human life, but the Holy Spirit gives birth to spiritual life. So don't be surprised when I say, 'You must be born again.' The wind blows wherever it wants. Just as you can hear the wind but can't tell where it comes from or where it is going, so you can't explain how people are born of the Spirit"* (John 3:3-8).

All men are body and soul. The believer is body, soul, and spirit (see 1 Thess. 5:23). The body is the part of you that interacts with the physical realm. The soul is the mind, will, emotions, and personality. The soul is where free will is exercised. The spirit is the part of you that experiences oneness and fellowship with the Holy Spirit.

Before you were born again, your spirit was dead. You had no connection with God. Since your spirit was dead, you had no sense of God, no desire for God, and no true awareness of God. You came to God because you were called by God.

Salvation occurs when you are born, not in a physical body, but born *again* of the *Spirit*. Your spirit man, your innermost being, the part of you that connects with God, was brought to life at salvation. That life came about by the Holy Spirit.

He gave you a new life, a new nature, new knowledge, and new desires.

Salvation is a miracle. No amount of eloquence can explain it. No level of curiosity or diligence can understand it. It is a work of the Holy Spirit. He is the breath of eternal life, and only He can transform the spirit of a man—only He can dwell so deep that everything about a person is truly changed forever—for all time and eternity. The transformation is so profound that the one who experiences it is said to be "born again." You cannot be physically born again, but you can begin to exist as a new creation in the spiritual realm.

The change begins in the spirit and eventually comes to affect the body and the soul of a person. When you are saved, your spirit is brought to life, and your spirit changes the way you live in soul and body. The Holy Spirit unites with your spirit, and transformation happens from the inside out. Religion demands that you change from the outside in. But true salvation is a work of the Holy Spirit. Religion says, "Change the behavior." The Spirit says, "Transform the being." The Holy Spirit doesn't merely change your actions. He changes your nature and your desires. The Holy Spirit is the Spirit of salvation.

THE RIVERS OF LIVING WATER—*John 7:38-39*

"He who believes in Me, as the Scripture said, 'From his innermost being will flow rivers of living water.'" But this He spoke of the Spirit, whom those who believed in Him were to receive; for the Spirit was not yet given, because Jesus was not yet glorified (John 7:38-39 NASB).

The Holy Spirit is a surge of life. Deep from within your Spirit, He floods over into your soul and body—He proceeds from your innermost being. Wherever He flows, life flourishes. In the springs of His presence, hope, joy, peace, and love are refreshed. The force of the rushing river washes away the filth of the flesh, making you clean and blameless. Don't just drink from the river; dive into the river. Let the river take you.

THE POWER OF GREATER WORKS—*John 14:12*

The Holy Spirit enables greater works.

As I explained when covering the Holy Spirit in the Book of Isaiah, the same Holy Spirit who was upon Jesus is upon you. It is our responsibility as followers of Christ to do as Jesus did. It is our mandate to carry on His work and ministry.

But beyond that—and I really want to stretch your faith here—Jesus not only said that we would do the works He did but that we would do greater works:

> *I tell you the truth, anyone who believes in Me will do the same works I have done, and even greater works, because I am going to be with the Father* (John 14:12).

Who will do the greater works? Anyone who believes on Jesus. Do you believe on Jesus? Then you can do those works.

So what does it mean to do greater works than Jesus did? This is difficult to imagine, let alone believe. It's possible that the greater works are our multiplied efforts as a church. In other words, we can do more works collectively, and that collective power is what makes the works greater.

A greater work could be the sharing of your testimony. Jesus could never say, "Once I was lost, but now I am found." Perhaps a creation so broken being used so powerfully is what makes your preaching a greater work.

Whatever one concludes regarding the definition greater works, we should all aim to do our utmost in obeying the leading of the Holy Spirit.

But I want to address the question of why these greater works are even possible in the first place.

Jesus Himself told us: "*…because I am going to be with the Father*" (John 14:12). Now why is that important? Why does Jesus going to His Father mean that we will be able to do the works He did?

> *But in fact, it is best for you that I go away, because if I don't, the Advocate won't come. If I do go away, then I will send Him to you* (John 16:7).

Jesus going to His Father coincided with the sending of the Holy Spirit. So Jesus is in essence telling us, "I tell you the truth, anyone who believes in Me will do the same works I have done, and even greater works, because

I am sending you the Holy Spirit." (Connect the truths of John 14:12 and John 16:7.) The Holy Spirit had always been working on the earth, as we clearly see in the Scripture, but now He works in a greater capacity than ever before.

OUR HELPER—*John 14:16-17*

I will ask the Father, and He will give you another Helper, that He may be with you forever; that is the Spirit of truth, whom the world cannot receive, because it does not see Him or know Him, but you know Him because He abides with you and will be in you (John 14:16-17 NASB).

The Holy Spirit demonstrates His humble nature in helping the very ones who are sustained by His breath. He abides with you to help you in everything you face in life—big and small. When you feel overwhelmed by something, just pause and whisper, "Holy Spirit, I need Your help." He will help you.

THE TRUSTED SPIRIT—*John 16:7*

But in fact, it is best for you that I go away, because if I don't, the Advocate won't come. If I do go away, then I will send Him to you (John 16:7).

The Father trusted the Spirit to guide His Son. The Son trusts the Spirit to guide His Church. Therefore, you should trust the Holy Spirit to guide your life. He's never failed, and He won't fail you. Trust the Holy Spirit.

Chapter 45

THE HOLY SPIRIT IN ACTS

THE SPIRIT OF POWER—*Acts 2:1-4*

The Church needs the Holy Spirit.

If the Gospels are a record of the life and ministry of Jesus, then the Book of Acts is a record of the ministry of the Holy Spirit. The Book of Acts is a narrative about the birth and growth of the early Church. The book begins with Jesus instructing the believers to wait in Jerusalem for the Holy Spirit:

> *And, being assembled together with them, commanded them that they should not depart from Jerusalem, but wait for the promise of the Father, which, saith He, ye have heard of Me. For John truly baptized with water; but ye shall be baptized with the Holy Ghost not many days hence (Acts 1:4-5 KJV).*

The believers were united in their obedience to the command of Jesus, and they received the Holy Spirit.

> *And when the day of Pentecost was fully come, they were all with one accord in one place. And suddenly there came a sound from heaven as of a rushing mighty wind, and it filled all the house where they were sitting. And there appeared unto them cloven tongues like as of fire, and it sat upon each of them. And they were all filled with the Holy Ghost, and began to speak with other tongues, as the Spirit gave them utterance (Acts 2:1-4 KJV).*

The Holy Spirit was the One who birthed the early Church and has sustained the Church throughout the centuries. He is the power of the

Church. The Holy Spirit is the ultimate church growth expert. He is not a liability that needs limiting but the only One who can truly make an eternal impact. We need to let Him run our ministries and churches.

I am of the belief that there needs to be more of an emphasis placed on the Holy Spirit and His power. I love the Holy Spirit, and I love to talk about the Holy Spirit. In fact, some think that I talk about the Holy Spirit too much.

You see, in an effort to become more "relevant," many parts of the church are beginning to neglect the Holy Spirit and His ministry. Some knowingly, most unknowingly. Especially in the American church, there has been a culture shift away from the supernatural. Wanting to be celebrated on the secular platforms of influence, Christian leaders often make the mistake of limiting the expressions of the Spirit.

Ministries that welcome the Holy Spirit are criticized for being different. People who welcome the Holy Spirit are many times dismissed as "weird."

But if I had to choose between being cultured or being anointed, I'd tell you to keep your trendy clothes, catchy sermon titles, hyped crowds, and tweetable catch phrases. Give me the presence and power of the Holy Spirit.

Without the Holy Spirit, a church is just a club, our preaching is just motivation, and our outreaches are just temporary acts of charity. The work of the Holy Spirit is not supplemental; it's primary. Demonstrations of His supernatural power are not to be occasional but prolific. We must emphasize His saving power by preaching the Gospel of salvation and allowing people to testify of His transforming work. We must proclaim His delivering power by boldly claiming that addictions can be broken. And it must go beyond that. Many ministers stop there and work up clever-sounding excuses like, "Isn't salvation the most important work of the Holy Spirit? Lives are being transformed. That means we allow the Holy Spirit to move." What they're really saying is, "We have some of His work, but we don't need the rest. We'll take it from there."

The Holy Spirit is a gentleman. He'll go only as far as you allow Him to go. Of course, salvation, deliverance, and emotional healing are works of the Holy Spirit. But we must allow Him to do more than what we think makes us look good in front of our secular onlookers. We must permit Him to go further than just what allows us to maintain a savvy or sophisticated image.

When was the last time a demon was cast out in your church? When was the last time you laid hands on the sick? I don't mean when did you offer a corporate prayer for someone sick—I mean when was the last time you laid hands on the sick with the expectation that they'd recover right then and there in front of many witnesses?

When was the last time a prophetic tongue was spoken aloud? When was the last time people were filled with the evidence of speaking in tongues at your church? When was the last time you saw words of knowledge in operation at your church? We see it all over the Book of Acts. Has the Holy Spirit changed? Have the needs of the people changed?

Or has the Church changed its approach?

Then he said to me, "This is what the Lord says to Zerubbabel: It is not by force nor by strength, but by My Spirit, says the Lord of Heaven's Armies" (Zechariah 4:6).

In a church that He helped to begin, the Holy Spirit is being minimized and neglected. The Holy Spirit is not just the greatest evangelist; He's the greatest pastor, teacher, prophet, and apostle. When we carry out our ministry tasks with His aid and are conscious of our need for His enabling, a profound and powerful grace comes upon us. There is a certain unique dynamic to Spirit-led ministry. So we must model our approach, not after the approach of men and women who have gone before us, but after His unique and responsive direction as it pertains to each moment.

Without the Holy Spirit, we begin to rely upon systems and strategies. Yesterday's revival can so easily become today's religion. Men have a way of systemizing everything.

But there is no substitute for the genuine power and presence of the Holy Spirit. You cannot duplicate His craftsmanship. We have to stop limiting His timing to our church calendars and schedules. We need to stop confining His power to private meetings and "special services." Methods cannot replace miracles. Programs cannot replace power. Structure cannot replace Spirit. And our pursuit of attendance should never become more important than our pursuit of the anointing.

The truth is that the world is hungry for the very thing away from which much of the Church has shifted. People want the supernatural, and only the Holy Spirit can bring it to the Church.

The Holy Spirit is the greatest church builder. Nobody can win souls, build a church, or expand God's Kingdom better than He can. If we will embrace His leading, humbly submit to His expertise, and seek His guidance, then we will embrace a better way to build God's Kingdom. For He is not a liability; He's our only hope at drawing men to salvation. He's our only hope of building disciples. He's our only hope at properly presenting Jesus. Why would we want to receive any less than all than Holy Spirit has for us?

Be practical, yes. Gain wisdom from leaders, yes. Be organized and orderly, yes. But never prioritize any of that over what the Spirit of God can do.

Want to build people in the faith? Follow the greatest pastoral anointing in the earth—the Holy Spirit.

Want to draw crowds? Obey the enabler of the miraculous, the Holy Spirit.

Want to build a church? Consult with the One who built the church of Acts, which is the model church. Consult with the Holy Spirit.

The Holy Spirit is the Power of the Church.

THE SPIRIT OF BOLDNESS—*Acts 2:38*

Peter replied, "Each of you must repent of your sins and turn to God, and be baptized in the name of Jesus Christ for the forgiveness of your sins. Then you will receive the gift of the Holy Spirit" (Acts 2:38).

The same Peter who denied the Lord was the very same one who stood before thousands and boldly proclaimed the Gospel. What made the difference? The Holy Spirit did. The Holy Spirit is the One who gives us a holy boldness.

THE SENDER—*Acts 13:4*

So Barnabas and Saul were sent out by the Holy Spirit. They went down to the seaport of Seleucia and then sailed for the island of Cyprus (Acts 13:4).

God appoints through man, but the one who enters into ministry is sent *by* the Holy Spirit. The Holy Spirit is ultimately the One who sends every minister or servant of the Lord. Only He can so stir the spirit that one is moved to do a heavenly work; only He can so anoint a person that one is ready to do a heavenly work. The Holy Spirit is the Sender.

Chapter 46

THE HOLY SPIRIT IN ROMANS

THE ONE WHO LOVES JESUS—*Romans 5:5*

The Holy Spirit loves Jesus and helps us love Jesus.

Many believers are caught between the two unhealthy extremes of legalism and liberalism. Some are bound to one; others sway between the two. Legalism comes from fear. Liberalism comes from the flesh. Legalism births religion. Liberalism births perversion. Those who are caught in legalism have no joy or peace. They doubt their salvation. Those who are caught in liberalism have no holiness or power. They abuse their salvation. For many, it's difficult to find the place of power and peace, joy and holiness.

Legalistic Christians are burdened by a constant sense of shame, a paranoid dread of losing their salvation, and an angry perception of God. They are stoic, joyless, lifeless, and celebrate the preaching of a mean Gospel. They view any and all pleasure as sin and, deep within, believe that pain is itself the key to salvation. For them, the ministry is tiring, the Christian life is tedious, and the mind is tormented. They never find rest, and they come across as angry.

Liberal Christians are blinded by a deception, a view of God's grace that is a perversion of the truth. They doubt the power of the Holy Spirit to change hearts and minds. They embrace the ungodly customs of this world in the name of grace. They are shallow in the Word, irreverent toward worship, and ignorant of the deep things of the Spirit. They view any and all sacrifice as a religious burden. They hesitate to acknowledge God's holiness, righteousness, wrath, and judgment.

What is the key to freedom with holiness? How does one walk in both joy and commitment? The key is understanding that everything God requires of us can be accomplished in this: love.

> *Jesus replied, "'You must love the Lord your God with all your heart, all your soul, and all your mind.' This is the first and greatest commandment. A second is equally important: 'Love your neighbor as yourself.' The entire law and all the demands of the prophets are based on these two commandments"* (Matthew 22:37-40).

If we will simply love God with all that we are, everything else will flow naturally. When you perform out of love, ministry is powerful, holiness is joyful, and your Christianity is natural. When you do things out of a love for God, you are energized, not weighted.

A love for Jesus is the key to true living. Love doesn't become exhausted. Love never feels burdened to serve its beloved. Your love for Jesus is a powerful force that moves you to fulfill the will of God. Yes, the key to doing all that God asks and becoming all that God desires is a pure, simple, and devoted love for Jesus.

And the source of that love is the Holy Spirit.

> *And hope maketh not ashamed; because the love of God is shed abroad in our hearts by the Holy Ghost which is given unto us* (Romans 5:5 KJV).

Love is all God requires of us. If you love God, you will keep His commands. If you love God, you'll find it difficult to do that which offends Him. Love is the motivator, the key to all. Love causes holiness. Love causes fellowship. Love inspires your prayer life, your worship, and devotion to God's Word. And this sort of love comes from the Holy Spirit.

So think about this: not only does the Holy Spirit draw you to Jesus and give you the grace to serve God—He also gives you the love that makes your devotion natural, enjoyable, and electrified.

In giving you His love, the Holy Spirit gives you everything you need to fulfill the will of God in every possible way.

Nobody loves Jesus like the Holy Spirit loves Jesus. The Spirit exalts, magnifies, glorifies, intensifies, and will always emphasize the Son. And, if you'll surrender to Him, the Holy Spirit will cultivate that love within you. I often tell the Holy Spirit, "Help me to love Jesus like You love Jesus." Oh, that we might love Jesus like the Holy Spirit loves Him! The Holy Spirit is the fire of first love. The Holy Spirit is the One who loves Jesus.

THE ONE WHO LEADS GOD'S CHILDREN—*Romans 8:9,14*

But you are not controlled by your sinful nature. You are controlled by the Spirit if you have the Spirit of God living in you. (And remember that those who do not have the Spirit of Christ living in them do not belong to him at all.) ...For all who are led by the Spirit of God are children of God (Romans 8:9,14).

Those who are truly children of God are led by the Holy Spirit. His presence is what distinguishes God's children from all others.

THE RESURRECTION SPIRIT—*Romans 8:11*

The Spirit of God, who raised Jesus from the dead, lives in you. And just as God raised Christ Jesus from the dead, He will give life to your mortal bodies by this same Spirit living within you (Romans 8:11).

The resurrection life of the Holy Spirit that raised Jesus from the dead will also give life to our mortal bodies. Notice the Scripture says, "mortal bodies." This means that He inhabits and graces the mortal body you possess now. He helps your current mortal body to function in its new nature. So His resurrection power gives us life unto holiness now and new eternal bodies in the future (see 1 Cor. 15:51-53).

MIGHTY INTERCESSOR—*Romans 8:26-27*

The Holy Spirit prays for you.

Over the years, I have sought impartation from mighty men and women of God. I lost count of how many ministers of the Gospel have prayed or prophesied over me. There is something powerful about receiving prayer from multiple different servants of God. Something in the spirit is transferred from each one of them. I am convinced that each prayer has accomplished something deep within my spirit.

Aside from my heroes in the faith, my ministry supporters, family members, friends, and spiritual leaders pray for me regularly. I'm sure that you too have people praying for you. Perhaps you have a praying mother, father, friend, or pastor. If not, I suggest you surround yourself with more people who pray.

You can feel the strength that comes from a prayer backing.

One time, while watching my grandfather preach, under my breath I began to pray for him. I asked the Lord to guide him as he ministered. After he finished preaching, my grandfather walked up to me and said, "Thank you for your prayers. I could feel them."

And at my miracle services, I have a prayer team that prays throughout the entirety of the service. They arrive hours before the event to lay hands on each and every chair. They walk the property with anointing oil and spiritually consecrate the grounds. I can feel the difference between the services backed by a prayer team and the services not backed by a prayer team. We need the backing of prayer from our loved ones and spiritual family.

Think of the purity and power of a mother's prayer—a spiritual mother or a natural mother. Think of the effectiveness of a father's prayer. How much is accomplished in the prayers of our friends and church family members? Much, I'm sure. But did you know that the Holy Spirit prays for you?

And the Holy Spirit helps us in our weakness. For example, we don't know what God wants us to pray for. But the Holy Spirit prays for us with groanings that cannot be expressed in words. And the Father who knows all hearts knows what the Spirit is saying, for the Spirit pleads for us believers in harmony with God's own will (Romans 8:26-27).

That's right, the Holy Spirit Himself lifts your needs before the Father. He knows you better than anyone knows you. He knows you better than you know yourself. He knows your needs, your desires, your failures, your potential, your gifts, and your strengths. And He prays for you constantly.

Yes, it's wonderful to have mighty servants of God pray over you, but the Holy Spirit wants to lay hands upon you Himself!

The Holy Spirit prays prayers that are so deep, so effective, that they cannot be expressed in words. The truth and power behind His every prayer for you are so abundant that they cannot fit into the expressions of human breath.

By the way, that's why speaking in tongues is so key. Speaking in tongues is the Holy Spirit praying for you, through you. I wrote extensively on speaking in tongues in my book *Carriers of the Glory.*

The Father understands the Holy Spirit's prayers. There is no deeper communication between you and the Father than the spirit-to-Spirit intercession that occurs within your inner being. The Holy Spirit pleads for you "in harmony with God's own will." This means that His prayers help cause you to become who God wants you to become. His prayers strengthen your willingness to obey, heighten your faith to believe, and increase your desire to know God. All that God wills for you, through you, and in you is made manifest in the spirit through the prayers of the Holy Spirit.

The Holy Spirit is your most vital prayer backing. The Holy Spirit is your mighty Intercessor.

THE GIVER OF SIGNS AND WONDERS—*Romans 15:19*

They were convinced by the power of miraculous signs and wonders and by the power of God's Spirit. In this way, I have fully presented the Good News of Christ from Jerusalem all the way to Illyricum (Romans 15:19).

When you are filled with the Spirit, you don't have to follow signs because signs will follow you. The Holy Spirit confirms the Gospel message through signs and wonders. If what you're preaching isn't backed by the Holy Spirit's signs and wonders, then it's time to start preaching the Gospel.

Chapter 47

THE HOLY SPIRIT IN
FIRST CORINTHIANS

THE SPIRIT OF GOD—*1 Corinthians 2:10-12*

He gives us all of that which is of God.

The Holy Spirit searches the eternal depths of God and knows them fully. He understands the Father's nature, mind, will, and attributes.

> *But it was to us that God revealed these things by His Spirit. For His Spirit searches out everything and shows us God's deep secrets. No one can know a person's thoughts except that person's own spirit, and no one can know God's thoughts except God's own Spirit. And we have received God's Spirit* (not the world's spirit)*, so we can know the wonderful things God has freely given us* (1 Corinthians 2:10-12).

Except for God, nobody knows you as deeply as you know yourself. In the same way, nobody knows God quite like His own Holy Spirit. The Holy Spirit takes God's deep secrets and makes them known to you.

But the Holy Spirit doesn't reveal these things to your intellect or even your heart; He reveals them to your spirit. It is in the spirit that you are united with God—not *being* united but already united.

> *But the person who is joined to the Lord is one spirit with Him* (1 Corinthians 6:17).

Your inner man is one with God's Holy Spirit. The depths of you are one with the depths of God. The Holy Spirit is the Spirit of God. He takes all that He knows of God and deposits that revelation and reveals it to your spirit. Deep connects with deep.

Deep calleth unto deep at the noise of Thy waterspouts: all Thy waves and Thy billows are gone over me (Psalm 42:7 KJV).

What should take you an eternity to discover you know the moment the Holy Spirit comes to live in you. Because you are one with the Spirit of God, you know God, you understand God, you are connected with God. Your spirit knows God fully.

When we pray, "Lord, I want to know You more!" we are actually crying out for understanding to be given to our minds and hearts—understanding that we already possess in the spirit. All spiritual growth is really just becoming aware in the soul of what we already know in the spirit. When that which is of the spirit begins to connect with that which is of the soul, we experience revelation and transformation.

The eternal nature of God is revealed to us by the Spirit of God. All that may be known of the Father is ours to know, for the Spirit reveals it to us. We know God fully and are one with Him by the Spirit, for the Holy Spirit is the Spirit of God.

GOOD JUDGMENT—*1 Corinthians 2:15*

The person with the Spirit makes judgments about all things, but such a person is not subject to merely human judgments (1 Corinthians 2:15 NIV).

The Spirit-filled believer has the advantage of seeing through the eyes of the Spirit and thinking with the mind of the Spirit. The Holy Spirit's wisdom, discernment, and judgment influence the one who stays near to Him. This is why friends of the Holy Spirit make the best decisions.

THE MIND OF CHRIST—*1 Corinthians 2:16*

For, "Who can know the Lord's thoughts? Who knows enough to teach him?" But we understand these things, for we have the mind of Christ (1 Corinthians 2:16).

Who can know the Lord's thoughts? The Holy Spirit can. He searches out the deep things of God and makes those deep things known to us. The

Holy Spirit is the mind of Christ. He knows the thoughts and thinking patterns of the Lord. The Holy Spirit is the same mind Christ uses, and we have that same mind. Not only can you know about Jesus by the Holy Spirit; you can know *like* Jesus by the Holy Spirit.

THE TRANSCENDING SPIRIT—*1 Corinthians 5:3*

Even though I am not with you in person, I am with you in the Spirit. And as though I were there, I have already passed judgment on this man (1 Corinthians 5:3).

Paul knew that, though he was physically separated from the Corinthian church, he was with them in the realm of the spirit. When we commune with the Holy Spirit, we are all united. The Holy Spirit's presence, which transcends time and space, miraculously joins us together as one—in one moment and in one place. Every believer from every culture, nation, place, and time is one together in the heavenly realm.

THE INDWELLING SPIRIT—*1 Corinthians 6:19*

The Holy Spirit abides in the believer.

The Holy Spirit dwells within you. He does not abandon you. He abides.

Don't you realize that your body is the temple of the Holy Spirit, who lives in you and was given to you by God? You do not belong to yourself (1 Corinthians 6:19).[1]

Your physical body is the temple of the Holy Spirit. You are a carrier of the very glory of God. Everywhere that you go the atmosphere changes. When you walk into rooms, demons run out. When you enter a place, sickness loses its hold in that very place.

You don't have to waste another second begging for more of God. All that God is dwells in you by the Spirit. You don't have to pull on God to draw Him nearer. He cannot come any closer than within you. You don't have to yell for Him to hear you; He's close enough to hear you whisper. He's close enough to know your thoughts.

---

1   See also First Corinthians 3:16.

What's more, you can hear Him too. You can know His thoughts too. In the deepest part of who you are, you are united with God, for the Holy Spirit dwells in you.

THE GIFT GIVER—*1 Corinthians 12:11*

It is the one and only Spirit who distributes all these gifts. He alone decides which gift each person should have (1 Corinthians 12:11).

The spiritual gifts are special abilities that believers are given to help build the Church and evangelize the world. These gifts include prophecy, healing, miracles, faith, the word of knowledge, and more.

Chapter 48

THE HOLY SPIRIT IN
SECOND CORINTHIANS

THE TRANSFORMING SPIRIT—*2 Corinthians 3:18*

True transformation is by the Holy Spirit.

Nobody is made righteous by the law. The law revealed the holiness of God and the sinfulness of men, but it did not provide a permanent solution to man's sinful state. It acted as a placeholder, a guide. The law of Moses was a mirror in which man could see that he was sinful.

> *For no one can ever be made right with God by doing what the law commands. The law simply shows us how sinful we are* (Romans 3:20).

The law was written upon stone, but the new covenant is "written" upon the hearts of those who believe.

> *Clearly, you are a letter from Christ showing the result of our ministry among you. This "letter" is written not with pen and ink, but with the Spirit of the living God. It is carved not on tablets of stone, but on human hearts* (2 Corinthians 3:3).

> *He has enabled us to be ministers of His new covenant. This is a covenant not of written laws, but of the Spirit. The old written covenant ends in death; but under the new covenant, the Spirit gives life* (2 Corinthians 3:6).

In other words, the law addressed the sinful behavior of man, but the New Covenant addresses the sinful nature of man. The law reforms behavior, but the Spirit transforms the heart.

The law was certainly from God. It was given with such glory that the face of Moses shone brightly after Moses received it. The glory, however, would wane. But if the law was glorious, how much more glorious is the New Covenant that is by the Spirit?

> *Shouldn't we expect far greater glory under the new way, now that the Holy Spirit is giving life?* (2 Corinthians 3:8)

The Holy Spirit is the Spirit of the New Covenant, the one who gives us life under a new way of living. Under the New Covenant, there is true transformation.

Nothing stands between you and God. You can see Him by the Spirit, and seeing Him brings about true transformation—transformation not just of behavior but of nature as well.

> *So all of us who have had that veil removed can see and reflect the glory of the Lord. And the Lord—who is the Spirit—makes us more and more like Him as we are changed into His glorious image* (2 Corinthians 3:18).

The key to real and lasting transformation is the Holy Spirit. Transformation does not come about by human effort; it's a miracle of the Spirit.

> *Let me ask you this one question: Did you receive the Holy Spirit by obeying the law of Moses? Of course not! You received the Spirit because you believed the message you heard about Christ. How foolish can you be? After starting your Christian lives in the Spirit, why are you now trying to become perfect by your own human effort?* (Galatians 3:2-3)

The Holy Spirit continues to transform us—from glory to glory—until we look like Jesus. The Holy Spirit truly is the Spirit of transformation.

THE SPIRIT OF FAITH—*2 Corinthians 4:13*

> *It is written: "I believed; therefore I have spoken." Since we have that same spirit of faith, we also believe and therefore speak* (2 Corinthians 4:13 NIV).

Paul the apostle calls the Holy Spirit "the Spirit of faith." We need Him. We are helpless without Him. He is our strength to believe. When doubt and fear tether your hopes to the lowly places of human limitation, the

Holy Spirit breaks the cord and sends your faith soaring. I've witnessed the Holy Sprit's faith-stirring power in action. I have seen the sick and the oppressed, wishing to be free of their suffering, receive a faith to believe for the miraculous. Though dejected and hurting, those in need of God's power somehow find the inspiration to expect something wonderful. In the atmosphere of the Holy Spirit's presence, faith is sent climbing to new heights. Doubt dissolves, fear becomes powerless, and miracles are obtained in the midst of the Spirit of faith.

Chapter 49

THE HOLY SPIRIT IN GALATIANS

THE CHRIST-LIKE SPIRIT—*Galatians 5:22-24*

The Holy Spirit is Christ-like.

The Holy Spirit is Christ-like in all His attributes. You cannot give what you don't have, and this is what the Holy Spirit gives us:

> *But the Holy Spirit produces this kind of fruit in our lives: love, joy, peace, patience, kindness, goodness, faithfulness, gentleness, and self-control. There is no law against these things! Those who belong to Christ Jesus have nailed the passions and desires of their sinful nature to His cross and crucified them there* (Galatians 5:22-24).

Like Christ, the Holy Spirit is loving, joyful, peaceful, patient, kind, good, faithful, gentle, and self-controlled. He makes us the same.

You can't know the Spirit and be bitter and hateful; He's loving. You can't be in fellowship with the Holy Spirit and live in a constant state of misery; He's joyful. You can't live in chaos and fear, because He's peaceful. The more time you spend with Him, the more patient, kind, and good you become. Those who are Spirit-filled are not unreliable; they are faithful. They are not apathetic and aimless; they are self-controlled and disciplined.

The Holy Spirit is like Jesus, and He makes you like Jesus.

For example, the Holy Spirit makes you as joyful as Jesus.

People also think that the more spiritual people are, the more stoic and serious they become. Sure, spirituality often calls for stillness and reverence, but that doesn't mean that the spiritual are unapproachable or lifeless. In fact, joy is an attribute of the Christ-like Spirit. The Holy Spirit produces such joy in your life that you become magnetic and vibrant—people become drawn to you.

The Holy Spirit is the river of joy.

A river brings joy to the city of our God, the sacred home of the Most High (Psalm 46:4).

The Holy Spirit fills us with joy.

At that same time Jesus was filled with the joy of the Holy Spirit, and He said, "O Father, Lord of heaven and earth, thank You for hiding these things from those who think themselves wise and clever, and for revealing them to the childlike. Yes, Father, it pleased You to do it this way" (Luke 10:21).

And it doesn't stop at joy. Every attribute that Jesus had the Spirit has and shares with you.

The Holy Spirit is the Christ-like Spirit.

THE MIRACLE-WORKING SPIRIT—*Galatians 3:5*

The Holy Spirit works miracles.

I ask you again, does God give you the Holy Spirit and work miracles among you because you obey the law? Of course not! It is because you believe the message you heard about Christ (Galatians 3:5).

Wherever the Holy Spirit moves, miracles happen. A true move of the Holy Spirit will result in things that cannot be explained outside of divine intervention. More than just unlikely outcomes or favorable results, the Holy Spirit causes the actual miraculous to occur—the healing of the sick, the deliverance of the demon-possessed, and the suspension of the natural laws of the physical world. Miracles, signs, and wonders follow the presence of the Holy Spirit. Miracles bring visible, notable results. Signs make His presence and intentions known. And His wonders simply leave us standing in awe.

We mustn't stifle any part of His work. And if we are offended or uncomfortable with any aspect of His ministry, rest assured that the problem lies with us. We cannot deny Him the freedom to move for fear of what skeptical minds might think. Many imagine that the work of the Spirit is superficially spiritual and primarily practical. It's not. All true ministry of the Holy Spirit is fundamentally miraculous, supernatural, and spiritual.

Miracles make up the core of the Christian faith. The Holy Spirit's miracle-working power did not wane with time. His miracle-working power is just as strong as it always has been. Wherever the power of the Holy Spirit moves, the sick are healed, the oppressed are freed, and the lost are saved.

And why does the Holy Spirit work such miracles? The Bible says that, *"It is because you believe the message you heard about Christ"* (Gal. 3:5).

No tricks. No gimmicks. No methods, systems, programs, or human efforts. It's simply the power of the Holy Spirit that works miracles, and the Holy Spirit releases that power through this simple thing: belief.

Only believe.

The Holy Spirit is the miracle-working Spirit.

Chapter 50

THE HOLY SPIRIT IN
EPHESIANS

THE SUSTAINING POWER—*Ephesians 5:18*

The Holy Spirit wants to fill us consistently.

I am not immune from seasons of spiritual dryness. I need to be mindful to keep my friendship with the Holy Spirit and prayer life fresh. I too can become distracted. This is why even the believer is commanded to be filled with the Holy Spirit.

> *Don't be drunk with wine, because that will ruin your life. Instead, be filled with the Holy Spirit* (Ephesians 5:18).

In the verse above, the word *filled* is the Greek verb *plerousthe*. It literally means "to be continually filled." The infilling of the Holy Spirit is both an occurrence and a continual state of being.

The Holy Spirit doesn't just come upon us once and then leave us alone. He abides. He continually refreshes and fills your inner man.

Let's say that you are like a mobile phone. You can be plugged into the power outlet and then charged to 100 percent, but the moment you unplug from the source, you begin to lose power. Your charge begins to drop. In order the keep the phone at 100 percent charge, it has to be charged up and then *remain* plugged into the power source.

In the same way, the believer can be "filled" and be "being filled."

The key to receiving this daily, fresh empowering of the Holy Spirit is to think in terms of moments. Realize that the Holy Spirit and His power are available to you on a moment-by-moment basis.

The Holy Spirit's empowering is not limited to ministry and special church services. He is available to you in every moment. We need His involvement down to the very last second of every hour. He's available to you when you're sorrowful, joyful, confused, confident, busy, or resting. His strength can be accessed from your home, your car, your work place—anywhere, anytime.

We need to be filled consistently. The Holy Spirit's infilling is like wind in a sail, a rushing river, or the breath in your lungs. There is a constant flow, a consistent rhythm to His empowering presence. Don't settle for the now-and-then infilling—take advantage of the power that is available for your every moment.

Plug into the sustaining Power.

THE SPIRITUAL ARMOR BEARER—*Ephesians 6:17*

Put on salvation as your helmet, and take the sword of the Spirit, which is the word of God (Ephesians 6:17).

True to His humble nature, the Holy Spirit serves as an armor-bearer to equip the believer with the sword of the Spirit, which is the Word of God. It's the very same weapon that He Himself uses against the enemy. The sword belongs to Him. He, the Spirit of Truth, wields the Word to devastate the deceptive work of the enemy. He lends you His weapon so that you can resist the lies of the enemy.

Chapter 51

THE HOLY SPIRIT IN
PHILIPPIANS

THE PERSONAL SPIRIT—*Philippians 2:1-2*

The Holy Spirit is a Person.

When I first learned the wonderful truth of the Holy Spirit's personal nature, I desired to cultivate a friendship with the mysterious third Person of the Trinity. I found everything about His essence to be alluring, magnetic. As I examined the Scriptures, I sought for clues and insights to His nature and personality. I wanted to understand His every nuance and familiarize myself with His every quality.

In search of the Spirit, I turned the pages of the Bible. My inner being would become lit with joyful anticipation. My eyes enjoyed the glimmer of every truthful word. In the Old Testament, I saw the Spirit hovering over the face of the deep and so gloriously displaying His power that men trembled in fear and awe. In the New Testament, I saw this same Spirit gently descend upon Christ as a dove, raise Jesus from the dead, and assist the apostles in the Book of Acts.

As a student of the Spirit, I've learned this simple yet powerful truth: the Holy Spirit is not an "it"; He is a Person. He has feelings, a will, and a mind. The Holy Spirit is not an influence, though He is influential, and He is not a force, though He possesses immense power. He is a Person that can be loved and known. We can fellowship with the Holy Spirit.

If there be therefore any consolation in Christ, if any comfort of love, if any fellowship of the Spirit, if any bowels and mercies, fulfil ye my joy, that ye be likeminded, having the same love, being of one accord, of one mind (Philippians 2:1-2 KJV).

The Holy Spirit is personal. Therefore, it is our goal, not to obtain the Holy Spirit, but to fellowship with Him—to befriend Him. And when we are given to this friendship, everything changes and progressively becomes as it should be. The entirety of our spirituality is summarized in our interaction with God's Holy Spirit.

In fact, Paul the apostle encourages this personal fellowship with the Holy Spirit:

May the grace of the Lord Jesus Christ, the love of God, and the fellowship of the Holy Spirit be with you all (2 Corinthians 13:14).

The Holy Spirit is a Person—just as divine as the Father and the Son. I don't mean that He is a human. I mean that He is a personal Being.

As simple of a thought as this may be (that the Holy Spirit is a Person), I still believe that it's important to demonstrate it through Scripture. The Scriptures I am sharing with you in this section demonstrate that the Holy Spirit is personal.

In the case of the original language, the Greek refers to the Holy Spirit with a masculine pronoun in the following portions of Scripture:

But I will send you the Advocate-the Spirit of truth. He will come to you from the Father and will testify all about Me (John 15:26).

But when He, the Spirit of truth, comes, He will guide you into all the truth; for He will not speak on His own initiative, but whatever He hears, He will speak; and He will disclose to you what is to come. He will glorify Me, for He will take of Mine and will disclose it to you (John 16:13-14 NASB).

The Bible refers to the Holy Spirit as a "who," not a "what":

And Jesus Christ was revealed as God's Son by His baptism in water and by shedding His blood on the cross—not by water only, but by water and blood. And the Spirit, who is truth, confirms it with His testimony. So we have these three witnesses—the Spirit, the water, and the blood—and all three agree (1 John 5:6-8).

Why then is the Holy Spirit referred to as "the" Holy Spirit?
Consider this verse:

Therefore, go and make disciples of all the nations, baptizing them in the name of the Father and the Son and the Holy Spirit (Matthew 28:19).

The Father…

The Son…

The Holy Spirit…

The word *the* doesn't take away from one's personal nature. We refer to persons all the time using the article *the*. For example: the president, the police officer, the teacher, etc.

Furthermore, the Holy Spirit has a will.

But all these worketh that one and the selfsame Spirit, dividing to every man severally as He will (1 Corinthians 12:11 KJV).

The Holy Spirit can speak.

The Holy Spirit said to Philip, "Go over and walk along beside the carriage" (Acts 8:29).

Finally, we are to walk in fellowship with the Person of the Holy Spirit.

May the grace of the Lord Jesus Christ, the love of God, and the fellowship of the Holy Spirit be with you all (2 Corinthians 13:14).

The Holy Spirit can commune with us because He is a Person.

Chapter 52

THE HOLY SPIRIT IN
COLOSSIANS

THE SPIRIT OF LOVE—*Colossians 1:8*

He grows our love for one another.

This is a simple verse with a profound application:

He has told us about the love for others that the Holy Spirit has given you (Colossians 1:8).

Not only does the Holy Spirit enflame your love for God; He also helps you to love others. Every relationship you will ever have is ultimately shaped by your capacity to love others. Therefore, the Holy Spirit can work in every godly relationship.

He helps you love your spouse, children, parents, siblings, family, and friends with a deeper love. In doing so, He helps you become a better parent, a better spouse, and so forth.

Something you'll notice about Spirit-filled believers—I mean truly Spirit-filled believers: they are forgiving, they don't hold grudges, and they make people feel important. I don't care if you speak in tongues, cast out devils, or even raise the dead—you don't know the Holy Spirit if you cannot love others.

The Scripture doesn't say that we'll be known for our power, our preaching, or our projects. What does it say?

Your love for one another will prove to the world that you are My disciples (John 13:35).

The closer you become to the Holy Spirit, the more you will love others, for He is the Spirit of love.

Chapter 53

THE HOLY SPIRIT IN
FIRST THESSALONIANS

THE DELICATE FIRE—*1 Thessalonians 5:19*

Don't quench the Spirit.

I was ministering at a church in Southern California, and the service was prophetically anointed. I mean the prophetic was activated with such intensity that I was shocked at some of the things that were coming out of my own mouth! People's very thoughts were being revealed, and I could see and hear into the spirit with an unusual clarity.

I continued to prophesy over people, and each person receiving a word would either break down into tears or gasp at the detailed words of knowledge. I said something like, "I'm in a whole different place in the spirit now! I can see so clearly." The people were captivated by the Spirit, and the room was silent with anticipation.

As I scanned the crowd with my eyes, I noticed a woman walking in from the very back of the church. She walked all the way from the back, moved down the aisle, and sat directly in the front row, right in front of me. The way she entered was so distracting that I watched her take her seat. Then, as if my eyes were released from a locked position, I readjusted my vision. Right at that moment, I felt normal again. The weight of power lifted from my shoulders, and I could no longer see with that astonishing clarity. The flow was broken. Immediately, I said, "Well, that's it. I'm done." Then I handed the microphone back to the pastor and left.

That woman disrupted the move of the Holy Spirit. She came in and distracted me—as well as the people.

I learned a long time ago that nothing breaks the flow of the anointing like distraction. It's possible to disrupt a move of the Spirit.

Quench not the Spirit (1 Thessalonians 5:19 KJV).

The Holy Spirit is a fire, and He can be quenched. Remember, in us, He only goes as far as we allow Him to go.

I'm not suggesting that the Holy Spirit is a weak and easily frightened Person. We are the ones who can be easily distracted. Distraction doesn't stop the Holy Spirit from moving; distraction stops us from recognizing and receiving that move.

We can stifle Him with distraction, rejection, and foolishness. Be careful to reverence and embrace the Holy Spirit. Don't disrupt His moving. Don't despise His ways.

Don't quench the Holy Spirit.

Chapter 54

THE HOLY SPIRIT IN
SECOND THESSALONIANS

THE RESTRAINER—*2 Thessalonians 2:7-8*

The Holy Spirit restrains the antichrist and the last days.

Every so often, series of cataclysmic events incite panic among the spiritual masses. Claims to knowledge of the Lord's return and end time calculations pour onto the social media landscape. Whether it be a string of natural disasters or the threat of powerful nations rising against each other, anything resembling a pattern of consistent danger will rouse speculations about the end of all things.

The threat of a war, an eclipse, a strange celestial sighting, a timely blood moon—you name it. Almost anything can stir the people to prepare for Armageddon. Of course, I acknowledge that the Lord can return at any moment—even while you read this very sentence.

But I think it's important to consider what Jesus said about the last days. Among all of the apocalyptic imagery and cryptic prophetic passages, we find a very clear and direct address to the question of the Lord's return and the earth's final moments. The disciples put the question to Jesus directly. And Jesus answered directly. We must use the clear end-time teachings of Jesus to serve as a foundation upon which we assemble and understand the relatively unclear passages of Scripture that deal with the end times.

> *Later, Jesus sat on the Mount of Olives. His disciples came to him privately and said, "Tell us, when will all this happen? What sign will signal your return and the end of the world?"* (Matthew 24:3).

Jesus responds to their questions by revealing the signs of the end times—false messiahs, wars, rumors of wars. Then Jesus makes it perfectly clear that such signs are not cause for panic. In fact, those signs are only the preliminary signs.

> *...but don't panic. Yes, these things must take place, but the end won't follow immediately* (Matthew 24:6).

The Master further describes a time of trouble and devastation. He predicts earthquakes and famines in many places around the globe. He describes the state of a catastrophic world while again accentuating His description with a call for reservation. Neither are earthquakes and famines the final signs of the end. They too are only the prelude of the shaking of the nations.

So what does Jesus clearly say is the sign of the end? In Matthew 24, Jesus is recorded as mentioning worldwide persecution of the Church (Matt. 24:9), a great falling away from the faith (Matt. 24:10), the rise of false prophets (Matt. 24:11), and the viral spread of sin (Matt. 24:12). But what ultimately is the triggering event, the harbinger of the return of the Lord?

> *And the Good News about the Kingdom will be preached through-out the whole world, so that all nations will hear it; and then the end will come* (Matthew 24:14).

What is the indication of the Lord's return? The spreading of the Gospel. You see, it's not the chaos in the world that dictates the coming of the Lord; it's the commission of the Church—the preaching of the Gospel in every part of the world. God, not destruction, is in control. It is the fulfillment of the commission of the Church that marks the beginning of the end.

The fulfillment of the commission of the Church is a priority for God. In fact, it's a primary reason why He sent His Holy Spirit upon us:

> *But you will receive power when the Holy Spirit comes upon you. And you will be my witnesses, telling people about me everywhere— in Jerusalem, throughout Judea, in Samaria, and to the ends of the earth* (Acts 1:8).

Once the commission of the Church has been fulfilled, a major part of the Holy Spirit's work has been completed. The fulfillment of the commission is a mark of completion in the Holy Spirit's ministry.

As we continue to examine what the Scriptures say regarding the end times, keep this in mind: once the Gospel has spread far enough, once enough people have heard the Gospel, the end will come.

But what other event marks the final days? The arrival of the antichrist.

Don't be so easily shaken or alarmed by those who say that the day of the Lord has already begun. Don't believe them, even if they claim to have had a spiritual vision, a revelation, or a letter supposedly from us. Don't be fooled by what they say. For that day will not come until there is a great rebellion against God and the man of lawlessness is revealed—the one who brings destruction (2 Thessalonians 2:2-3).

So far, we see two signs that mark the end of days: the fulfillment of the commission of the Church and the arrival of the antichrist. Since the Bible tells us that these two events both signal the end times, we know that these two events must occur close to one another. In fact, they are connected. The arrival of the antichrist and the finishing of the commission of the Church both have to do with the Holy Spirit.

Pay close attention here:

And you know what is holding him back, for he can be revealed only when his time comes. For this lawlessness is already at work secretly, and it will remain secret until the one who is holding it back steps out of the way (2 Thessalonians 2:6-7).

The Holy Spirit is the restrainer of the antichrist. It's interesting that when the Holy Spirit steps in, Christ is revealed; when He steps out, the antichrist is revealed.

The series of events that bring about the end of the world cannot spring into motion until the antichrist is revealed. And the antichrist cannot be revealed until the Holy Spirit steps out of the way. The Holy Spirit's work has placed a hold on the end time chain reaction. The Holy Spirit suspends the calamity and chaos until His work is complete.

Furthermore, not only does the Holy Spirit restrain the antichrist from entering the world stage, but He also destroys him at the coming of Christ.

Then the man of lawlessness will be revealed, but the Lord Jesus will kill him with the breath of his mouth and destroy him by the splendor of his coming (2 Thessalonians 2:8).

Who is the Breath? That's the Holy Spirit. The Holy Spirit's power pins the antichrist into inaction, moves out of the way for a time, and then destroys the antichrist at the right moment.

Think about it. The fulfillment of the commission and the arrival of the antichrist run parallel to one another. Once the great commission is fulfilled, the Holy Spirit steps out of the way, the antichrist arrives, and then the end comes. That's how this all connects. The Holy Spirit's stepping out of the way marks both the fulfillment of the commission and the coming of the antichrist—both are events that simultaneously mark the end.

In the last days, the Holy Spirit will step out of the way and allow wrath to come upon the earth.

After that, the day of destruction is upon the earth. There will come a time when Holy Spirit will no longer convict the conscience of mankind, when the flickering light within humanity's soul no longer lights the path to salvation. When the commission of the Church is fulfilled, the Holy Spirit will step out of the way and allow chaos to invade the earth.

The Holy Spirit suspends the judgment of God that's coming to the earth, and He pleads with every heart, "Seek Me while I still may be found." Dear reader, the Holy Spirit has frozen the divine clock of wrath; He holds open the door of salvation and calls out to all who will hear and enter. But the door is closing.

There will come a moment of untold horror when the Spirit—the moral sense of the human race—will no longer guide. In that day, no one will call upon the name of Jesus because no one will see the need to call. His still small voice, His patient leading, His striving with the sinful nature of man will cease.

Until then, the Holy Spirit continues to restrain the antichrist and empower the Church to fulfill the commission. The man of lawlessness will be revealed and the Gospel will be preached to the ends of the earth—then comes the end.

Chapter 55

THE HOLY SPIRIT IN
FIRST TIMOTHY

THE PROPHETIC SPIRIT—*1 Timothy 4:1*

The Holy Spirit inspires the prophetic.

An expecting couple approached me for prayer. They wanted me to pray over their baby—that there would be no complications with the delivery. Within just a few minutes of praying, I sensed the Holy Spirit press this message upon my spirit: "Before the baby is born, the doctors will say that there are major complications." I thought to myself, "That can't be the Holy Spirit, can it?" Still, I couldn't get past the Holy Spirit. He wasn't going to change His mind about what He wanted me to say. "You better be hearing God," I thought to myself.

Reluctantly, I looked up at the couple and told them, "Before the baby is born, the doctors will say that there are major complications." The couple looked perplexed and upset.

Thankfully, as soon as I prophesied about what the doctors would declare, the Holy Spirit gave me the rest of the message, "But the baby will be born without any complications." The couple still seemed bothered by that prophetic word, but I wasn't going to say anything outside of what God was speaking.

Sure enough, at their next appointment, the doctors told them that the baby was going to be born with complications. Most couples would have been frightened by such news, but this couple had the full picture. The word that had previously brought them discomfort had now brought the couple peace—they knew the end result was good.

Sure enough, the baby was eventually born in perfect health, and that couple was spared months of anxiety because of the prophetic word of the Lord.

The Holy Spirit knows and predicts the future; He is the prophetic Spirit.

> *Now the Holy Spirit tells us clearly that in the last times some will turn away from the true faith; they will follow deceptive spirits and teachings that come from demons* (1 Timothy 4:1).

I did not understand why the Holy Spirit would speak something so negatively into what was an otherwise happy situation. It was a simple two-part prophecy: "Before the baby is born, the doctors will say that there are major complications, but the baby will be born without complications." However, it wasn't until I opened my mouth and gave the first portion of the message that the Holy Spirit gave me the second part of it. He likes to reveal things progressively.

The Holy Spirit often does that to me. This progressive giving of prophetic revelation is partly why Paul said:

> *For we know in part, and we prophesy in part* (1 Corinthians 13:9 KJV).

The Holy Spirit is the power behind prophetic insight. He moves men to declare the oracles of God and know the naturally unknowable—past, present, and future. He stirs the spirits of people to prophesy.

> *And the Lord came down in a cloud, and spake unto him, and took of the spirit that was upon him, and gave it unto the seventy elders: and it came to pass, that, when the spirit rested upon them, they prophesied, and did not cease* (Numbers 11:25 KJV).

All prophetic communication between God and man is by the Holy Spirit. When God reveals the details of people's lives, it's by the Holy Spirit, for the Holy Spirit is the omnipresence of the Father God. When God reveals the future, it's by the Holy Spirit, for the Holy Spirit searches the mind of God and reveals what He finds to us.

The Holy Spirit is the prophetic Spirit.

Chapter 56

THE HOLY SPIRIT IN
SECOND TIMOTHY

THE SPIRIT OF PEACE—*1 Timothy 1:7*

The Holy Spirit gives us peace.

If ever I get into the flesh, I can be very controlling. The need to control is rooted in fear and anxiety. That's my primary battle with my flesh. Whenever one is in the flesh, their carnal attributes begin to surface. For me, anxious thinking is a sign that I need to hide myself in the presence of God for a little longer than usual. Sometimes God will use the surfacing of my weakness as an invitation to go further into the depths of prayer.

In fact, my anxious way of thinking, my overthinking, began when I was a kid. My grandmother, who is a Spirit-filled woman of God, would often sing to me a cheerful song of biblical truth:

God has not given you a spirit of fear
But of power and of love and a peace of mind
So don't be afraid anymore
He'll be there to hear your prayers every time.

The lyrics, I would come to find, were not just words; they were Scripture. The song she would sing to me came from this powerful verse:

For God hath not given us the spirit of fear; but of power, and of love, and of a sound mind (2 Timothy 1:7 KJV).

We've been given a spirit of power. A spirit of love. A spirit of a sound mind. Your spirit becomes peaceful, powerful, and loving. From where does your spirit receive these attributes? How are these traits manifested? The Holy Spirit, of course.

He is the Spirit of power (see Acts 1:8). He is the Spirit of love (see Rom. 5:5). And He is the Spirit of peace.

> *For the kingdom of God is not meat and drink; but righteousness,*
> *and peace, and joy in the Holy Ghost* (Romans 14:17 KJV).

He gives to us a soundness of mind. I've noticed that the most spiritual people I have ever met know how to be relaxed during crisis. They are calm, collected, and level-headed. They do not panic or become irritated easily.

That's what the Holy Spirit does for you. As a citizen of the Kingdom of Heaven, you have a right to the Holy Spirit's righteousness, peace, and joy. When troubles arise, call upon the Holy Spirit. As your fears approach, cling to the Holy Spirit. He will strengthen you. He will keep you in perfect peace.

> *Thou wilt keep him in perfect peace, whose mind is stayed on Thee:*
> *because he trusteth in Thee* (Isaiah 26:3 KJV).

Let the Spirit of peace have dominion in your life.

Chapter 57

THE HOLY SPIRIT IN
TITUS

THE GIVER OF NEW LIFE—*Titus 3:5-7*

The Holy Spirit has given you a new life.

Being a follower of Christ is about so much more than "not sinning." It's the embracing of a whole new life. In His mercy, God has washed your sin-stained soul by the blood of Jesus and has given you a brand-new life by the Holy Spirit.

> *But—When God our Savior revealed His kindness and love, He saved us, not because of the righteous things we had done, but because of His mercy. He washed away our sins, giving us a new birth and new life through the Holy Spirit. He generously poured out the Spirit upon us through Jesus Christ our Savior* (Titus 3:4-7).

Because of the empowering presence of the Holy Spirit, you are able to function in your new way of existing. What does it mean to have a new life?

It means your past is erased, your mind is renewed, your nature is transformed, and your future is reset. There is a new path that has been set before you. Your destination has changed. Embrace the adventure of the journey ahead. Don't look back anymore. The miracle of new life has been accomplished in your life.

The Holy Spirit gives you new life.

Chapter 58

THE HOLY SPIRIT IN PHILEMON

THE SPIRIT OF FORGIVENESS—*Philemon 1:25*

The Holy Spirit helps us forgive.

Paul wrote a letter to a man named Philemon in hopes that he would forgive his brother in Christ, Onesimus. Philemon is a very short book of the Bible, but in the pleading of Paul the apostle, who was moved by the Holy Spirit to write the letter, you can feel the pleading of the Holy Spirit. The Holy Spirit pleads with believers to be reconciled with one another.

After instructing Philemon to choose forgiveness, Paul writes an interesting concluding remark:

> *May the grace of the Lord Jesus Christ be with your spirit* (Philemon 1:25).

The grace that would be with Philemon was the very same that would enable him to forgive Onesimus. That grace came, of course, by the Holy Spirit. The Holy Spirit graces you with the ability to forgive others. Forgiveness is not a feeling; it's a work of the Holy Spirit.

Perhaps someone has done something terrible to you, something that still affects you to this very moment. The horrors that you may have experienced may be lingering in your emotions, thoughts, and self-view. You may *feel* that it's difficult to forgive them. You may *feel* like it's not possible to be released from the pain of being wronged or violated.

Be encouraged in knowing that the strength to forgive does not come from your own power; it comes from the Holy Spirit. You may say, "I've tried to forgive before, but the pain still lingers." So how does one overcome the sting of bitterness?

Allow the Holy Spirit to fulfill His desires for that person through you. Pray for the one who wronged you. Declare blessings over the one who wronged you. In doing this, you are releasing that individual to the will of the Holy Spirit. He may vindicate you, and He may restore the other individual.

The Holy Spirit can and will remove the pain from your heart, but you have to first give Him the situation. Tell Him, "Holy Spirit, whenever a thought of bitterness arises in me, remind me to not dwell on that thought." In time, the Spirit of forgiveness will overcome you, and you'll be free.

Chapter 59

THE HOLY SPIRIT IN
HEBREWS

GOD—Hebrews 9:14

The Holy Spirit is God.

The Holy Spirit is God. He is just as divine as the Father and the Son. The following verse from Hebrews is, in my opinion, one of the most supportive of the Holy Spirit's divinity (and of the trinity).

> *Just think how much more the blood of Christ will purify our consciences from sinful deeds so that we can worship the living God. For by the power of the eternal Spirit, Christ offered Himself to God as a perfect sacrifice for our sins* (Hebrews 9:14).

We see that the verse makes a clear distinction between the Father, the Son, and the Holy Spirit—Christ offered Himself to God by the Eternal Spirit. The Son offered Himself to the Father by the Spirit. The three are distinct from one another.

Think of how often the Scripture mentions the three members of the Trinity as distinct from one another.

> *And Jesus, when He was baptized, went up straightway out of the water: and, lo, the heavens were opened unto Him, and He saw the Spirit of God descending like a dove, and lighting upon Him: And lo a voice from heaven, saying, This is My beloved Son, in whom I am well pleased* (Matthew 3:16-17 KJV).

> *Go ye therefore, and teach all nations, baptizing them in the name of the Father, and of the Son, and of the Holy Ghost* (Matthew 28:19 KJV).

The grace of the Lord Jesus Christ, and the love of God, and the communion of the Holy Ghost, be with you all. Amen (2 Corinthians 13:14 KJV).

Here, the Son speaks from His distinct voice of the Father and the Holy Spirit:

And I will ask the Father, and He will give you another Advocate, who will never leave you. He is the Holy Spirit, who leads into all truth (John 14:16-17).

So are they each divine?

Well, every Christian acknowledges the deity of the Father and the Son. Not a single Christian doubts the divinity of the Father. Not a single Christian doubts the divinity of the Son. By definition, if one doesn't believe in the divinity of Christ, they are not a Christian. However, for some believers, there is, for some reason, a hesitation to acknowledge the Holy Spirit's divinity.

But Hebrews describes the Holy Spirit as eternal. If the Spirit is eternal, then the Spirit is divine. In fact, the Bible describes the Spirit as having many divine traits.

He is referred to as the Lord.

Now the Lord is that Spirit: and where the Spirit of the Lord is, there is liberty (2 Corinthians 3:17 KJV).

He is referred to as being one with Christ.

They passed through the Phrygian and Galatian region, having been forbidden by the Holy Spirit to speak the word in Asia; and after they came to Mysia, they were trying to go into Bithynia, and the Spirit of Jesus did not permit them (Acts 16:6-7 NASB).

He is omniscient.

But it was to us that God revealed these things by His Spirit. For His Spirit searches out everything and shows us God's deep secrets. No one can know a person's thoughts except that person's own spirit, and no one can know God's thoughts except God's own Spirit (1 Corinthians 2:10-11).

He is omnipresent.

I can never escape from Your Spirit! I can never get away from Your presence! (Psalm 139:7).

The Book of Isaiah tells us that God spoke to the prophet:

Then I heard the Lord asking, "Whom should I send as a messenger to this people? Who will go for us?" I said, "Here I am. Send me." And He said, "Yes, go, and say to this people, 'Listen carefully, but do not understand. Watch closely, but learn nothing'" (Isaiah 6:8-9).

In the Book of Acts, we see that it was the Holy Spirit who spoke to Isaiah, but the Book of Isaiah calls the Holy Spirit "the Lord":

And after they had argued back and forth among themselves, they left with this final word from Paul: "The Holy Spirit was right when He said to your ancestors through Isaiah the prophet, 'Go and say to this people: When you hear what I say, you will not understand. When you see what I do, you will not comprehend'" (Acts 28:25-26).

The truths in Hebrews paired with the clear teachings of Scripture settle the discussion. The Holy Spirit is God.

That the Father, Son, and Holy Spirit are all distinct from one another and just as divine as one another is the basis of the belief in the Trinity. If the doctrine of the trinity is true, then the Holy Spirit is God. To conclude that the trinity is biblical, one simply has two answer two questions:

Does the Bible make distinctions between the Father, the Son, and the Holy Spirit?

Does the Bible attribute divinity to each the Father, the Son, and the Holy Spirit?

If the answer to both of those questions is affirmative, then there you have it. In fact, the Bible describes one God and three Persons who are equally divine. The Holy Spirit is the third member of a divine Trinity that is one God. The Holy Spirit is His own distinct Person who is just as divine as the Father and the Son. The Holy Spirit is God—as is revealed in Hebrews 9:14.

Chapter 60

THE HOLY SPIRIT IN
JAMES

THE JEALOUS SPIRIT—*James 4:5*

The Holy Spirit gets jealous.

So I was sitting in the car with one of my ministry's largest donors. I got to telling him a story about a woman who had called my ministry office. Within the first few minutes of talking to her, my brother Michael knew that she was an ungodly woman. She kept asking about the ministry's stance on certain things—only to try to persuade my brother to contradict the Bible. My brother was adamant that our stances were biblical ones and that we would not compromise that for anyone. She then became angry and told my brother, "How stupid are you? Don't you realize how much money I could drop into the ministry? You're very, very stupid."

To be honest with you, neither me nor my brother believe that the woman actually had any money. And even if she did, we are not a ministry controlled by our donors. We obey the Lord and His Word, and if someone wants to stop funding us because of that, so be it.

So my donor and I began to laugh at the strangeness of the story I told him. I said, "I don't care who stops giving. I'm not going to compromise what I believe." Then I turned to the man and said, "Besides, if she won't give, I know we have you as our source."

Immediately, I felt a heat fill the car, and I became uneasy. In my jovial mood, I had spoken something quite foolish. Of course, I appreciate the generosity of my donors, but no donor, no matter how much they give, is the source of the ministry. I sensed the Holy Spirit rebuke me and say, "I am your source."

The man looked at me. I looked at him. I'm not sure if he felt what I felt in that moment, but I believe he did. There was a tension that came into that car.

The Holy Spirit gets jealous.

> *What do you think the Scriptures mean when they say that the spirit God has placed within us is filled with envy?* (James 4:5).

Isn't jealousy a sin? Not necessarily. Jealousy, like anger, can become sinful but isn't sinful of its own accord. Does not a wife have the right to be jealous should her husband cheat on her? Does not God have the right to be jealous when we choose the world over Him?

Godly jealousy is based in love and demands what rightfully belongs to it. Ungodly jealousy is based in insecurity and demands what does not belong to it.

The Holy Spirit gets jealous when we befriend the world, rely on others more than we rely on Him, and choose to neglect our time with Him. The Holy Spirit is the jealous Spirit.

THE OIL OF HEALING—*James 5:14-15*

> *Are any of you sick? You should call for the elders of the church to come and pray over you, anointing you with oil in the name of the Lord. Such a prayer offered in faith will heal the sick, and the Lord will make you well. And if you have committed any sins, you will be forgiven* (James 5:14-15).

The Holy Spirit's presence brings healing to the sick. There is no "secret" to miraculous healing; it simply is the healing power of the Holy Spirit. This is why, in my meetings, I don't emphasize miracles. I emphasize the presence of the Holy Spirit. And when the Holy Spirit's presence becomes more real to the afflicted than their own sickness and pain, they are healed. Wherever the Oil of Healing touches, sickness leaves.

Chapter 61

THE HOLY SPIRIT IN
FIRST PETER

THE SPIRIT OF JESUS—*1 Peter 1:11*

The Holy Spirit is Jesus without physical limitations.

The Holy Spirit is, in every sense of the description, the Spirit of Jesus. He is Christ-like.

> *They wondered what time or situation the Spirit of Christ within them was talking about when He told them in advance about Christ's suffering and His great glory afterward* (1 Peter 1:11).

When Jesus walked the earth, He was, in many ways, bound to the limitations of a physical body. Jesus, of course, willingly subjected Himself to these limitations. He only visited one city at a time, had to travel, needed rest, got hungry, and so forth.

In my opinion, very few Bible stories illustrate Jesus's physical limitations better than the story of Jairus (see Mark 5:21-43). Jairus's daughter was dying. In desperation, Jairus approached Jesus on behalf of his dying little girl and asked Jesus to come to his home and heal his daughter. Jesus responded to Jairus's request and began to head toward his house. It was just then that a woman, who had been bleeding for twelve years, took the opportunity to touch Jesus's robe. The woman with the bleeding issue was healed the moment she touched it. The problem was that Jesus had to stop in order to talk to the woman who was healed. If I were Jairus, I would have been furious with the woman who stopped Jesus.

Imagine that. Your daughter is dying—she could pass at any moment. Jesus is finally on his way to your house. Then a woman with a non-life-threatening medical problem stops Jesus. I'd be thinking, "Lady, you waited twelve years. Surely you can wait another hour!"

While Jesus was interacting with the woman who was healed, a messenger delivered the tragic news—Jairus's daughter had died. Of course, Jesus later raised the little girl to life, but you can see that Jesus was limited to a physical body.

But think about the ways in which Jesus overcomes such physical limitations. He ascended on a cloud.

After saying this, He was taken up into a cloud while they were watching, and they could no longer see Him (Acts 1:9).

Jesus was transfigured in a cloud.

But even as He spoke, a bright cloud overshadowed them, and a voice from the cloud said, "This is My dearly loved Son, who brings Me great joy. Listen to Him." The disciples were terrified and fell face down on the ground (Matthew 17:5-6).

Jesus will return on a cloud.

Then everyone will see the Son of Man coming on the clouds with great power and glory (Mark 13:26).

Jesus overcomes His physical limitations by the cloud. We, of course, know who the cloud is. The cloud is the Holy Spirit. We see that the cloud removed physical limitations from Jesus.

To illustrate my point, I'll use this analogy: our smart phones have become a necessity in life. We use them to connect with others, schedule our days, purchase goods, track finances, and so much more. I use my smart devices to store sermon notes, outlines, book ideas, and preaching material. I also like to save photos. I am very sentimental when it comes to pictures. I don't like to delete photos.

My point is that there is a lot of important irreplaceable data on my phone. My vulnerability doubles along with my convenience. Were I to ever misplace or break my phone, I would lose a lot of precious data. That would be it. Some things just cannot be recovered.

Another disadvantage to having everything on my phone is that I cannot access that data unless I have the phone.

These problems are why I store all of the data from my phone online. I store all of the data in what is called the "cloud." The cloud not only allows me to access my data from any device at any time, it also serves as a backup if ever my phone were to become lost or destroyed.

The Holy Spirit is Jesus on the cloud.

The Master is no longer bound to a physical body. He can be accessed anytime, anywhere, by as many people that need Him. His body was destroyed, but He wasn't—because He is one with the Holy Spirit.

Not only can we access the Lord from the cloud of the Spirit; we can also download Him. The Holy Spirit makes us more like Jesus. You are Adam 2.0. You received a software upgrade because you have access to Jesus on the cloud. Jesus can be accessed by anyone at any time through the Holy Spirit. Jesus is no longer limited to a physical body. The Holy Spirit is the omnipresent form of Jesus, while also a distinct Person.

Then coming to the borders of Mysia, they headed north for the province of Bithynia, but again the Spirit of Jesus did not allow them to go there (Acts 16:7).

For the Lord is the Spirit, and wherever the Spirit of the Lord is, there is freedom (2 Corinthians 3:17).

For I know that as you pray for me and the Spirit of Jesus Christ helps me, this will lead to my deliverance (Philippians 1:19).

This means that the Holy Spirit will do anything for you and through you that Jesus would and could have done standing before you in physical form. The Holy Spirit is the Spirit of Jesus.

THE GLORIOUS SPIRIT—*1 Peter 4:14*

So be happy when you are insulted for being a Christian, for then the glorious Spirit of God rests upon you (1 Peter 4:14).

The Holy Spirit is spectacular and wonderful in nature. There is nothing dull about Him. He is colorful, lively, beautiful, and magnificent. He is the Spirit who is the full weight of God. He shines like the bright morning star. He is glorious. The Holy Spirit is the Spirit of glory.

Chapter 62

THE HOLY SPIRIT IN SECOND PETER

THE BREATH OF THE SCRIPTURES—*2 Peter 1:20-21*

The Holy Spirit inspired the Scripture.

The Holy Spirit inspired every word of the Scripture.

> *Above all, you must realize that no prophecy in Scripture ever came from the prophet's own understanding, or from human initiative. No, those prophets were moved by the Holy Spirit, and they spoke from God* (2 Peter 1:20-21).

It was by the breath of God that the Scripture came to be.

> *All Scripture is God-breathed and is useful for teaching, rebuking, correcting and training in righteousness* (2 Timothy 3:16 NIV).

What does it mean for something to be "God-breathed"? It means that it originated within God. Remember that "breath" or "wind" is a symbol of the Holy Spirit. The Word of God is carried upon the breath of God. The Word represents Jesus Christ (see John 1:1) and the breath represents the Holy Spirit (*Ruach*). The Son is made manifest by the Spirit.

Every truth, every narrative, and every word was written by the Holy Spirit. The Holy Spirit is the breath of the Scriptures.

Chapter 63

THE HOLY SPIRIT IN
FIRST JOHN

THE WITNESS OF THE INCARNATION—*1 John 4:1-2*

The Holy Spirit testifies of the Incarnation.

Because the Holy Spirit was the power of the incarnation of Christ, it means that He was also a witness of that incarnation.

> *Dear friends, do not believe everyone who claims to speak by the Spirit. You must test them to see if the spirit they have comes from God. For there are many false prophets in the world. This is how we know if they have the Spirit of God: If a person claiming to be a prophet acknowledges that Jesus Christ came in a real body, that person has the Spirit of God* (1 John 4:1-2).

There are some who say that Jesus did not come in bodily form. The Holy Spirit would vehemently disagree with them. He makes it known to us that Jesus came in the flesh.

Nobody has to convince you that you're saved. You know it by the Spirit. Nobody has to convince you that Jesus rose from the dead. You know it by the Spirit. You know by the Spirit that you belong to God. You know by the Spirit that you are forgiven. You know by the Spirit that Jesus is coming again. And you know by the Spirit that Christ came in bodily form. That deep knowing is the inner witness of the Holy Spirit. He convinces you of everything He has witnessed.

> *For when we brought you the Good News, it was not only with words but also with power, for the Holy Spirit gave you full assurance that what we said was true. And you know of our concern*

for you from the way we lived when we were with you. So you received the message with joy from the Holy Spirit in spite of the severe suffering it brought you. In this way, you imitated both us and the Lord (1 Thessalonians 1:5-6).

And the Holy Spirit also testifies that this is so. For He says, "This is the new covenant I will make with My people on that day, says the Lord: I will put My laws in their hearts, and I will write them on their minds" (Hebrews 10:15-16).

But I will send you the Advocate—the Spirit of truth. He will come to you from the Father and will testify all about Me (John 15:26).

The Holy Spirit was a witness of the Incarnation and He assures you of what He saw. He speaks assurance to your heart. He has personally verified every work. He has personally witnessed all that God wants you to believe.

Chapter 64

THE HOLY SPIRIT IN SECOND JOHN

MASTERFUL TEACHER—*2 John 1-3*

The Holy Spirit reveals truth.

The Holy Spirit, the Spirit of truth, lives within every believer.

This letter is from John, the elder. I am writing to the chosen lady and to her children, whom I love in the truth—as does everyone else who knows the truth— because the truth lives in us and will be with us forever. Grace, mercy, and peace, which come from God the Father and from Jesus Christ—the Son of the Father—will continue to be with us who live in truth and love (2 John 1-3).

The Holy Spirit lives in us, giving us, not information, but revelation of the Word of God and the truths of God. He teaches us.

The difference between information and revelation is like the difference between looking at a photo of a moment and actually being there to experience that moment.

The Holy Spirit is a masterful teacher of the Word of God because He doesn't just give you information; He brings forth revelation. He doesn't just help you process the information; He helps you appreciate the revelation. Information is the depositing of facts into your mind, but revelation is the impartation of truth into your spirit. Information informs. Revelation transforms.

When we tell you these things, we do not use words that come from human wisdom. Instead, we speak words given to us by the Spirit, using the Spirit's words to explain spiritual truths (1 Corinthians 2:13).

The Holy Spirit leads us into the truth of the Word of God. We cannot fully appreciate what God is communicating to us without the guidance of the Holy Spirit. Sure, anyone—even the carnal man—can retain the factual information of Scripture. However, knowing what God's Word says and experiencing the truth of God's Word are two separate things.

One can know of God's love and still never yield to it. One can know of the Holy Spirit's power and still never walk in it. One can read about Jesus and still never meet Him. The information of the Word comes by reading the Word, but the revelation of the Word—the full experience and understanding of it—comes only with the help of the Holy Spirit. The Word of God becomes an experience when the Holy Spirit breathes upon it.

You sent Your good Spirit to instruct them, and You did not stop giving them manna from heaven or water for their thirst (Nehemiah 9:20).

The Holy Spirit is our Instructor.

He is the Holy Spirit, who leads into all truth. The world cannot receive Him, because it isn't looking for Him and doesn't recognize Him. But you know Him, because He lives with you now and later will be in you (John 14:17).

Perhaps you have become frustrated with what you feel is a lack of understanding. Perhaps you have attempted several times, to no avail, to receive from the Word of God on your own. Maybe you have seen others expound upon the Word of God with powerful insight and have thought, "Why didn't I see that in the Word?" or "I wish I could receive revelation like that."

If you're like me, then there are times when you're reading the Word and the information seems scattered. You have a difficult time putting the pieces together. My secret is simple: I just ask for the Holy Spirit to teach me as I read the Word.

Yes, it really is that simple. The Scripture says:

If you need wisdom, ask our generous God, and He will give it to you. He will not rebuke you for asking (James 1:5).

Without His help, I am absolutely unable to truly understand the deeper things of God. I don't want to just learn theology; I want to access spirituality. The Holy Spirit helps me do that. I simply and slowly move through the text. As I am diligent to give myself to the discipline of research and reading, He is faithful to remind and reveal. You do the difficult work, and the Holy Spirit will do the supernatural work. You take time for the Word, and He will meet you there to teach you.

So, as you read the Word of God, relax, be still, and with child-like faith, ask for the guidance of the masterful Teacher, the Holy Spirit.

Not only is truth deposited by the Holy Spirit; it's also guarded by the Holy Spirit.

> *Through the power of the Holy Spirit who lives within us, carefully guard the precious truth that has been entrusted to you* (2 Timothy 1:14).

The Holy Spirit is your masterful Teacher.

Chapter 65

THE HOLY SPIRIT IN
THIRD JOHN

THE SPIRIT OF UNITY—*3 John 1:1-3*

The Holy Spirit calls for unity.

Nothing can slow down the work of the Kingdom quite like competition or resistance from our own brothers and sisters in the faith. When we refuse to help one another out of spite or competition, we offend the Holy Spirit.

The Book of Third John is John's letter to Gaius, a brother in the faith who welcomed the traveling teachers with loving hospitality. John commends Gaius for his hospitality and tells him that he is *"living according to the truth"* (3 John 1:3). In the same letter, John also condemns the actions of Diotrephes, a man who not only refused to welcome the traveling teachers, but who encouraged others to close their doors to them.

Again, in welcoming traveling teachers, Gaius was said to be *"living according to the truth"* (3 John 1:3). We know that the truth is made known by the Holy Spirit. John also told Gaius that he was *"strong in spirit"* (3 John 1:2). The kind of actions that Gaius was taking were born in the spirit by the Spirit. His acts of unity came from spiritual maturity.

So what ultimately is the theme here? The theme is hospitality toward and unity with one another. Those who are strong in spirit and live according to the truth walk in both.

The message from the Holy Spirit is made clear in the Book of Third John. Through John's letter, the Holy Spirit is pleading for unity and peace among His children. The Holy Spirit loves unity and condemns the rejection of brothers and sisters in Christ. The Holy Spirit is the key to unity.

In fact, the Book of Ephesians confirms this truth:

Endeavouring to keep the unity of the Spirit in the bond of peace (Ephesians 4:3 KJV).

Those who live in the truth are united by that truth, made one by that truth. The Holy Spirit of truth is our common ground. The Holy Spirit in me is one with the Holy Spirit in you. Therefore, all who have the Holy Spirit are united as one and should act accordingly, for the Holy Spirit is the Spirit of unity.

Chapter 66

THE HOLY SPIRIT IN JUDE

THE SPIRIT OF PRAYER—*Jude 1:20*

The Holy Spirit helps us pray.

I had an interesting vision. In my vision, I saw myself. Within me was a glowing pulsating orb of light. That light would grow in size as it intensified in brightness. It would also shrink in size as it dimmed. On top of the orb rested a layer of soil. That soil had structures upon it. Whenever the light would shrink, the soil would shift and the structures would collapse. Whenever the light would grow, the soil would become even and the structures would stand again.

The Holy Spirit told me, "That orb of light represents the power of your prayer life. The soil represents your life, and the structures represent everything in your life—relationships, ministry, finances, health. When you pray, the light grows, your life stabilizes, and the structures of your life stand. When you become inconsistent in your prayer life, the light shrinks, the soil shifts, and the structures collapse. The stronger your prayer life, the more stable your life. When your prayer life is in place, the soil remains even, the structures stand tall, and you can handle more weight on the soil."

Prayer is the foundation of life, and the Holy Spirit is the power behind your prayer life.

Jude writes to all who have been called by God:

> *But ye, beloved, building up yourselves on your most holy faith, praying in the Holy Ghost* (Jude 1:20 KJV).

We are instructed to pray in the Holy Ghost because prayer without the Holy Spirit is powerless. Yes, it's possible to pray without power. Jesus Himself instructed us not to pray like the hypocrites:

> And when thou prayest, thou shalt not be as the hypocrites are: for they love to pray standing in the synagogues and in the corners of the streets, that they may be seen of men. Verily I say unto you, They have their reward (Matthew 6:5 KJV).

The hypocrites desired to be admired by men. They wanted to be seen as spiritual. So they would pray in public places. That was what they wanted from their prayer lives, and that was all they got from their prayer lives. Jesus said, "... They have their reward" (Matt. 6:5). In other words, "That's all their prayers will accomplish." Nothing more would come of their prayers other than the fact that they were seen praying. What power is there in that?

Religious people pray, but there is no *real* power in their prayers. Even sincere believers can find themselves praying without power. Remember this: prayer only becomes effective when it's inspired and sustained by the Holy Spirit. He is the Spirit of prayer. When it comes to Spirit-inspired prayer, it is impossible to accomplish nothing in prayer.

Yet so many believers struggle to connect with God. They exhaust themselves, straining their emotions and tiring their minds. Some even wear out their physical bodies with ritualistic movement and noise. And what is earned for all the struggle? What is gained in such straining? Nothing but discouragement and confusion.

Prayer is a spiritual act, and spiritual acts can be accomplished only with the Holy Spirit's help. You cannot access the spiritual by means of the flesh.

So how does one cooperate with the Holy Spirit in prayer? How exactly are we to benefit from His help in this area? The key is stillness. Stillness is the quieting of the soul and the mind. It is the art of meditation upon the Word of God and total trust in His grace. We cannot receive the help of the Holy Spirit if we are too distracted with self.

Do you know why we struggle so much in prayer? We are too distracted by worry. Worry is our attempt at prayer. Worry is the flesh's substitute for the Holy Spirit's zeal to pray. How is the Holy Spirit supposed to be the power of your prayers if you're too busy relying upon the power of your worry?

We imagine that by worrying about something or analyzing a situation, we can bring about the results we wish to see. We imagine that our emotions will get God's attention or that our noise will create power. However, we must resist the urge to overthink and to obsess about the many things that call for our attention. We must stop striving so much, as if our ability to pray comes from ourselves. Inner chaos distracts us from the Holy Spirit's gentle leading, and it is caused by giving our attention to anything else but the face of Jesus.

Be still, and know that I am God: I will be exalted among the heathen, I will be exalted in the earth (Psalm 46:10 KJV).

Be still and know. In other words, relax. Stop asking so many questions. Stop worrying about so many things: "Can God hear me? Is God angry with me? Am I praying right? What's going to happen in this situation? Why don't I feel God?" All of those questions and others like it should have no place in your mind as you pray. If you fill your mind with such questions, you'll not be able to hear the Holy Spirit's instructions.

Just go somewhere that's quiet and private. Sit down. And then wait. Really, just wait. Ask the Holy Spirit to help you pray, and then *wait*. Be still. Be still in your mind, soul, and body.

Often, I'll tell people to be still and they'll come back and say, "It didn't work for me." However, each and every time—and I do mean *every* time—it is revealed that the individual wasn't actually relying on the Holy Spirit. Here's how their inner chaos of worry looks:

"Lord, I love You. Help me to seek You."

Fifteen minutes go by.

"Lord, are You there? Why don't I feel anything? What did I do wrong? This always happens to me. I never feel God's presence. This isn't working."

Then the individual is right back at frustration.

Or prayer can sometimes look like this:

"Lord, I love You. Show me Your glory. Let me experience Your presence."

The enemy reminds them of something shameful from their past.

"Lord, I'm so sorry. Forgive me."

Guilt enters. The person becomes distracted with how they feel instead of trusting in God's forgiveness.

"Lord, please!"

The individual begins praying out of emotions.

Now I don't have to describe your situation specifically in order for this to apply to you. I assure you, whatever it is that goes through your mind when you pray, if it robs you of the peace of God, it needs to be ignored when you pray. The analyzing of our own issues, as noble as it may seem, kills prayer because it is ultimately self-reliance and not reliance on the Holy Spirit.

The Holy Spirit can't lead you if you're trying to lead yourself. So determine to fill your mind with the truth of God's Word, and allow the Holy Spirit to help you pray. Ask Him to help you; then be still. Trust Him. Listen to Him.

Once He begins to influence your prayer life, not only will you pray more effectively, but you'll pray more passionately. The Spirit of prayer gives you the desire to pray. Exchange your worry for the power to pray. Rely not upon your mind but the Spirit of prayer.

The Holy Spirit is the Spirit of prayer.

Chapter 67

THE HOLY SPIRIT IN REVELATION

THE REVEALER OF CHRIST—*Revelation 1:10-11*

The Holy Spirit reveals Jesus.

Revelation is all about the revealing of Jesus. It wasn't until John was in the Spirit that Jesus was revealed to Him.

> *I was in the Spirit on the Lord's day, and heard behind me a great voice, as of a trumpet, Saying, I am Alpha and Omega, the first and the last...* (Revelation 1:10-11 KJV).

> *And immediately I was in the spirit: and, behold, a throne was set in heaven, and one sat on the throne* (Revelation 4:2 KJV).

> *And He carried me away in the spirit to a great and high mountain, and shewed me that great city, the holy Jerusalem, descending out of heaven from God* (Revelation 21:10 KJV).

The Holy Spirit makes Jesus real to us. He intensifies the Master, vivifies Him. As the Holy Spirit reveals Jesus to the eyes of your heart, you will become more aware of the presence of Jesus than ever before. The Holy Spirit wants to make Jesus more real to you than even your own physical body is to you. He wants to present Christ to you with perfect clarity. He wants the presence of Jesus to be potent to you.

And once you begin to know Jesus in this way, the reality of Christ surrounds your very being. Just your nearness can cause others to become hungry for the things of God. Just the way you talk can inspire people to want to love Jesus more. Your words will become backed by the weight of His presence. Truly, the glory will rest upon you. People will begin to recognize Jesus in you.

> *The members of the council were amazed when they saw the boldness of Peter and John, for they could see that they were ordinary men with no special training in the Scriptures. They also recognized them as men who had been with Jesus* (Acts 4:13).

The Holy Spirit wants to make Jesus more real to you than you ever knew possible. This sort of revelation of Jesus comes only by the Holy Spirit. Let your faith be stirred, and whisper, "Holy Spirit, reveal Jesus to me."

THE SEVENFOLD SPIRIT—*Revelation 3:1*

> *Write this letter to the angel of the church in Sardis. This is the message from the one who has the sevenfold Spirit of God and the seven stars: "I know all the things you do, and that you have a reputation for being alive—but you are dead"* (Revelation 3:1).

In the Book of Revelation, a mysterious name for the Holy Spirit is mentioned. He's called the "sevenfold Spirit of God." Now, there are many ideas as to what that means, but I think there is a correlation between the verse in Revelation and this portion of Scripture from Isaiah:

> *Out of the stump of David's family will grow a shoot—yes, a new Branch bearing fruit from the old root. And the Spirit of the Lord will rest on him—the Spirit of wisdom and understanding, the Spirit of counsel and might, the Spirit of knowledge and the fear of the Lord* (Isaiah 11:1-2).

These could very well be the seven aspects of the sevenfold Spirit of God:

1. The Spirit of the Lord
2. The Spirit of Wisdom
3. The Spirit of Understanding
4. The Spirit of Counsel
5. The Spirit of Might
6. The Spirit of Knowledge
7. The Spirit of the Fear of the Lord

Conclusion

WHO IS THIS HOLY SPIRIT?

So often we read portions of the Scripture without considering their full weightiness. So often we become familiar with the truths of the Word. At times I wish that I could again read the Bible or learn a truth for the first time. What we lose in familiarity can be regained in deeper contemplation of and meditation on the truth. So think upon this truth:

> *The Spirit of God, who raised Jesus from the dead, lives in you...* (Romans 8:11).

The Holy Spirit already dwells in you. The believer does not need more of God. All that God was, is, and ever will be came to dwell in the believer at the very instant of salvation! When the Holy Spirit comes, He comes in fullness, not in partiality. For how can the eternal be divided?

The issue is not how much the believer has of the Spirit but how much the Spirit has of the believer. You don't need more power; you need more surrender.

Think about that wonderful truth! The Holy Spirit lives in you. Who is this Holy Spirit?

He's the same Spirit who, in Genesis, hovered over the face of the deep at the dawn of time, brooding over creation and moving upon the creative declarations of the Father, causing all things to come into existence. He's the same Spirit who gave dreams to Joseph and who gives favor to those who dare to dream godly dreams.

In Exodus, He's the fire in the bush that called forth Moses and delivered a people from the miserable oppression of slavery. He's the precious oil that anointed priests, kings, and prophets. He's the One who empowered men for the crafting of the Ark of the Covenant, the gold lampstands, the incense altar, and other furnishings of the tabernacle. He empowers us to do the practical.

In Leviticus, He's the sovereign fire that could only be started by God. In Numbers, He's the different Spirit that separated men of faith from men of fear. Deuteronomy calls Him the cloud by day and the fire by night. In the Book of Joshua, He's the *Ruach* of God's people, the breath that came forth upon shouts and trumpets, the sound that caused the walls to crumble, the Spirit of breakthrough. He's the discernment of Joshua that exposed the destructive power of sin in the camp.

He was the same Spirit upon the judges that enabled them to lead God's people away from deception and back into God's ways. He was the supernatural strength of the mighty man Samson. The Book of Ruth reveals Him as the Spirit of adoption and the oil of favor. In First Samuel, the Spirit is the One who appoints, anoints, and removes people. In Second Samuel, He's revealed as the One who spoke through David and the One who now speaks through you.

First Kings calls Him the "still small voice." He's hidden in Second Kings as the pervasive oil that fills only what we surrender to Him. In First Chronicles, He's the kindred Spirit. Second Chronicles reveals Him as the fortifying Spirit, the One who leads us to correct compromise and spiritual breaches. Ezra reveals His convicting power—He truly is the Spirit of conviction, the only One able to draw the hearts of men toward repentance.

In Nehemiah, the Holy Spirit is revealed as the Comforter. In Esther, He is the voice of destiny. In Job, He's the life-giving Spirit, the One who sustains the breath of all. In Psalms, He is the Spirit of worship. In Proverbs, He is the Spirit of wisdom. In Ecclesiastes, we find Him as the Spirit of purpose, eternity in our hearts.

His hiding nature is captured in the Song of Solomon—He is the hidden dove among the rocks. There, He is also the unquenchable fire and the alluring wind. Isaiah reveals Him as the Spirit who rested upon Jesus and who performs through you with the same power today. Jeremiah called Him a fire in his bones, One who ignited a passion for the Word of God.

Lamentations reveals Him as the One who grieves deeply over sin. Ezekiel shows us that the Holy Spirit is the Spirit of oneness with God. In Daniel, He's the excellent Spirit. In Hosea, He's the patient Spirit. In Joel,

He's the Promise of the Father. In Amos, He's the consuming fire, the flames that devour our false perceptions of God.

Through the prophetic words of Obadiah, it becomes apparent that the Holy Spirit fights for the ones He loves—He's the vindicating fire. In Jonah, He's the wind that redirects —He's the Protector of the call and your guide in the perfect will of God. He won't let you go too far. In Micah, He is shown to be stubborn as the unchanging Spirit—He won't change His mind about what He's telling you to do.

Nahum's words reveal the Holy Spirit as the One who warns the sinfully stubborn of God's wrath. In Habakkuk, He's the Spirit of righteous indignation. In Zephaniah, He is the Spirit of hope. In Haggai, He is the enemy of fear. In Zechariah, He is the Spirit of Grace—He empowers us to do and become all that God desires.

In Malachi, He's the refiner's fire. Matthew reveals Him as the power behind the incarnation of Christ and the unstoppable power against the demonic forces of darkness.

In Mark, He's the beloved Spirit whom we should not even dare to blaspheme. In Luke, He's the threshing wind. In John, He's the secret to greater works. In Acts, He's the power of the Church, and He's the mighty rushing wind. We can't build the Church without Him. In Romans, He's the One who loves Jesus as well as your mighty Intercessor. In First Corinthians, He is the Spirit of God. In Second Corinthians, He is the transforming Spirit. In Galatians, He is the Christ-like Spirit. In Ephesians, He is the sustaining power. In Philippians, He is the personal Spirit—He can be known as a friend.

Colossians reveals Him as the Spirit of love. First Thessalonians describes Him as a fire that we should not stifle. Let Him do His work. Second Thessalonians tells us that He is the One who holds back the coming of the antichrist. He holds back the motion of all end-time events until the preaching of the Gospel is complete. When He leaves, chaos comes.

In First Timothy, He's the prophetic Spirit. In Second Timothy, He's the Spirit of peace. In Titus, He is the Giver of new life. In Philemon, He is the Spirit of forgiveness. Hebrews reveals that He is God; James, that He is the jealous Spirit; First Peter, that He is the Spirit of Jesus; Second Peter, that He is the Breath of the Scriptures; First John, that He is the witness of the Incarnation; Second John, that He is the masterful Teacher; and Third John, that He is the Spirit of unity.

In Jude, He is the power of prayer. And in Revelation, He is the One who reveals Jesus.

And that same Spirit, that powerful and holy Spirit, lives in you.

Epilogue

WELCOME, HOLY SPIRIT

Would you believe that there are still many things concerning the Holy Spirit that I did not include in this book? He truly is the fountain that never runs dry, the eternal river of living water. I pray that you are hungering more than ever before for the presence of the Holy Spirit. I hope that a new level of understanding of, a deeper appreciation for, and a greater friendship with the Holy Spirit has been given to you.

Dear reader, all that you have read of the Holy Spirit in this book is yours for the asking! But you might be wondering how to keep track of all His benefits. Some might even feel a little overwhelmed by all that is available to them by the Holy Spirit. I know you don't want to miss a thing.

So let me give you the good news: all of the benefits from the Holy Spirit are received by simple faith. When you welcome the Holy Spirit, you welcome His presence, as well as all that He brings with Him and does. You don't have to toil for each and every blessing He offers. You just need to embrace Him. When you embrace Him, you get it all.

So how do you welcome the Holy Spirit? How do you involve Him in your life? It's so simple that it brings me joy to tell you: you welcome the Holy Spirit through time.

Time…

Just spend time with Him, and all that He offers becomes yours. We're so busy and distracted that we neglect the simplicity of time with the Holy Spirit. Yet all He needs is your time, because as you spend time with Him, you become one who learns to surrender, to obey. He loves to spend time with you. He welcomes you. Do you welcome Him?

Prayer is the act of depending on the Holy Spirit.

So, dear reader, I encourage you to welcome the Holy Spirit through spending time with Him as often as you are able to. Let nothing come between you and that precious time in His presence. Speak to Him. Acknowledge Him. Listen for His voice.

In your ministry, in your home, in your life, welcome the Holy Spirit.

ABOUT THE AUTHOR

David Diga Hernandez is an evangelist, healing minister, author, and TV host. He has an uncommon grace to guide believers into closeness with the Holy Spirit. Based in Southern California, David travels worldwide to preach the gospel of Jesus Christ and heads an anointed evangelistic healing ministry. The ministry's weekly TV program, *Encounter TV*, is available in millions of homes globally and features highlights from David's Miracle Services. His ministry is distinctly marked by the presence and power of the Holy Spirit. David is a unique and emerging spiritual leader, called to take God's saving and healing power to this generation.

Made in the USA
Columbia, SC
25 July 2019